Forgiveness:
The Key
to Happiness

Dear Norman, for your
So grateful friendship on
warm journey home!
our journey appreciation,
With love & appreciation,
Susan
(And the happiest of
birthdays!!! :)

Also by Susan Dugan

Extraordinary Ordinary Forgiveness
Forgiveness Offers Everything I Want
Safe Haven

Forgiveness:
The Key
to Happiness

SUSAN DUGAN

Cover design: Sven Upsons

Reviews

"There is no doubt in my mind that Susan Dugan is going to burn to a crisp in hell for this book!"
The ego, best-selling author of, well, that would be *Everything!*

"This book cracks me up!"
Jesus, author of the Indie sleeper, *Seriously?*

Contents

Author's Note

Many of these selected and heavily edited (occasionally completely rewritten) essays first appeared temporarily as drafts on my blog at www.foraysinforgiveness.com. Read consecutively, they reflect another leg in my seeming journey home through practicing *A Course in Miracles'* extraordinary forgiveness of what never was in the ordinary "classroom" of my daily life.

In reading this collection, please note that *A Course in Miracles* uses the character of Jesus (but you could use any enlightened figure) as a *symbol* of the part of our one, shared mind that remembered (and remembers) to laugh at the "tiny, mad idea" that we could separate from our true, non-dualistic nature or would possibly want to. By choosing this *completely* non-dualistic inner teacher in the classroom of our lives, our belief in the ego thought system's illusion of differences and separate interests is gently undone for us. We gradually become more kind and loving, beginning to recognize our own mind in need of healing in our wish to perceive ourselves unfairly treated. Learning, from moment-to-moment, that choosing the inner teacher of fear hurts, while choosing the inner teacher of kind forgiveness heals, yields peace that defies understanding, and includes everyone and everything in its warm embrace.

Acknowledgments

I remain eternally grateful to Dr. Kenneth Wapnick, whose presence and teachings continue to offer the light in our dream that is leading us home, to Gloria Wapnick for venturing to so generously share this light in the first place, and to the teachers and staff members at the Foundation for *A Course in Miracles* in Temecula, California (www.facim.org). Inspired by Ken and Gloria, they continue to gracefully stand for the alternative to separate interests, speaking the message of true forgiveness that will heal the mind and mend the heart of all who choose to listen.

Finally, I'd like to extend my continuing gratitude to Kevin and Kara for enabling me to learn the meaning of love beyond guilt, blame, and need. Thank you from the bottom of my heart!

> Here is the answer to your search for peace. Here is the key to meaning in a world that seems to make no sense. Here is the way to safety in apparent dangers that appear to threaten you at every turn, and bring uncertainty to all your hopes of ever finding quietness and peace. Here are all questions answered; here the end of all uncertainty ensured at last. (*A Course in Miracles* Workbook lesson 121, Forgiveness Is the Key to Happiness, paragraph 1)

Bridge Over Troubled Water

Shhhh … Lean in a little closer, OK? I have a confession to make. I killed a spider the other day in cold blood. I spotted it immediately on entering my bathroom to prepare for bed. A large, brown, hairy creature; it appeared to have rappelled into the center of my bathtub on its way to some sinister, top-secret mission. It froze as I flipped on the light. To me, it seemed a no-brainer. I turned on the forceful faucet to wash it away, watching, detached, and lost in thought about a problem I was unsuccessfully trying to solve by myself, as it fought for its apparent life. It wasn't until the suction of the eddying water actually forced it down the drain that a wave of horror, followed by remorse, shuddered through me.

The charms of *Charlotte's Web* notwithstanding, I have always feared spiders, and long ago made a bargain in an effort to achieve a certain détente with their kind. I would not bother them, I vowed, if they would not bother me. I would not approach them, interfere with them, trash them in everyday conversation or on the page, or harm them in any way, provided they stayed in their own territory: the great outdoors. I have remained faithful to my end of the agreement (coerced by my family, I once even hiked— *really* fast!—for hours in New Mexico among tarantulas without a single murderous thought). They, alas, have repeatedly broken their side of our pact with often tragic results. But as the water continued to run, spider-free, it struck me, like a blow to the solar plexus, the degree to which I had completely disassociated the killing of the spider from practicing forgiveness *A Course in Miracles*-style.

Allow me to explain. I had been listening again (it takes a lot of listening for me to begin to hear) to (premier Course scholar, teacher, and author) Ken Wapnick's lengthy, meaty, ever-so-challenging and helpful CD series *Cast No One Out*. In which he explains that we need to learn to extend forgiveness not only to humans, but also to animals, vegetables, minerals, insects, amoebas, protozoa, bacteria, computers, and even members of the U.S.

1

House of Representatives! We need to generalize the Course's message to *everything* we imagined to stand in opposition to our singular truth. To join with our right mind and allow the comfort of its all-knowing vision to help us dissolve the "hierarchy of illusions" we have constructed to obscure our awareness of our undifferentiated, eternally whole, loved and loving nature.

My robotic reaction to the crawling "intruder" in my bathtub helped me see once again how falsely, madly, deeply defended I am against the idea of seeing everyone and thing as sharing the same mind split over the terrifying belief that our wish to experience separation from our source was more than a momentary fantasy. But only learning to see that everyone and thing apparently "out there" shares the same split mind—the same fear that they/it will never be accepted back into the loving fold—and therefore deserves the same compassionate response, will ultimately heal my mind. Allowing me to awaken to the one and only loving, capital S Self I really want.

It struck me as I gazed down at the blank, white, tub—cleansed of my projection of a spider out to get me but nonetheless soiled by guilt over my perceived "crime"—that my resistance to what this Course was really saying—that there is *no* individual named Susan in conflict or collusion with other "out there" beings—went so much deeper than I could ever wrap my puny, little ego head around. In truth, the trouble I was having again holding my brother harmless in a special relationship in which I continued to perceive myself misunderstood and unfairly treated, the trouble I was having being kind and gentle with my own body, the trouble I was having refraining from cursing out my computer, the irritation I felt toward the wind-born dust and pollen assaulting my nostrils, lungs, and eyes, was no different from my perception of, and reaction to, a spider that had accidentally wandered, as spiders (wittingly or unwittingly, who the hell knows?) will, into enemy territory.

And it struck me as I stood there, once again dropping the ego's hand and reaching instead for the hand of the inner teacher of true forgiveness, that resisting doing what the Course was asking us to do hurt so much more these days. Because I now knew I always had a choice of which inner teacher—the ego or Jesus/Holy Spirit/right mind—I wanted to follow. I could choose peace instead of this, if only I wasn't so terrified of going home.

As Chapter 16, VI. The Bridge to the Real World, paragraph 8 tells us:

> ... Delay will hurt you now more than before, only because you realize it *is* delay, and that escape from pain is really possible. Find hope and comfort, rather than despair, in this: You could not long find even the illusion of love in any special relationship here. For you are no longer wholly insane, and would soon recognize the guilt of self-betrayal for what it is.

As I stood watching myself watching the empty tub with Jesus—that *symbol* of the part of our mind that never took the "tiny, mad, idea" of separation seriously and patiently guards the jewel of our uninterrupted completeness—I realized my fear of losing the self I see in the mirror, the self I still believe enables me to have my Course and my special identity, too—was at an all time high. My mind was still split. And although I knew I felt so much better when I chose the inner teacher of love over fear, I still subconsciously believed I was losing something real, and remained unconvinced I was gaining anything at all.

But with Jesus beside me, I could take hope and comfort, rather than despair, in knowing I am no longer wholly insane. Learning more and more, as I am willing from moment-to-moment to admit I am wrong about everything, that seeking for love outside myself has, and will, never work. But extending kindness and gentleness (and forgiving myself when I forget), even to spiders, even to their human equivalents, even to computers and politicians, even to the unworthy self I still think I am, will always bring peace. And continue to heal our one fractured mind in ways I can't possibly, and thankfully don't need to, understand.

The Holy Spirit asks only this little help of you: Whenever your thoughts wander to a special relationship which still attracts you, enter with Him into a holy instant, and there let Him release you. He needs only your willingness to share His perspective to give it to you completely. And your willingness need not be complete because His is perfect. It is His task to atone for your unwillingness by His perfect faith, and it is His faith you share with Him there. Out of your recognition of your unwillingness for your release, His perfect willingness is given you. Call upon Him, for Heaven is at his Call. And let Him call on Heaven for you. (Paragraph 12)

Truth or Cake?

I have stored in my bodily memory an image from early child-hood of a perfect autumn Sunday afternoon. Burnished maple leaves still wanton on their branches waving in a spicy breeze, the scent of engorged apples nearly ready to relinquish their final grip. I am six or seven years old. We are visiting parents of my parents' friends. I careen about the still lush grounds of a modest farmhouse anchoring acres of green, perched on the edge of the mighty, mythic Hudson River forging forth thousands of feet below toward Manhattan.

About to execute another somersault, I catch a glimpse, through the open kitchen door, of a vision so exquisite, I pause, and gasp. A beam of sunlight illuminates the white caps of boiled frosting on a just-baked Devil's Food cake, perched on a pedestal-stand in the center of a kitchen table. I freeze, immobilized by desire to taste it, yet suddenly and painfully aware that it can't possibly deliver on its promise. The anticipation of it, the desire, the meaning I have given it, cannot possibly be realized. Not in a single bite. Not in a million.

And so I stand perfectly still, savoring a longing I somehow can't help but realize can never be filled, has never been filled, will never be filled. Not by the cake on the counter. Not by the church where each Sunday I drag a self, already dense with accumulating sins, for absolution that never comes. Not by my parents sitting inside in the adjoining dining room, drinking yet another cup of coffee; acting like everything is OK. Not by the life I've imagined for myself, the trip to the moon I plan to make, the stories I will write, the end to the Cold War I plan to negotiate; the frog I will transform into royalty and protect from all possible harm with a single, sweet kiss.

And still I stand, transfixed, struggling to prolong a lingering hope that I am wrong. Waiting and waiting for some kind of sign I somehow know will never come. I bite down hard on my fist to keep from weeping, only babies do that—my younger brothers, my many little cousins—but I am strong. I seize control of myself, and stuff the unwelcome thought back down into the Pandora's Box from which it sprang, uninvited, clown-like, before the old woman calls us in to sample her latest confection.

Lately, I have been once more aware of what I have always known, but struggled to deny: that nothing in this world—however promising and tantalizing—will ever satisfy the longing for love I came in with and continue to crave. For decades I did a pretty good job burying that awareness whenever it once more crept, uninvited, into my peripheral vision. But it never worked for long. My life has been a half-hearted effort to give all the world's offerings one more shot. You know, in case I missed that one remaining treasure that might yet perfectly slip like a missing puzzle piece into the hollow space in my heart.

A Course in Miracles does a really good job explaining why the world we made ultimately fails us, why we need to see that, and why we must ultimately quit trying to drag an all-inclusive, loving God (who doesn't know about pretend kingdoms) into the mess we think we made. According to the Course's creation myth, in the beginning, we experienced ourselves seamlessly fused with our creator in a manner that defies our current, seemingly differentiated understanding. Into that state of perfect unity and boundless joy—for reasons that also defy our current comprehension—there crept a "tiny, mad, idea" that we should somehow separate from our source to experience ourselves individually.

Had we remembered to laugh at the impossibility of fragmenting infinite, indivisible wholeness we would never have experienced ourselves as fugitives from the one love "joined as one" we remain. Instead we took it seriously, and perceived ourselves figuratively cast out of heaven, believing we had forever forsaken our real Self. The one mind then appeared to split over the crushing guilt of that belief into the ego, the part of our mind that believed we pulled off the separation, and the right mind/ Holy (Whole) Spirit that remembered to smile. In our fear and guilt and continuing desire to taste what individuality might offer, we followed the ego into an entire projected universe of fragmented forms to hide out in. And to ensure we never got back to the "scene of the crime" in the mind, we figuratively fell asleep, and now find ourselves dreaming a dream of exile that—like our apparent sleeping dreams—seems very real, but in no way affects our waking, united reality.

Yet here we seem to find ourselves, adrift in an illusory world attempting to satisfy our longings by bargaining with other selves to get our physical and emotional needs met, to fill ourselves up with promising substances that never deliver, all the while recognizing, if we are deeply honest, that it does not, has not, and will never work. Even though we study and may intellectually grasp *A Course in Miracles*' challenging metaphysics, we continue to want to have our cake and our Course, too. We spin out our days attempting to entice the Holy Spirit into an illusory world to help us cook up a sweeter dream to satisfy our perpetual hunger. Rather than asking for help to heal our minds of the belief in separation that led to dreaming up all these futile substitutes, and prevents us from experiencing true nourishment.

Today, in my classroom, I am that child again, watching my temptation to reach back into the illusion to satisfy my desire for assurance that I am still loved and loving, my craving to have my cake and my Course, too. Even though I know, with growing, welcome clarity, as I again reach for the memory of my right mind; that the cake can never deliver on its promise. The anticipation of it, the desire, the meaning I have given it, cannot possibly be realized. Not in a single bite. Not in a million. And in that recognition, outside the circular bondage of time in which innocence for one and all prevails, I am once more cured of all craving, completely completed, along with you. A little less invested in the allure of the world's confections; a little closer to opening my eyes on all I ever wanted, and never really threw away.

Today we pass illusions by. And if we hear temptation call to us to stay and linger in a dream, we turn aside and ask ourselves if we, the Sons of God, could be content with dreams, when Heaven can be chosen just as easily as hell, and love will happily replace all fear. (From *A Course in Miracles* workbook lesson 272, paragraph 2)

It Is Impossible to See Two Worlds

The day began to the grating tune of NPR reporting yet another round of polls indicating a shocking drop in support for Barack Obama in the upcoming U.S. presidential race resulting from his—how to put this kindly?—less than stellar performance in the first debate right here in Denver, Colorado. Although I had done my best to suspend judgment of opponent Mitt Romney during and following that travesty, and, upon failing to do so, at least offer the critical differences the ego tallied in its 24/7 rant between two opposite ways of viewing the role of government and civilized society (mine and theirs) to the perception of the inner teacher of forgiveness, enough was enough!

"Welcome to another freaking day in paradise," the ego whispered, in its best pretend-flight-attendant voice.

My heart raced as I allowed the panic afflicting roughly half of the American electorate who identify themselves as one of the president's supporters to infect the body I still think I am. The welcome sting of the familiar drug of judgment coursed through my ravenous veins as I realized "we" could actually lose this race. I could literally feel myself salivating, as if at the scent of a favorite, long-denied meal. Seemingly of their own accord, my fingers began dancing across the keyboard; unloading my outrage in pithy detail in an email to a friend certain to fire back immediately with kindred ire. About to hit "send," I paused, gazing at the computer monitor and considering banging my head against it.

"There has to be another way!" I thought, *A Course in Miracles'* collaborator Bill Thetford's famous words that had invited its scribing by Helen Schucman into the world, echoing in my empty skull. And, of course, there is. I had been studying and practicing that better way for almost nine years, for Christ's sake, no pun intended. I knew just how fleeting this current fix of projection would prove, could already taste the crushing pain of its hangover. Did I really want to hurt myself like this again? Enough really was enough!

I cancelled out of the email and opened the big, blue book instead to *A Course in Miracles* workbook lesson 130: It is impossible to see two worlds, paragraph 4, lines 1-7:

> Fear has made everything you think you see. All separation, all distinctions, and the multitude of differences you believe make up the world. They are not there. Love's enemy has made them up. Yet love can have no enemy, and so they have no cause, no being and no consequence. They can be valued, but remain unreal. They can be sought, but they can not be found.

Welcome to freaking paradise, indeed.

I thought about how my judgments kept cropping up all over the place recently, along with a heightened awareness that I used them as shields to defend against a growing experience of an abstract, singularly loving force that embraces us all—regardless of political affiliation or philosophy—when I am willing to choose the inner teacher of love over fear. To align with the part of our mind that responded correctly to the preposterous idea that we could have severed our connection to indestructible, all-encompassing oneness from the seeming beginning and continued gently smiling; certain our gloom-and-doom dreams of "one or the other" had no effect.

I thought about how the ego seemed intent on enticing me to believe that awakening to an unwavering, peaceful wholeness that included everyone and thing was not attainable in this lifetime. There were simply too many enemies "out there" to thwart me. Not enough years left to look at all the defenses I invented to block my awareness of our one true identity with our right mind, that I might see them for the nothingness they remain. Look past their disguises to the same fearful heart we share as imaginary fugitives from our one loving source. Expressing ourselves in ostensibly different ways that nonetheless serve the same purpose of keeping the real abstract love we no longer think we deserve away. Desperately clinging to, and defending, whatever dogma we think will keep us safe, while attacking what we perceive as its opposite, even though real love knows no opposites.

Funny, the ego would like me to believe peace is not attainable in this world but it would also like me to believe peace is attainable right now, right here in the dream, to prevent me from employing the means offered to attain it. I don't have to forgive, the spiritual ego tells me. No need to look at my judgments. Since I never really left my home in God, I just need to smile a lot, step away from the disturbing radio and TV images, the alarming pollsters, the nut cases in my kitchen, and affirm "God is." But that doesn't serve my only real goal of awakening from this dualistic nightmare of separate interests. It merely plunges me more deeply into it. The ego is a sneaky bastard, speaks out of both sides of its proverbial mouth, always lies, and smiles the ultimate politician's smile.

Peace *is* attainable in this lifetime. I know it because I have experienced elongated instants in which all individual and collective differences fall away (along with the awareness of an individual story line) and only the common interest of healing our mind prevails. I have attained it through my willingness to forgive what never was. But sometimes it feels like trying to hold onto water. Because a part of me still wants to indulge those oh-so-solid-seeming judgments that preserve the delusion of me at the same time, and it is impossible to grasp two worlds.

And so it is not enough to smile and say I love God. I need to forgive my belief in something external to judge as well as my belief in the person I identify with doing the judging and smiling, one illusion at a time. To offer my addiction to this *me*-ness, expressed through my runaway judgments, to the part of my mind that sees only the vast, infinitely kind truth of our eternal *we*-ness, that field of healed awareness in which delusions of separate interests reveal themselves for the nothingness from which they sprang.

When I am willing to do this I see that despite the differences that seem so insurmountable to this *me* that identifies with *my* tribe, we all share the same split mind, the same crushing belief that the wild thought of separation had real consequences. We're all terrified here; fighting for what we think will protect us, operating on the basis of false information. Although that fear manifests differently in our individual and collective worlds, frightened people still deserve love, not condemnation. And the only way I can experience the love I am seeking to soothe my fear is to learn to love instead of hate in all circumstances.

And so, despite my continuing strong opinions and preferences, my sanity does not depend on which candidate wins the next debate or the next or even the election. My sanity depends on which inner teacher I am willing to choose again and again, right now, to experience this world with, until all perceived differences disappear for good. Forgiveness is not done by me, but by:

... asking for strength beyond your own, and recognizing what it is you seek. ... emptying your hands of all the petty treasures of this world. You wait for God to help you, as you say:

It is impossible to see two worlds. Let me accept the strength God offers me and see no value in this world, that I may find my freedom and deliverance. (From paragraph 8)

Chutes and Ladders

I sat in the plane beside my daughter on our way back from attending a memorial service for my mother-in-law in Maryland. I was just finishing up reading the last of a stack of cooking magazines purchased to distract me from the physically and emotionally enervating events of the past few days, including helping my husband finish emptying the house he grew up in and ready it for rent or sale, attending to his parents' friends and family members, and preparing his elderly father for the impending difficult move to an independent living facility in Denver. Although I had appealed to my right mind each morning for help in looking at my urge to make the dream of separated bodies vying for survival real, I nonetheless had became once more entwined and engrossed in the many dream forms and figures appearing to live, decay, and perish on the screen of my perception.

Over the past few days, I had gradually succumbed to a mixture of sadness, regret, and helplessness as I attempted to navigate the complicated scenario confronting us combined with my profound empathy for my husband's seemingly unrelenting predicament. Then, too, I had moments in which I observed myself outraged and arguing with "external" reality, once again convinced I had no choice about the way I was feeling, and judging myself harshly for lack of greater compassion. Now and then I conversed in my head with Jesus; that memory of our one, awakened mind that refused to believe the preposterous idea that we could shatter eternal wholeness. That shred of sanity that continues to serve as a beacon of light whenever we choose again to offer it our dark illusions. Those shadows of guilt and fear we secretly cherish that—according to the ego—culminate in bodily death and destruction; thereby at least proving we once existed as separate, vulnerable entities.

I know this is crazy. I understand what the Course is saying. And yet, when it comes to my body or the bodies of loved ones, my "stuff" and their "stuff" of all kinds; I still can't always side with the light. (Not by a long shot.) I am able to practice the Course's forgiveness—looking with Jesus/Holy (Whole) Spirit/right mind at the unconscious guilt I robotically project "out there" in the form of all these "incoming distractions and attacks"—more and more in my daily classroom. At least when I seem to encounter a fairly reasonably paced curriculum. But when seemingly thrust into accelerated learning situations, like this one, the seeming circuits overload and I regress; begging Jesus to meet me here on this dangerous fantasy island, in the vulnerable embodied condition I still think I'm in.

And so I found myself, toward the end of our flight home, in a complete ego meltdown as the captain came on the loudspeaker to announce we faced weather in our final descent into Denver. We would experience turbulence coming in, forcing the flight attendants to immediately return to their seats. My daughter— all too familiar with my fear of flying—smiled, and reminded me we would soon be safe on the ground. *Teenagers.* I dug my fingers into the pulse point my Chinese Medicine doctor recommended for anxiety and began inwardly bargaining with Jesus, explaining I simply had not come as far as I thought and had too many other forgiveness issues still on my plate to deal with this one. I promised to attend an extended review session in his office in the morning if he would just, *please*, meet me right here, right now, in the frightened condition I found myself in.

I did not want to push his love away, but I was freaking out, and too tired to weather this particular storm, to entertain the possibility that my safety lay elsewhere even though I believe that learning and practicing forgiveness will lead me to my real home. My rationalizations and pleas continued in this vein as we made it safely to the ground, seemingly without an untoward bump. Driving home, I thanked him profusely in my head, gazing up at a horizon of bruised, anvil-shaped clouds and a circular patch of blue sky, carved like a tiny portal through which I imagined we had been gently guided.

This got me to thinking about the way in which we seem to go forward and backwards on this fantasy return to the one love we never left; now and again retreating into fear. As very young children, my brother Michael and I often played the board game *Chutes and Ladders.* In which players who make "good choices" proceed toward the finish line by climbing up ladders while those who make "bad choices" plunge backwards down chutes; a crafty attempt at socialization via behavior modification that sneaks in rudimentary arithmetic skills for good measure.

I have to wonder if Jesus had this game in mind with the scribing (through Helen) of *The Song of Prayer* pamphlet, written soon after the Course's publication, partly to help correct and clarify the misinterpretations of the Course already running rampant in the world we think we inhabit, in the separated condition we think we're in. The publication explains how the Course figuratively reaches down to us here in the dream where we find ourselves perched at the bottom of the ladder of prayer, recognizing there must be a better way of living in this world but still completely clueless about what that could possibly mean. Still convinced we require divine intervention to rescue us here in our impossible dream of exile from perfect wholeness, completely unaware we are the dreamers (rather than heroes) of the dream. As explained in II. The Ladder of Prayer:

> ... for in this world prayer is reparative, and so it must entail levels of learning ... It is possible at this level to continue to ask for things of this world in various forms, and it is also possible to ask for gifts such as honesty or goodness, and particularly forgiveness for the many sources of guilt that inevitably underlie any prayer of need. Without guilt there is no scarcity. The sinless have no needs. (From paragraph 3)

Like the Course itself, *The Song of Prayer* invites us to experience ourselves, not as differentiated egos, but as one decision-making mind, outside the dream of time and space. The part of our *mind* that chose to side with the ego's story of sin, guilt, and fear at the seeming beginning, but can learn to choose for the part of our mind that remembered to smile at that impossible idea. By learning to choose for a different, sane inner teacher when we find ourselves frightened and confused, we join with the one, unalterable peace we have never left. We begin to rely more and more on that inner teacher of truth as we practice looking with it at the smaller seeming illusions in our lives, eventually expanding to the greater, at whatever pace our fear allows.

But when fear overwhelms us, we again stumble backwards down a chute, appealing to Jesus to help us here in the dream. If most healing to our mind at the moment, we may imagine that help. Because increasing our fear is never helpful; while relieving it enough to reconnect us with the direction we really want to go always is. And so this morning I am heading to my imaginary Jesus' office to request the help with undoing the blocks to my awareness of love's presence I really want, the direction I really want to go, and the real prayer for a unique forgiveness I want to learn to apply in all circumstances. Again aware, as I draw breath into lungs I still believe sustain me, that all urgency springs from the ego, and I can only move up this ladder as quickly as my unconscious fear permits. That time, itself, is an illusion of the ego I can instead learn to kindly use to heal my mind of all illusions. We are, in truth, already home; an occasional tumble down another imaginary chute notwithstanding.

> ... Prayer in its earlier forms is an illusion, because there is no need for a ladder to reach what one has never left. Yet prayer is part of forgiveness as long as forgiveness, itself an illusion, remains unattained. Prayer is tied up with learning until the goal of learning has been reached. (From paragraph 8)

Bad Baby

"I will not hurt myself again today," I read, closing—OK; slamming—the big, blue book shut, the words from *A Course in Miracles* workbook lesson 330 echoing in my head. Since returning from Temecula, California, where I'd attended a workshop with Ken Wapnick at the Foundation for *A Course in Miracles*, I'd been haunted by newfound awareness of an insatiable appetite for hurting myself (as opposed to the usual awareness of my desire to hold *others* responsible for my inner suffering). Worse, the distinction between the two had begun to blur. I could suddenly see how the spate of recent attacks on my own body (a bad fall carrying my dog down the stairs resulting in bruising on my leg severe enough to rob me of sleep for weeks, another sinus infection, seemingly accelerated symptoms of an aging form, and an ongoing, internal rant of self-judgment about all my less than desirable traits) were no different from the attack thoughts I projected on other bodies.

The Course tells us we must learn to make no distinctions between attacking the dream figure we believe we inhabit or any other dream figure (since in truth, we are non-differentiated dreamers of the dream, rather than its stars and co-stars) if we ever hope to learn once and for all that we are not these vulnerable bodies we cling to and robotically defend. But right now I was not a happy learner. The realization only raised the hair on the back of my neck as I gazed out the window at the last blaze of glory in an autumn hell-bent on mocking me with its gaudy, pre-death splendor, trying to come up with some words worthy enough to place on the illusion of a blank page.

I headed for the kitchen hoping another cup of Joe might help me return to a state of caffeinated mindlessness deep enough to blunt a nagging dread and was startled by the creepy gurgles of a plastic zombie baby we had purchased for Halloween and temporarily hung on the back of a kitchen chair. I had forgotten to turn her off and the sound of my footsteps had reactivated her eerie lament. She clung by her little green fingers and bloodied nails, a mixture of infantile laughter and sobbing gurgling forth from her life-size, pink-night-gown-clad form. Her eyes flashed on and off like ambivalent brake lights as she reared back and arched forward, banging her bald baby head against the back of the metal chair. "Bad, bad, bad!" she cried, over and over again.

My little dog cowered, gazing up at me for some explanation. I sighed.

I had been reading and teaching The Obstacles to Peace again in chapter 19, in which Jesus gets uncomfortably up close and personal with us about the real purpose of the body and our attraction to its seemingly meteoric rise and descent. My fear of death was up, big time. But it paled beside the dawning realization that there is no life in bodies; only in the one mind outside the ego's apparent body of evidence, the one place we're absolutely terrified to seek, and find, our real, uninterrupted life. We tell ourselves that's where the grim reaper of a God we created to punish us for our imaginary bolt from all-inclusive oneness lies in wait, poised to annihilate us in return for our insubordination. It's a bad, bad, bad setup. Fortunately, it doesn't exist. It's merely a rerun of an old horror flick seemingly produced and immediately tossed on the cutting room floor with a knowing smile long, long ago.

"Bad, bad, bad," the zombie baby cried.

Jesus was smiling, too, as we returned to his imaginary office in my head for a little review. "I'm laughing with you," he said.

"Yeah, right. Anyway, I thought it was the other way around?"

"What other way would that be, again?"

He was so funny. I squeezed his hand and sat down beside him. It had been a terrifying few days really, retreating into fear again as I tried to integrate the workshop's wisdom all by my false, little, lonesome. But I was back in school again, thank God, the only teacher I really wanted right there at my side, where he'd been waiting all along.

"I know what you're thinking," I said.

"You always do."

"We're all head-bangers here. Just a bunch of zombie cry babies intent on proving our inherent badness. Punishing ourselves for what we did not do. See, it doesn't matter if I see you as bad or me as bad because it's always *my* bad. Punishing the self I think I am, or punishing you, serves the same purpose of keeping the guilt alive. Keeping the idea that we deserve God's punishment real and proving we exist as separated zombies! Our guilt over believing it feeds on blame of any kind. The particular objects of our projections are actually irrelevant."

Jesus nodded. "Tell me more."

"It's like, I secretly believe that if I can convince this avenging God I made up, hot on my trail, that you're the guilty one, he'll leave me alone and go after you. But then, because I've been practicing the Course's forgiveness and have begun to see I feel better when I stop attacking you, I start to quit doing it. That's when the ego gets really sneaky and starts attacking the body I think I am instead. And I totally forget I have to forgive that, too. And all that means is looking at it with you. So I can see it through your eyes as the same unreal "problem" of guilt, but not take it seriously, not be afraid of it anymore."

Jesus raised his thumb.

I pressed my thumb against his in a little thumb toast.

"Nothing personal, but it's really just because I became afraid of *you* again, isn't it? What you symbolize, I mean; the abstract love that will ultimately save me from this dream of separate interests. But my mind is still split. I still believe I'm a body. Even though I know I feel much better when I choose you as my inner teacher. So that's all I need to focus on: choosing you. Practicing that, from moment to moment, whenever I catch myself secretly hating me or anyone or thing else, pulls the plug on the guilt in my mind. Eventually it dies of malnutrition. Then I open my eyes, and all that's left is love?"

I looked up and Jesus was gone. In imaginary form that is. But I could still feel his smiling presence. I did hope he'd caught that last analogy, though. I thought it was pretty damn good. I went back into the kitchen to warm up my coffee. The zombie baby started banging her head against the chair again; go figure. I turned her off, picked up the dog, and headed back to my computer.

What Do You Ask for in Your Heart?

"I'm not talking about this now," I said, barricading myself in the fox hole of my office against incoming verbal shrapnel like any self-respecting ego. Feeling once more misunderstood, manipulated, unfairly treated, and falsely accused in a special relationship; just when I thought things were humming along benignly enough in my dream. The sudden, toxic turn of my projections left me licking my wounds, delicate feelings shredded, boundaries trampled; blah, blah, blah.

Ken Wapnick's sage advice to simply remember *A Course in Miracles* workbook lesson 5: "I am never upset for the reason I think" and 34: "I could see peace instead of this," seemed a lifeline, dangled in mockery, just beyond my reach. "So you became afraid again; just don't take it seriously," I could hear my right mind cooing. "Seriously?" I wanted to shriek. Because unlike that cock-eyed optimist, I knew only too well that if I left this room I would find myself back in the fray; one or more dream figures in my face again, waxing thunderously eloquent about my many failures.

And so I turned, as I often do, to the big, blue book itself, for solace. Ironically, I had been reading workbook lesson 185: "I want the peace of God" again, and, as usual, had conjured my attraction to its opposite. My reaction to the ensuing drama in a close relationship illuminated just how much I must secretly want to prove the reality of this guilty, unloving self I *really* hold close, a shield against the punishment we're all convinced we deserve for coveting individuality in the first place and participating in the ego's collective cover-up. Still, a part of me really does want the peace of God, really does want to experience itself as worthy of all-inclusive, unwavering love. Only I can't experience it *and* still hold on to these trippy, painful dreams of persecution.

See, I want the peace of God, but I want it *my* way, right here, right now, in my kitchen. I want to gracefully negotiate it, if you know what I mean, to bring these wayward others in line with my elevated reasoning, in a civilized conversation involving wild blueberry muffins and well-brewed cups of dark-roast Joe. I want agreement among my costars, to serve as a silent ambassador for peaceful behavior they will happily and gratefully emulate.

But apparently, it doesn't work that way. To say I want the peace of God means I relinquish all attachment to private, separate interests and outcomes. And there's the rub. Because the body I still think I am fears for other bodies unwilling to cooperate with its higher understanding and expanding clarity. The body I still think I am longs to take literally passages in this lesson that seem to allude to a human joining that belies everything *A Course in Miracles* says about the world and its seeming inhabitants vying for survival:

> Many have said these words. But few indeed have meant them. You have but to look upon the world you see around you to be sure how very few they are. The world would be completely changed, should any two agree these words express the only thing they want. (Paragraph 2, lines 6-9)

But the agreement, of course, is never among other dream figures, considering the startling fact that, well, there are no dream figures! The agreement is always and only about *my* sincere willingness to *disagree* with the one ego's dire, hateful interpretation of events, thereby agreeing with the one right mind's certainty that only truth remains. "Not one note in Heaven's song was missed" by an insane desire to experience ourselves other than whole and eternal; loved and loving. The agreement is merely my decision to align with the one right mind we share; to join in the only relationship truly available, our relationship with the memory of wholeness within the one mind capable of teaching us to heal our mistaken belief in the sin of separation realized.

> Two minds with one intent become so strong that what they will becomes the Will of God. For minds can only join in truth. (Paragraph 3, lines 1-2)

And that means it is always only *my* seemingly separated mind in need of joining with the truth held and protected in our one right mind. Because here in the broken condition I find myself in I cannot ever completely agree with anyone or anything. My very seeming survival depends on protecting the illusion of our differences, the strength of our vying positions, our dependencies and declarations of independence, that shore up the illusion of our very existence.

> In dreams, no two can share the same intent. To each, the hero of the dream is different; the outcome wanted not the same for both. Loser and gainer merely shift about in changing patterns, as the ratio of gain to loss and loss to gain takes on a different aspect or another form. (Paragraph 3, lines 3-5)

A Course in Miracles does not mince words about what our minds on ego are really up to here in our relationships within the dream we call our lives. We compromise and sacrifice, bargain, manipulate, and seduce to get our needs met. When our negotiated agreements are inevitably reneged upon, all hell breaks loose and we self-righteously brandish our betrayal. Or, we learn to stop and recognize there is a better way of relating in this so-called world, that we haven't a clue about what we really want, but are willing to learn from a new inner teacher that does. We can stop, and sincerely ask that teacher to tell us what we really want to learn.

> What do you ask for in your heart? Forget the words you use in making your requests. Consider but what you believe will comfort you, and bring you happiness. But be you not dismayed by lingering illusions, for their form is not what matters now. (Paragraph 8, lines 2-5)

What do I really ask for in my heart? I ask for peace. I ask for healing. I ask to learn I feel better when I release you from the bondage of my opinions and the conditions of my love. I ask to see you and me as the same, regardless of the gory details of our ego meltdowns. To remember we still love each other, even when our behavior speaks otherwise. To remember we share the same split mind made mad by guilt and the same reassuring inner teacher that knows we are already home, our seemingly broken heart still beating as one.

Let not some dreams be more acceptable, reserving shame and secrecy for others. They are one. And being one, the question should be asked of all of them. 'Is this what I would have, in place of Heaven and the peace of God?' (Paragraph 8, lines 6-8)

Even though these dreams of our deep fissure rattle me to the seeming bone and almost convince me once more that love is gone for good, I know that underneath it all I want the peace of God. And I am learning, from moment to moment, to withdraw my hopes of finding answers in an illusion that has never delivered on its promises, and listen to that inner cockeyed optimist instead. Because it remains certainly grounded in vital information I have forgotten.

It is this one intent we seek today, uniting our desires with the need of every heart, the call of every mind, the hope that lies beyond despair, the love attack would hide, the brotherhood that hate has sought to sever, but which still remains as God created it. With Help like this beside us, can we fail today as we request the peace of God be given us? (Paragraph 14)

Not very God-damn likely!

I Want It, I Want It, I Want It, No, Wait; What Is It Again?

I'd been working with making inner peace my goal from moment to moment in what Ken Wapnick refers to as the "classroom" of our lives, in which we learn to release ourselves from the bondage of the ego thought system of individual differences and separate interests by making forgiveness, ACIM-style, our new life's purpose. Although feeling victimized by a special relationship's seemingly manipulative ways days earlier, I'd at least been able to look with my inner imaginary Jesus—that *symbol* of the one, awakened mind we all share—at the specious nature of my reasoning. And enjoy, if not yet exactly peace, at least the helpful, theoretical awareness that I was the director of the movie of this so-called life and not the beleaguered protagonist. I could claim my saved seat in the theatre's audience beside the inner teacher of kindness whenever I was ready. But I knew I had not yet done so because I found myself still hooked on what to do in form. Still puzzling over how to express love while remaining firm about my position; still certain of a *me* doing the puzzling, a position to defend, and—in this case—a child to protect from her own (in my humble opinion) wayward wishes.

In an effort to entertain myself while awaiting the inevitable return to right-mindedness, I randomly opened the big, blue book to *A Course in Miracles'* Teachers Manual—a practice I refer to as "The Course as Ouija Board"—trusting that the answer I really needed to the question I was really asking would reveal itself as it always does (no matter what page I turn to). "What Is the Peace of God?" I read, the powerful, welcome realization that I did not know of peace washing over me, anew, filling me with gratitude that only from this place of total resignation on behalf of the self I still think I am could I begin to embrace the Self I truly want to remember, regardless of seeming circumstances. A Self that includes the entire imaginary cast of characters I've invented in my ultimately feeble efforts to push the reflection of real, all-inclusive love, from far beyond these bodies we think we interact with, away.

The section clearly describes the attributes of God's peace versus the occasional pauses in our dramas we sometimes experience, usually as a result of acute exhaustion from the battles we robotically wage in the dream and the decision to reach for yet another tempting "fix" in one form or another. Conversely, God's peace—the memory of which our right mind holds in its gentle embrace—has absolutely no reference here in the condition we think we're in, and nothing to do with the adrenaline spikes or tranquil interludes we deem pleasure. Its characteristics are—in every way and without exception—*other* than anything we have experienced in a seeming world of linear time we invented to act out our secret wish to exist at our creator's expense. Rather, God's peace:

> ... calls to mind nothing that went before. It brings with it no past associations. It is a new thing entirely ... The past just slips away, and in its place is everlasting quiet. Only that. (From *A Course in Miracles* Manual for Teachers, 20. WHAT IS THE PEACE OF GOD, paragraph 2)

Only that. *I know*; easy for Jesus to say, right? But how can "I" access a peace I don't even know exists? How can I make it my goal throughout my day when its nature completely eludes my current understanding? Funny I should ask.

> ... No one can fail to find it who but seeks out its conditions. God's peace can never come where anger is, for anger must deny that peace exists. Who sees anger as justified in any way or any circumstance proclaims that peace is meaningless, and must believe that it cannot exist. In this condition, peace cannot be found. Therefore, forgiveness is the necessary condition for finding the peace of God. (From paragraph 3)

I smacked myself upside the head! I was still trying to justify anger, still trying to conceal it behind a façade of non-judgment.

But only the Course's forgiveness—looking at our tumultuous lives, our addiction to anger and hallucinations of unfair treatment at the hands of imaginary others with the part of our mind eternally grounded in the quiet center of all-inclusive union within—will free us. Only the Course's gentle forgiveness of what never was will teach us that nothing we do in form will solve the problem because nothing exists outside the mind that dreamed it up.

Despite our elaborate attempts to rationalize and defend our positions, the problem remains within the one mind that mistakenly believed its experiment in individuality had real effects. When I willingly return to the inner teacher that knows otherwise, all the complexity of how to respond to seemingly external situations dissolves, all worry about the most loving thing to do vanishes, and any action I take in form springs only from the eternally loving present. I will automatically say or do whatever is most truly helpful for all concerned. Certain of healing and no longer bound by whether or not the object of my projection heeds my advice.

Reading these words helped remove the stubborn stain of darkness obscuring my vision in this apparent situation, along with all urgency to "talk it out" (how well has that ever worked out?) or decide for them or me. In fact, I found it impossible to recall what had so frightened me to begin with and could only smile at the folly of it all. Still, I knew from experience that this was an ongoing scene in my dream, likely to challenge me again. So how to hold onto my peace? The author of the passage had anticipated the question; go figure. (How does he do that?)

How is the peace of God retained, once it is found? Returning anger, in whatever form, will drop the heavy curtain once again, and the belief that peace cannot exist will certainly return ... Now must you again lay down your sword, although you do not recognize that you have picked it up again ... Stop for a moment now and think of this: Is conflict what you want, or is God's peace the better choice? Which gives you more? (From paragraph 4)

√

Until we have allowed the undoing of all the unconscious guilt in our mind through practicing forgiveness, day in and day out, with whatever appears to arise in our classroom, our attraction to anger—our desire to see the problem as we set it up outside the mind instead of as it really is within—will inevitably return. But we can learn to stop ourselves as we reach for that muscle of judgment, condemnation, and false self-defense. Simply, stop and ask ourselves honestly what we really want. What choice will further our reunion with wholly eternal love, and what choice will delay it?

And so, today, again in this moment, I choose to catch myself reaching to exercise the muscle of dueling interests and victimization, stop, and reach instead for the muscle of forgiveness. Knowing that doing so furthers the former's atrophy and the latter's power. I am thereby enveloped once more in the peace that always waits for us just beyond our limited field of vision, offering us all we have ever really wanted.

What is the peace of God? No more than this; the simple understanding that His Will is wholly without opposite. (From paragraph 6)

Amen to that.

Confessions of a Gentleness Wannabe

Although I'd fallen asleep the night before praying for help in finding my AWOL inner teacher of kindness, I awoke painfully aware I'd been harshly judging someone in my dream. A person I'd just met, a beautiful, young woman with perfect hair whose intellectual prowess I'd been delighting in inwardly questioning. She might have strolled off the pages of one of those celebrity rags amply available at the fitness center where I work out. The ones I relish mindlessly flipping through while furiously pedaling nowhere on a stationary bike, inwardly rejoicing in the latest news of Hollywood's finest, dressed to the gills, as they posed on the red carpet, entered rehab, signed divorce papers, or struggled to conceal their latest botched rendezvous with a plastic surgeon.

"Damn," I thought, pulling the covers up over my head as if to hide from my inner bully. Ever since I'd attended a workshop with Ken Wapnick in October I really had tried to put gentleness at the forefront of my practice with this Course. To remember that everyone was fighting the same hard battle here in this illusion of exile from perfect love, suffering under the same delusion of a mind made mad by guilt. Split over its failure to smile at the ridiculous idea that we could separate from the eternal wholeness of our true nature. After all, as *A Course in Miracles* Teachers' Manual reminds us in 4. WHAT ARE THE CHARACTERISTICS OF GOD'S TEACHERS? IV. Gentleness:

> ... No teacher of God but must learn,—and fairly early in his training,—that harmfulness completely obliterates his function from his awareness. It will make him confused, fearful, angry and suspicious. It will make the Holy Spirit's lessons impossible to learn. Nor can God's Teacher be heard at all, except by those who realize that harm can actually achieve nothing. No gain can come of it. (From paragraph 1)

Although I often succeeded in recognizing my same split mind at work in everyone and thing I seemed to encounter—compassion welling up within for all—just as often I veered uncomfortably close to my hard-wired gentleness-resistance. At times, the more I sought to kindly respond to everyone and thing (ignoring the ego's distinction between animate and inanimate), the more my urge to attack—and justify doing so—seemed to flourish.

Besides, real shit happened! I *know*. But still, I'm just saying, my computer crashed again. The ATM machine ate my debit card. I slipped and fell on a patch of ice. I stubbed my toe, cut my finger while making dinner; was inexplicably assaulted by random, searing nerve pain in my jaw, ear, neck, shoulders, and ribs. One day I ran a fever, the next I couldn't stay warm. Presidential contenders just kept flooding the airwaves with their dubious economic solutions. Meanwhile, an inner newscaster tallied up every lost opportunity to choose gentleness over murder, as one challenge after another in my special relationships appeared to catapult me back into that rawest of unloved and unloving places, mocking my doomed progress with this Course. And now—even in my sleeping dreams—I couldn't stop projecting!

Jesus stood in the corner waiting, I could tell. "What are you doing here," I mumbled, from beneath my worn comforter. After all, I'd dropped by his office quite a few times in the past few days, but he was always out to lunch. Chatting it up with all those other Course students out there, no doubt. Responding to something someone posted on Facebook.

"Hey," he said, reading my mind. How did he do that?

"I'm not coming out," I said.

There was a long silence. I mean *long*. The man had the patience of a saint.

"I know what you're thinking," I said, eventually.

"You always do."

"You'll wait here in hell with me until I'm ready. But, seriously, where were you Monday when I needed you, and Tuesday afternoon? OK, so maybe I wasn't quite ready to look at my curriculum with you but for just once in my life don't you think you might entertain the possibility of seeing *my* way? Just so you could understand what I'm talking about. You know; give and take; that's what relationships are all about, isn't it? Are you an Aries, by any chance? Taurus?"

"Ha!"

"OK, listen. This little Dalai Lama impersonation of mine is just not working out. All it makes me see is how violent I really am. I mean, storming through my days, pounding the pavement, having it my way, devouring the tasks on my plate."

"Wreaking havoc, plowing through."

"Exactly. Do you have any idea how many doors I slam on a given day?"

"Work day or holiday?"

"I'm being serious here."

"I can see that."

"I mean, what kind of advanced teacher of God in training do I think I am? It is so not OK not to look at the places in which I still think it's OK to project."

"Come again?"

"But then, when I finally do look, I see it everywhere! It's really discouraging! Because, to heal my mind of the idea of separation fueling my attachment to a mortal life filled with upholding and defending my individuality and secretly fed by a thought system of sin, guilt, and fear born of a tiny mad idea of murderous insubordination, I must see everyone and thing innocent first! And there's just too freaking many of them. It's exhausting!"

"When you put it like that ... "

"If we are one, and guiltless of our original attack on God that started this whole charade of a cover-up, then I must first hold you guiltless to experience it myself. I get that; I really do. There is no other way than this. All my blame and mindless cherishing of differences must go. But I mean, there are only so many hours in a day and I can't be expected to forgive while I'm sleeping! At this rate I'll never make it home this time around!"

"Well, actually ..."

"Yeah, yeah, yeah. I am home in capital T Truth—not Susan, but my real capital S self—blah, blah, blah. But we're talking about *awakening* to that awareness, and we're running out of time. So I have a better idea. Why not just get the hell out of Dodge right now; you know what I'm saying? Just forget about all these nut cases out there and blow this entire illusory pop stand. Sing Kumbaya, admit God is, and call it a final dream day?"

"Could you hum a few bars?"

"Ha. No, really. Please just take me home. Right now. I call, Uncle! You are right and I am so completely wrong. Just get me out of here." I reached my hand out of the covers to grab his and suddenly found myself in class again, seated beside him, staring at the big screen, the objects of my projection—animate and inanimate—flashing benignly by, along with photos of the dream figure I still think I am. Funny, in an instant, I could no longer tell one from the other ... and then they were gone.

"I know what you're thinking," I said.

"Go on."

"Maybe I could just try seeing with you in the first place. My thoughts are simply images I have made and all that jazz. Outward pictures of an inward condition that—in reality—has already been treated and healed, leaving only creation's invulnerable, robust gentleness. And then, when I forget, just not make such a big deal about it. No Course students in danger of never finding their way home. No stressing over failing electronic devices to avenge, bodies writhing in pain, bumbling, talking bobble heads vying for control of the never-really-actually-free-anyway world."

"Broken hearts, slamming doors," he said.

"Right." I looked back at the blank screen, and sighed. "Maybe I could just look with you at the ugliness of everything and simply smile at the silliness of it all."

"Well, no harm in that," Jesus said.

> ... What choice but this has meaning to the sane? Who chooses hell when he perceives a way to Heaven? And who

would choose the weakness that must come from harm in place of the unfailing, all-encompassing, and limitless strength of gentleness? The might of God's teachers lies in their gentleness, for they have understood their evil thoughts came neither from God's Son nor his Creator. Thus did they join their thoughts with Him Who is their Source. And so their will, which always was His Own, is free to be itself. (From paragraph 2)

Making It About Them

For weeks I'd been listening to a brilliant CD set of Ken Wapnick's entitled *Cast No One Out,* in which he recommends we "make it about them" in our relationships. By that I believe he means shifting our fixed focus from the perceived personal needs and interests of our seemingly separate selves to considering the needs and interests of others, as an interim step in beginning to recognize we share only one need: to remember our sameness within God. Wherein we remain eternally completed, loved, and loving, despite the separated, embodied condition we've dreamt up that appears to have cost us everything. Everyone here is fighting the same desperate battle; secretly begging to have someone else let them off the hook; include them in the loving gaze of right-minded forgiveness that transcends the ego's bogus body of evidence to the contrary.

I was excited at first, faithfully writing the words out on yellow sticky notes, one for my computer, one for my desk, and one for my purse. *Make it about them,* I reminded myself while walking my dog, catching my impatience rising as she sniffed about in the park tugging at her leash. After all, the holidays were approaching and already wreaking havoc with the beloved routines that kept her feeling safe. (I think I could relate to that.) *Make it about them,* I thought, asking a cashier how her day was going, and really listening. After all, she worked long hours for little pay, no doubt forced to endure all sorts of abuse from fellow dream figures. (I think I could relate to that.) *Make it about them,* I remembered, waving a driver aggressively nudging into my lane ahead, with a little right-minded smile. Probably late for work or dropping off the kids, poor guy. (I think I could relate to that.)

But as I continued to listen—my new mantra sinking deeper into the barren, fissured desert of my gray matter and the opportunities to apply it broadening from more trivial seeming encounters to special relationships—I realized I was not a happy camper. My inner ego feminist in particular had major issues with the whole make-it-about-them approach. Women, after all, had been making it about everyone else throughout the history of recorded time, for Christ's sake! Martyring themselves within their family and social units, manipulating to have their needs met through a vicious, self-defeating cycle of dependency and sacrifice. I had only recently begun to release this pattern in my own life, and couldn't quite grasp how Ken's approach differed from the compulsion to always put others first that had so long seemingly enslaved and secretly enraged my gender.

Then, too, as I strived to make it about them in my special relationships, the ego launched a retrospective film fest of the many ways in which they had failed to ever consider for once in their selfish little lives making it about *me*. The many ways in which they had failed to give any thought whatsoever to the hard battle *I* was waging here in this nightmare of exile from eternal wholeness, especially given my highly sensitive and spiritually inclined nature. As I sat watching past DVDs of our lives together while still struggling to make it about them, the ego upped the ante, narrating in booming voiceover a review of all the ways in which we had failed each other, illuminating the spectacular, glaring differences which made lasting peace between us impossible. In short, I caught myself once more red-handed, falsely, madly, deeply clinging to the notion that I could ace this freaking Course if only I didn't have to contend with these nut cases "out there," hell-bent on keeping me from ever finding my way home!

Jesus! I said, covering my eyes with my cupped hands in an effort to see no more evil, inwardly screaming for help. And then, in one hell of a holy instant, I got it. If there's no one truly "out there," as the Course insists over and over again there is not, then I am *only, always* looking at my own, insane, multiple, guiltily self-accused personalities! If there is truly no one out there (but I still imagine there is, and I do), then the only way I can heal the idea of separation in my mind and experience my own innocence, and thereby wholeness, is by first witnessing it in you. Although I had understood this most fundamental of Course concepts on an intellectual and occasionally practical level, I really got it this time in a difficult-to-describe, more visceral way that delivered a blast of relief and gratitude.

I randomly flipped open the big, blue, book for further clarity, trusting from experience that whatever page I turned to would offer the perfect reminder from the inner teacher of forgiveness I truly craved, a truth that thankfully transcended the highly sensitive, spiritually-inclined nut case holding the book.

"Today we are considering the will you share with God," I read, from *A Course in Miracles* workbook lesson 73, "I will there be light. This is not the same as the ego's idle wishes, out of which darkness and nothingness arise ... Idle wishes and grievances are partners or co-makers in picturing the world you see. The wishes of the ego gave rise to it, and the ego's need for grievances, which are necessary to maintain it, peoples it with figures that seem to attack you and call for 'righteous' judgment. These figures become the middlemen the ego employs to traffic in grievances. They stand between your awareness and your brother's reality. Beholding them, you do not know your brothers or your Self." (From paragraphs 1 and 2)

If I can learn to make it about the nut cases I've imagined to traffic in my grievances—recognizing the fear of real love masked by my idle wishes to exert another, fantasized will rather than allow the will I share with our Creator—I can learn to recognize and accept my true nature. To allow the healing of the one split mind that insists on a righteous hierarchy in which some dream figures deserve forgiveness (as if we were actually being asked to forgive imaginary individuals) while others continue to thwart my journey home. If I can learn to make it about them— recognizing the bad day they may be having within my dream, suspending my judgment of their behavior in a film I wrote, produced, directed, and hired them to costar in—I can learn to forgive myself for my wayward creations. And gently smile with an inner teacher who sees beyond all the special effects to the one and only capital T Truth that I am loved, you are loved; he, she, and it are loved, forever, always, and without exception.

We will succeed today if you remember that you want salvation for yourself. You want to accept God's plan because you share in it. You have no will that can really oppose it, and you do not want to do so. Salvation is for you. Above all else, you want the freedom to remember Who you really are. Today it is the ego that stands powerless before your will. Your will is free, and nothing can prevail against it. (Paragraph 7)

I guess making it about them means joining with my real will to remember my real Self by changing my mind about the cause and purpose of all the nut cases I cooked up to make me forget. I truly, madly, deeply want to learn to do that!

Kindness Created Me Kind; Oh, Never Mind!

I appeared to be battling another particularly nasty bout of what I've come to think of as *A Course in Miracles*-resistance flu, a malaise that strikes ever more viciously the closer I come to glimpsing our one, true, loving nature beyond this blockbuster nightmare of an especially traumatized separate self. A body I still believe I inhabit, beyond which lies only the great void left in the wake of my selfish decision to turn my back on God for good.

I had tried going to the movies again to cheer myself up and distract from the internal fray, but made the whack job decision to see the recently released *Melancholia*, in which Kirsten Dunst offers a harrowing performance as a woman devolving into the blazing inferno of depression followed by a family coping with the possibility of the end of the world via a rogue planet (who knew we had this to worry about, too?) colliding with earth in slow motion, delivered in Technicolor detail through the magic of special effects. Suffice it to say, I slept little for several nights, haunted by the gigantic orb inching closer in my inner sky, unloving thoughts about a cast of characters I know I created in my own little apocryphal movie but still take seriously swirling about my tiny little head.

Somehow, in my misery, the phrase "Kindness created me like itself" bobbed to the surface of my scant gray matter, causing me to turn to workbook lesson 67, "Love created me like itself," hoping revisiting that preposterous-to-the ego statement might somehow help dispel these haunting images. The lesson invites us to contemplate our true nature as perfectly, eternally completed within the non-dualistic, all-inclusive love of our source, versus the current, guilty, rogue bodily state in which we believe we find ourselves encapsulated. It asks us to begin by repeating the title statement, and then adding similar relevant thoughts about our true nature, such as "Kindness created me kind," despite all bodily evidence to the contrary the ego has amassed.

We are not asked to use these as robotic affirmations, but to genuinely allow their meaning to gently replace the ego's 24/7 rant of what the Course calls "specialness." The mindless allegiance we pay to a thought system based on the idea that we truly pulled off the "sin" of separation from our source, and must now struggle to preserve our new, mortal identities at the expense of everyone and everything seemingly at odds with us in a dualistic universe.

"Gentleness created me gentle," I said, unconvinced, but wishing to believe. "Wellness created me well."

"Sarcasm created you sarcastic," the ego countered, with a little, maniacal smile. "Self-righteousness created you self-righteous."

I covered my ears and resumed. "Love created me loving, Tolerance created me tolerant. Compassion created me compassionate." After all, everyone else seemingly here in this illusion of exile from perfect love was suffering under the same crushing guilt born of the delusion of specialness, frantically trying to prove they exist as individuals but it's not their fault.

"Self-deception created you self-deceptive. Ignorance created you ignorant. Neediness created you needy."

It had a point. I was one gigantic walking, talking bundle of needs when I chose the ego as my teacher. But I could choose otherwise. I had done it before and—by God—I could do it again.

"Completeness created me complete," I said, raising my voice in an effort to drown out you know who.

"Unworthiness created you unworthy. Superiority created you superior."

"Do you realize you just contradicted yourself?" I said. "I mean; how crazy is that?"

It yawned. "What can I say; insanity created you insane. Sue me."

I rolled my eyes and turned back to the lesson.

We are trying today to undo your definition of God and replace it with His Own ... try to reach past all your images and preconceptions about yourself to the truth in you. If love created you like itself, this Self must be in you. And somewhere in your mind it is there for you to find. (From paragraphs 2 and 3)

"Patience created me patient," I said. "Wholeness created me whole."

"Divisiveness created you divisive."

"Creativity created me creative!"

"Delusion created you deluded."

"Zip it," I said.

"Hey, don't forget who made you what you are today."

"Jesus!" I cried, in desperation, begging for the insight of another teacher, and was suddenly transported back to that classroom again, sitting across the desk from that *symbol* of the part of our mind aware of our hallucinations, but confident they are only a passing dream from which we have already awakened to find ourselves still wholly alive within our creator's love.

"You never write; you never call," he said.

"I know what you're thinking," I said.

"You always do."

"I've been trying to do this by myself again, haven't I?"

"How's that been working out for you?"

"Yeah. The thing is, I don't really believe love created me like itself, you know? I mean, the more I try to make kindness and gentleness the focus of my day, the more apocalyptic my dream becomes. But I know what you're thinking. That's what I need to look at. My attraction to the belief in annihilation, the erroneous thought that I traded my eternal, loving identity for this mess of insecure, misunderstood and misunderstanding protoplasm incapable of finding happiness where it doesn't exist."

"Well put."

"And that denying the ego's voice, or trying to shout it down, only gives it more power. Instead I should simply watch and listen with you, thereby remembering not to take it seriously."

"Humor created you humorous."

"Exactly. Like the lesson says, 'You need to hear the truth about yourself as frequently as possible, because your mind is so preoccupied with false self-images.' (Paragraph 5, line 2) But I can't let the false images go until I see them with you as my teacher. And that means not going to the movies by myself, *ever*; going only with you!"

"Funny; I just happen to be available."

I sighed. "You might want to put on some real shoes and a jacket," I said. "It's freaking freezing out there."

"Imagine that," he said.

I Am the Peace of God! (Who knew?)

I had fallen asleep the night before uttering the same prayer, the title of *A Course in Miracles* workbook lesson 185—*I want the peace of God*—I'd been invoking for weeks. It echoed in my head as I awoke and awoke again during the night in my restless way, finally opening my eyes at dawn on a class in progress with the inner teacher of wholeness, in which I must have nodded off. My imaginary Jesus—that *symbol* of our one mind healed of the thought of separation from our source—stood at the whiteboard scribbling variations on the theme.

"Repeat after me," he said. "I *am* the peace of God."

I rubbed my eyes—thinking I might still be dreaming—and sat up straighter at my imaginary classroom desk. "Seriously?" I asked. Because you could call me a lot of things lately, but not so much the peace of God. He must have mixed me up again with some other Course student.

He threw back his head and laughed. "Peace = God," he said, pointing at the block letters. "Joy = God. Peace + joy = God. Pain − guilt = innocence. Innocence = peace = joy = God."

Easy for him to say, but we both knew I never could stay focused on equations. Still, I sort of knew where he was going with this. Constantly chanting *I want the peace of God* had become its own kind of impediment to my awareness of real love. Implying, as it did, that the inner peace of everlasting wholeness lay always just beyond reach, available in an impossible-to-fathom future that never quite arrived. Leaving me vacillating between a state of extreme, ego-crafted darkness, in which the pain of a special relationship seemed more bottomless and impossible to transcend than ever, and a state of unspeakable grace, in which I experienced the vast certainty of our all-inclusive innocence and complete release from all thoughts of guilt, failure, and fear. But just as the Course warns us, each time I allowed myself to partake of the latter; the ego upped the ante again to convince me to pay attention to its illusory drama. Entreating me to immediately react, or perish. And I went charging toward the screen again to work it out with my costars, completely forgetting my real role as screenwriter/director.

"I know what you're thinking," I said.

"You always do."

"There's nothing to work out in an illusion."

"Well said."

"The thing is, the closer I get to believing I deserve the peace of God, the more I seem to suffer. No offense, but it's like crucifixion is my default position, you know what I'm saying?"

He smiled. "Not really."

"Jesus," I said. "I feel like I'm losing my mind."

"Imagine that."

"I mean, I want the peace of God, I really do. I've been around the block. I know this psycho world holds nothing that I want. I've tried it all, and yet, I still find myself blaming myself for failing at everything. You know, as if there were a real self to blame, a real crime committed."

He nodded.

I lay my throbbing head down in my folded arms. It was so exhausting. Over the last few weeks, I had caught myself again and again feeling unfairly treated by others, while fully aware I could be still at any moment and go home, that the judgment I was about to level, the comparison I was about to draw, the statement I was about to make, was not in my best interests. But forging ahead with it anyway, experiencing a nanosecond of satisfaction followed by obliterating guilt and self-judgment. Not to mention another ranting (albeit secretly gleeful) lecture from the inner teacher of separation realized about my dismal chances of ever awakening through forgiveness ACIM-style, given my glaring inability to consistently do what it says.

I sighed, and raised my heavy head.

Jesus was still smiling—go figure—pointer still hovering over the words: "I am the peace of God." The big, blue book lay open to *A Course in Miracles* workbook lesson 191: I am the holy Son of God Himself.

> What have you done that this should be your world? What have you done that this is what you see? Deny your own Identity and this is what remains. You look on chaos and proclaim it yourself. There is no sight that fails to witness this to you. There is no sound that does not speak of frailty within you and without; no breath you draw that does not seem to bring you nearer death; no hope you hold but will dissolve in tears. (Paragraph 2)

"Well, thanks for the little pep talk," I said.

"It was nothing."

"Ha! Anyway; I know what you're thinking. When I sided with the tiny, mad idea that we could separate from our source and assumed an imaginary body in which to act out that fantasy, I denied my true nature in an attempt to make the error of believing a preposterous thought real. To return to the peace I think I left, I need to 'deny the denial of truth.' That's how I remember I remain loved and loving; by looking at the chaos, the hopelessness, the frailty of this so-called life with you, and seeing it for the smoke and mirrors it is. That's how I eventually learn to experience the eternal state of unspeakable grace I am. But Susan can't wake Susan up. Only completely giving up on any investment in how the story of Susan will end can allow me to finally open my eyes on our one, true nature. That's how I experience peace. And joy. And innocence."

"Go on," he said

"God minus Susan's little guilty self; equals peace. But Susan can't subtract Susan from the equation. Only the part of my mind that made Susan up can release her in its own good time, when its fear of punishment for a crime that never happened finally abates. When its belief in the self it still sees in the mirror gently gives way to our real identity that lies beyond the body's eyes. Until then I need only admit I don't know what's in my own best interests whenever I find myself believing in the dream and its dire consequences again. Admit I don't know the answer to anything. Hell; I can't even remember the question. When I do that, the urgent, ego-hijacked struggle drops away, and faith that I will remember, when I'm ready to let the thought of Susan go, returns. "

He smiled. "I think you might be growing up."

"Seriously?"

He didn't answer.

"I know what you're thinking; seriously *not* seriously."

He just kept smiling that smile of his.

I had to smile, too.

My Home Awaits Me

"Close your eyes, and breathe deeply," I said. "As you inhale, focus on all that stress and worry you've been dragging around. As you exhale, imagine releasing all that baggage back into the nothingness from which it sprang. Now, see if you can visualize a solid root sprouting out the base of your spine and burrowing deeply downward, securing you firmly into Mother Earth, anchoring you into a well of perpetual safety."

I opened my eyes ever so slightly. Also sitting cross-legged, hands resting upward on knees, fingers pinched together just like mine; my imaginary Jesus had one eye open, and quickly shut it. I'd whisked him away for a little imaginary retreat. He'd had a lot on his plate over the last few weeks and, besides, I figured we'd been running in different circles too long and could use a little quality time together.

"Sit up straight," I said.

He threw back his shoulders.

We sat on cushions filled with beans in an open-air room high on a pristine mountain of unknown origin; a soft breeze rustling sheer curtains hung from carved wooden pillars. An alpine meadow embroidered with embryonic flowers fanned out to the East. A brook gurgled nearby. I had come here many times before in meditation, though always solo; and was looking forward to showing it off; hell, maybe even teaching him a thing or two about achieving serenity here in psycho land.

I paused, savoring the bellow-like action of my own lungs to the tune of Jesus breathing deeply and evenly beside me. "Now begin to feel a gentle but steady energy flowing from the earth and spilling into your root chakra at the base of your spine, symbolizing your foundation; your safety and security in this world."

Jesus caught his breath. I opened my eyes to find him watching me, mouth twitching to prevent him from busting out laughing like a kid caught firing spit balls in a middle-school classroom.

"Hey, Mister," I said, using my best middle-school teacher voice. Resurrected from my days of actually attempting to teach adolescents creative writing, a process akin to attempting to teach my small dog to read.

He pursed his lips and closed his eyes again.

"Now, try to imagine the energy beginning to spin in your root chakra, a vibrant red light rhythmically pulsing and energizing your entire body." Counter clock-wise or clock-wise? Damn, I couldn't even remember which way the chakras were supposed to spin. One way energized; the other de-energized. Hell, I couldn't even decide which one I wanted. In my post-New Year's hyper yet mysteriously depleted state, I had dipped back into my bag of magic tricks successfully used to calm the body down years ago. But it was so not working for me now. How could I expect it to work for Jesus?

"OK," I said, "just forget about that. Repeat after me, 'Om Namah Shivaya, Om Namah Shivaya.'" I began chanting the beautiful, haunting words to the Hindu mantra used in meditation I had participated in many times on visits to a nearby ashram and yoga training center. I think it translates as something like, "I bow to Shiva," or my supreme Self; an admirable sentiment that pointed to truth. But this time, my mind refused to surrender, still immersed in analysis of the seemingly complicated, trying events of the past few weeks, not to mention which way I wanted the freaking chakras to spin. I opened my eyes.

Jesus' other eye popped open, in unison.

I sighed, and dug into my pocket. "Crystal," I said, offering him a chunk of rose quartz.

He made no move to grasp it.

"Bordeaux chocolate?" I asked. I had stuffed a box of See's candy into my bag, just in case. "Glass of Marlborough sauvignon blanc?" This was my fantasy, after all; a choice bottle lay chilled in a bucket in the corner.

Jesus could no longer contain himself. He threw back his head, and merrily laughed, holding his sides and rocking back and forth.

I gave him my stone face—what the middle-school kids referred to as my "CIA agent" look—narrowing my eyes and drawing my lips together, but he just laughed harder (more kindly, of course, than they had, but still), tears rolling down his holy cheeks. And before I knew it, I was laughing hysterically, too, mysteriously born aloft and transported once more back to that imaginary inner classroom, in conference once more with our robed wonder.

I eventually managed to find my voice, albeit still quavering with contagious mirth. "I know what you're thinking," I said.

He nodded, wiping his eyes.

I had just begun the second part of *A Course in Miracles* workbook (offering a glimpse of our true identity within our creator beyond this hallucination of fragmented exile from all-inclusive love) again. In the past, my resistance to these brief, revelatory lessons had prevented me from allowing them to penetrate our one, true heart; even the lesson titles slipping away but seconds after reading them each morning. But this time around, I noticed a marked shift. Each lesson lingered with me throughout the day, hovering in my awareness, ever-ready to share its comfort and certainty. In fact, I had just read lesson 226: "My home awaits me, I will hasten there," and used it effectively to remind me: "If I so choose, I can depart this world entirely … If I believe it has a value as I see it now, so will it still remain for me. But if I see no value in the world as I behold it, nothing that I want to keep as mine or search for as a goal, it will depart from me …" (From paragraph 1)

Although physically retreating from the world with my bag of magic tricks had served me well in the past, I no longer really needed to dodge an ego thought system fraught with differences, judgments, comparisons, and bodies jockeying for favor, power, and exoneration. (Not that I didn't still plan to do so from time, to time.) I only needed to change my mind about the purpose of the world, to see it once more as a classroom instead of a prison. To resist making it real by attempting to fix, solve, or flee it.

Maybe I only needed to look at it with Jesus—that symbol of our one awakened mind that remembered to laugh at what the Course calls the "tiny, mad idea" that we could separate from indivisible love. And make up a world to briefly survive in as individual bodies, attempting to deny responsibility for our "sin" by blaming it on other imaginary bodies. A robotic habit the day-in and day-out work of forgiving all I believed about myself had taught me I really wanted to break. Because I always felt better when I resigned as my own teacher and admitted I didn't know squat about anything. At which point, I returned to the part of my one mind that did, and smiled at the silly meaninglessness of it all.

Jesus—eavesdropping on my thoughts again—nodded. "Let's call it a wrap," he said.

I got up and turned on the TV—more coverage of the upcoming Republican primaries.

We looked at each other and just lost it again.

The Rock of Salvation

I had just posted my most recent interview with Ken Wapnick and sat in my office on a Monday morning reviewing the copious notes I'd taken during the February workshop I'd attended at the Foundation for *A Course in Miracles*. "What Jesus is describing when he refers to us is paranoid schizophrenia," I read, quoting Ken. Sitting in the lecture hall in Temecula I'd laughed out loud at that observation. But it didn't seem all that hilarious this morning as I gazed out the window at dead grass crusted with dirty ice and snow in a seemingly endless winter. Another day of howling winds that last week had blown over a kid at a local school bus stop and hurled a Chihuahua into the tangled branches of a tree, leaving me fearful about walking my five-pound dog, Kayleigh.

I'd slept fitfully again. The blanket on my lap did little to assuage a deeper cold that seemed to have settled into my bones over the last few days as my mind on ego stepped up its chilly lobbying efforts, intent on convincing me once and for all that this Course was just *so not* working for me. Although I'd experienced remarkable inner healing since returning from California, my certainty that all was well in truth had once more wavered, and the ego's backlash at my decision for right-mindedness seemed particularly real, vicious, beyond my control, and completely independent of any choice I had made.

I knew I was back to wanting things to go my way in form, to thinking that if I put a troubled relationship under the guidance of Jesus/Holy Spirit–that *symbol* of the part of our mind that knew beyond all shadows of ego doubt that the separation never happened—a superhero Jesus would swoop down and deliver my special requests with an Oscar-worthy, leading-man smile. In short, I was once more convinced there was a special me in need of special saving from the especially twisted drama playing out in my tortured little head. Once more enthralled by the serial adventures of Susan in a world I made up in which I had visions and heard voices and seemed to suffer at the hands of insensitive, walking, talking costars intent on having things go *their* way.

"What makes this Course so impossible to practice?" someone had asked, during the February workshop. And Ken had talked about the fifth stage in the Development of Trust in *A Course in Miracles* Manual for Teachers, in which all hell breaks loose as we realize we still identify with a body even though we intellectually grasp that the Course is saying there is no body. We literally do not exist as separated selves. That means none of our special relationships, including our special relationship with the big, blue book and—hardest to swallow of all–our special relationship with the self we think we see in the mirror—will ever work. At least not to the satisfaction of my mind on ego, madly invested in a hallucinated world designed to prove I exist independently from my creator but it's not my fault.

I know this is ultimately good news; once we open our eyes, anyway. I know I just need to learn to treat myself with the same compassion I'd extend to the mentally ill. But right now, sitting in this chair, at this desk, with this computer–staring down another week in a dream that seemed so fraught with weighty responsibilities demanding sacrifices I don't want to make–it felt like loss. "Jesus," I muttered, aloud, and found myself once more transported into his office. "We need to talk," I said, settling into my chair.

He sat at his desk in his robe and sandals, completely oblivious to the wind rattling the windows. "I see," he said.

As if. "The thing is; I seem to have skipped the fourth stage in the Development of Trust, you know, where everything is all hunky dory. I was wondering if you could show me how to get there and just let me chill out for several thousand seeming lifetimes? You know, to recover from this last year in the dream. I don't know if you've been watching the whole time, but it's been a pretty bumpy ride."

"You don't say."

"I know what you're thinking. The Development of Trust is not linear and not literal and only meant to give us a sense of the process of climbing the imaginary ladder home with you. But my point is; I'm tired of this resistance, OK?" I pressed my palms together like the good little Catholic girl I once tried and failed to be, and shot him my best, pleading, Susan-of-Arc look. "Can't you do something about this dream? Can't you give me a better dream, just this once?"

His brows shot up. "You think I can give you dreams?"

I sighed. "It's my dream, is what you mean."

He nodded.

"I know what you're thinking. I don't want a teacher that tells me I'm the problem; I want a teacher that agrees with me that someone or thing else is the problem."

"Ah," he said.

"Except now I'm really screwed. Because, I'm far enough along on this imaginary journey home to the place we never really left to know I feel absolutely horrid when I choose the ego as my teacher; so unloved and unloving and anxious and scared; like I do right now. So, I really do want to look with you. I really do want to learn I'm a mind, not a body. Even though I think I'm reading this book with eyes that see and a brain that thinks, the book is just a *symbol* of the one love in the mind I really never left. A love that embraces all the nut cases seemingly out to get me in the dream, including the nut case I think I am."

"Well put."

"I just need to look with the sanity of your vision at the seeming problem as it is and not the way I set it up, is what you're saying. And I suppose that means it's time for another captivating episode in the long-running series *Desperately Seeking Susan*. Really, I could watch those reruns a thousand times."

"I think you have," he said, as we filed into the theatre.

"You really are funny. Oh, by the way; I have to go to Motor Vehicles this afternoon to try to get a duplicate title for that car I'm trying to sell. You available for a screening of that little adventure?"

"Wouldn't miss it for the world," he said.

"Ha!"

And we settled in for another afternoon at the movies.

The Holy Spirit has the power to change the whole foundation of the world you see to something else; a basis not insane, on which a sane perception can be based, another world perceived. And one in which nothing is contradicted that would lead the Son of God to sanity and joy. Nothing attests to death and cruelty; to separation and to differences. For here is everything perceived as one, and no one loses that each one may gain. (ACIM Text, Chapter 25, VII. The Rock of Salvation, paragraph 5)

Let Me Want to Want the Problem Solved

I sighed, another of the sighs for which I was justly famous; a gold-medal-caliber sigh, were sighing ever to gain its rightful status as an Olympic event. "Jesus," I said, head bowed, elbows resting on the edge of his office desk.

He handed me a box of tissues.

I blew my nose. "Don't make me go back out there," I said. "Promise?"

He smiled the way he does; a kind smile, but still.

I'm not going to lie to you. I had been spiraling downward with this Course all week, growing increasingly unable to apply what I had learned to the rapid-fire appearance of incoming problems in the dream apparently hurtling toward me like asteroids with an attitude in a nightmare video game. My reflexes were shot. Worst of all; my emotions appeared to have taken on a life of their own. They fluctuated wildly between fear, worry, and regret; finally unleashing a verbal round of shrapnel on an unsuspecting costar.

"The thing is, I haven't been this angry in years," I sniffed. "This convinced the problem was really out there aimed at me; you know what I'm saying? This convinced it could never be solved."

He smiled the way he does; a kind smile, but still.

"Jesus," I said, dabbing at my eyes. "I just can't keep up with the curriculum this semester; you know what I'm saying? I'm falling *seriously* behind."

"No kidding?"

I nodded. And sniffed. "Is it too late to take a couple of these classes pass/fail?"

He shrugged.

"I know what you're thinking," I said.

"You always do."

" 'No one can fail who seeks to reach the truth.' But you also say I have to 'only' want the peace of God. I'm in a body for crying out loud. I mean, go ahead—pinch me! What do I know from peace? Or God? Anyway this book contradicts itself all over the freaking place; no offense. And what's up with this passage right here about reluctance?" I cracked open the big, blue book. " 'To give reluctantly is not to gain the gift, because you are reluctant to accept it,' " I read. "I mean, seriously? Just look at me! How could I not be reluctant to forgive?"

He smiled the way he does; a kind smile, but still.

"I know what you're thinking," I said. "That passage in Chapter 25, IX. The Justice of Heaven, paragraph 2, goes on to say 'It is saved for you until reluctance to receive it disappears, and you are willing it be given you. God's justice warrants gratitude, not fear. Nothing you give is lost to you or anyone, but cherished and preserved in Heaven, where all of the treasures given to God's Son are kept for him, and offered anyone who but holds out his hand in willingness they be received. ...' I thought you said it just took a *little* willingness? I had a little willingness, right? I kept asking for your help—over and over and over and over—and just look what hit the fan anyway?"

I sighed, another gold-medal-worthy sigh. "Jesus," I said. "Let's be honest here. Keeping up with this Course, this torrent of forgiveness opportunities—the non-stop lab work required this semester—all this 'making it about them,' fielding these incoming demands; getting caught in these triangles and rectangles and freaking hexagons. I mean, all these nut cases seemingly out there I'm supposed to just see as the objects of *my* projection even as they continue to come at me in droves, venting, requesting, demanding, emoting. Expecting me to listen lovingly; advise and console. It's not like I'm in graduate school, for Christ's sake! But ever since I declared forgiveness as my major it's been a complete, 24-7 immersion. And not a graceful one; trust me."

"I always do," he said.

On a macro level, my curriculum seemed equally challenging. Wars raged on. Assassins continued to assassinate. Politicians continued to lie, attack their opponents, and promise the moon. Half of America was popping Xanax, for Christ's sake. The economy continued to make its death rattle noises. The earliest and worst allergy season on record loomed. (I had already succumbed to super pollens emitted by trees driven mad by the global warming certain pundits continued to insist did not exist.)

"I mean, I haven't even finished all my prerequisites," I said.

"Prerequisites?"

"You haven't been paying attention have you? They have really great medications for that these days, you know?"

"Seriously?"

"I'm talking about sorting out the valuable from the valueless, OK? I see you haven't read 'The Development of Trust' lately."

He smiled the way he does; a kind smile, but still.

"All I'm trying to say is can't we just slow this Course down a little so I can catch my breath? Because I seem to be regressing here. I've been filled with this sense of loss, you know? It really feels like I'm being asked to give up something real like, I don't know; *everything* I once cared about. And then, last night." I sighed, the sigh. "I don't suppose you caught that little meltdown of mine?"

His brows shot up.

I leaned toward him and lowered my voice. "Well, let's just say I definitely wasn't making it about them. I'm pretty sure my head might have spun around."

He threw back his head and laughed.

"I know what you're thinking," I said, gazing down at the big, blue book. "'To give a problem to the Holy Spirit to solve for you means that you *want* it solved. To keep it for yourself to solve without His help is to decide it should remain unsettled, unresolved, and lasting in its power of injustice and attack. No one can be unjust to you, unless you have decided first to *be* unjust.' (From paragraph 7) I get that; intellectually, anyway. The problem is these lessons are coming so fast and furious, I completely forget what the real problem is, right?"

He cocked his head, as if considering.

But I knew him better than that.

"I know what you're thinking," I said. "The problem is I don't really want the problem solved. I still want these incoming asteroids. It's not really the speed of the Course or the nature of the lessons or costars that's getting to me. I still want to try to solve it all myself so I can prove I am a real self. Because a part of me is just too terrified to consider the alternative. A part of me doesn't fully believe there's a home left to return to. A part of me doesn't want to give up on Susan. I mean, what would Susan be without these problems?"

"Go on."

"It really doesn't matter how well or poorly I seem to be doing with this Course, does it? I can't flunk out because in truth I'm already home. And every time I'm willing to really talk it out with you like this my split mind heals a tiny bit more. And for a moment—sometimes even an elongated moment—I know all minds are healed, too, forever and always."

He smiled the way he does; a kind smile. I'm pretty sure he has dimples under that beard.

"Anyway, this isn't a Course for the spiritually advanced," I said. "This is a Course for the spiritually challenged. The forgiveness-disabled. If I knew there was really no problem, I wouldn't be here, right? The best thing I can do in every circumstance is admit I don't know the problem, I don't know the solution, and ask for truth to reveal itself. Then I remember there really is no linear time in which to measure my progress in a program of mind healing from which I have already graduated."

He nodded.

"How do you always know just what to say to help me get my head screwed on right again?"

He smiled the way he does; a kind smile.

I smiled, too.

Personal Jesus

"Let me get this straight," I said, as my inner imaginary Jesus and I rode up the chairlift at Loveland Ski Area together last weekend. "You want me to make friends with my projections? You still haven't met them, have you?"

He just laughed, swinging his skis like he'd been doing this all his life. Minus ski boots, of course, sans helmet, same old nubby robe, those signature hot pink, sparkle-spackled shades I'd given him he'd grown so fond of last summer. He should have made quite the spectacle even among people whizzing by below in full spring-skiing, Colorado-style regalia: a man dressed as a banana on a ski board and another as a hot dog; women in bikini tops; Lady Gaga impersonators. But he must have borrowed Harry Potter's invisibility cloak again because obviously no one else but yours truly could see him.

I'd summoned him moments earlier as I boarded the lift solo having spun off from my husband and a friend who prefer to ski extreme terrain. A conversation with said friend on the ride up appeared to have re-activated my sense of victimization in a scene in my dream from the day before, a forgiveness opportunity I'd been grappling with, off and on, for more than 24 hours.

"Have I mentioned how much I just *love* forgiveness opportunities?" I muttered, as I related the story to Jesus.

Having risen that morning once more in a state of discontent about the way in which a dream figure seemed to be thwarting me, I headed for a fitness center I belong to at a nearby university—big, blue book in hand—in search of both endorphins and right-mindedness. I hit a stationary bike and opened *A Course in Miracles* to Chapter 27, IV. The Quiet Answer, in which we learn again that no problem is ever solved from within a thought system deliberately designed to keep the real problem (our belief in separation from our real source and Self) at the root of all problems perennially concealed.

... In conflict there can be no answer and no resolution, for its purpose is to make no resolution possible, and to ensure no answer will be plain. A problem set in conflict has no answer, for it is seen in different ways. And what would be an answer from one point of view is not an answer in another light. You *are* in conflict. Thus it must be clear you cannot answer anything at all, for conflict has no limited effects. Yet if God gave an answer there must be a way in which your problems are resolved, for what He wills already has been done. (From paragraph 1)

The wise words worked their magic on me as they almost always do. The ongoing conflict I was experiencing in this relationship—the sense that no alternative seemed likely or promising, no solution forthcoming—could only be healed when I chose against the inner teacher of separate interests and for the inner teacher of all-inclusive, innocent wholeness. The solution always and only lay in the mind of the dreamer, not the dream. By returning to the mind in the holy instant in which I admitted *I did not know* the real question let alone the answer and looking at the drama on the screen with Jesus—recognizing myself as merely another character in a dream created to prove I exist at God's expense but it's not my fault—I could experience peace instead of this.

As I continued reading the beautiful section my worries, needs, and fears dissolved, the imaginary credits to the most recent installment in the story of Susan on the imaginary screen rolled, and I smiled, certain as I headed for my brand new car in the parking lot that all was well. No one was guilty here. We were all truly awake within indivisible love, merely dreaming a trippy dream of exile.

I looked over my shoulder right, and left, scanning the rear view mirror as I slowly backed out of the parking spot and had almost made it when another, larger vehicle slammed into me. A woman got out and apologized, then moved her car back into the space she'd pulled out of and returned. I stood gazing at the side of my scratched and dislodged bumper, shaken. Just then, across the lot, a woman in an SUV (who happened to be a friend of the woman who hit me) got out of her car, came up, and declared it was no one's fault. We were both pulling out at the same time, she said, even though she had pulled into the lot after the incident. The woman who hit me, whose car had suffered no damage, then refused to give me her insurance information, and claimed she hadn't hit me hard enough anyway to have caused that much damage to my brand new car.

My hand shook as I wrote down her license plate number.

"Why are you so angry?" she asked.

What planet do you hail from? I thought, but, thankfully, did not say. Anyway, I *wasn't* angry, I hadn't berated her or raised my voice, had I? Who the hell was she to call me angry?

Right. I spent the next couple hours trying to figure out how I had shifted so abruptly from a state of seeming tranquility to this unexpected conflict in which I perceived myself once more unfairly treated and, well, treating? Her car hitting me had seemed so freaking random. I found it nearly impossible to see it as my own projection, completely forgetting that only the ego tried to enlist me in why I was projecting this, rather than simply focusing on my *reaction* to it, the only thing in need of correction from the condition I think I'm in. At any rate, I did at least recognize I had chosen the wrong teacher, and begged for help to want to choose again that I might feel better.

As I rode out the gap between asking for help from my right mind to see the situation differently—through the eyes of all-inclusive love instead of all-exclusive fear—and allowing/accepting the answer, I also recognized how my wrong-mindedness in this situation had broadened to include, well, everything. The "problem" upsetting me earlier in a special relationship seemed back in my face again, my allergy symptoms off the charts; the world at large on a tragic, downwardly spiraling trajectory.

And yet, as I called in Jesus this morning on a spring day under blueberry skies in the idyllic Rocky Mountains, upset anew about these and other projections, as I admitted I didn't know how to respond to or interpret anything, I kept hearing the same phrase in my mind: "Make friends with your projections."

"You seriously want me to make friends with my projections?" I repeated, as Jesus and I sailed off the lift at the top. "Be careful," I warned, as he skated from ski to ski, hair flying, beside me. "It's always icy in the morning this time of year. Ice can kill you. It will melt in a couple of hours and then turn into this slushy cement. Slush can kill you, too."

His brows shot up and down, up and down above the shades. He'd been watching those vintage Groucho Marx reruns again, I could tell.

"I'm not making this up. Well; never mind. Anyway, you have about a twenty-minute window around twelve-thirty/one where you're not dead meat. Of course, even then you might get taken out by that drunken banana man," I added, as said boarder fruit, as if on cue, crunched barely by us.

Jesus followed me down a winding catwalk leading to a fairly gentle run I'd chosen, given the less than stellar conditions. We paused near a stand of evergreens. "OK; I know what you're thinking," I said.

"You always do."

"Making friends with my projections is just another way of 'making it about them,' as Ken Wapnick likes to say. Which really means seeing their fear, their neediness, instead of just seeing mine? Seeing their fear, their neediness, as *the same* as mine, really. Like with that woman who hit me yesterday. How the hell do I know what was going through her mind? She might have had no insurance, or been terrified of losing it. Worried about money, her husband's reaction; who knows?"

Jesus shrugged and nodded.

"But the ego always speaks first. Of course I reacted out of ego; that's how projection works. I put it out there to prove I really do exist, but it's someone else's fault. Until all the guilt in my mind is gone, I will continue to want to see it in something external.

When that happens, all I need to do is remind myself I don't know the cause of anything and ask to look at and see it with you. When I do that I see that no one's guilty here. Everything seemingly 'out there' reflects the same inner fear. All problems, large and small—no matter the gory details—have the same solution because they're all designed to preserve the only 'problem': the *belief* that the 'tiny, mad idea' of separation from indivisible, eternally loving wholeness had any real effects."

Jesus smiled.

"Only, it didn't," I said.

I took off and he followed, but quickly passed me, gracefully dodging in and out of the wacky cast of spring-fevered characters descending around us. Frankly, it always worked out better when I followed him anyway.

At the bottom of the lift—I swear to God—they were blasting the Depeche Mode tune *Personal Jesus* from gigantic speakers.

Jesus and I looked at each other and cracked up.

Then he lifted his thumb in the air, and was gone.

Therefore, attempt to solve no problems in a world from which the answer has been barred. But bring the problem to the only place that holds the answer lovingly for you. Here are the answers that will solve your problems because they stand apart from them, and see what can be answered; what the question *is*. Within the world the answers merely raise another question, though they leave the first unanswered. In the holy instant, you can bring the question to the answer, and receive the answer that was made for you. (Paragraph 7)

Seek You No Further

All week long I'd been robotically watching the same old series of internal films starring yours truly, pausing to reflect on moments of glory interwoven among juicy tales of love lost, success stymied, and hopes diabolically dashed. Rewinding and zooming in on antagonists large and small, past and present, polluting the landscape of my so-called life, hell-bent on preventing me from capturing my fair share of hard-fought-for happiness and well-being here on planet crazy.

Then, too, under the ego's ever-willing tutelage, I'd been counting the many ways in which a special relationship continued to thwart me, without any discernible provocation on my puny part, the many ways in which plot twists and turns in *The Sorry Saga of Suffering Susan* seemed to throw me once more into chaos. As well as courting the possibility that new, unexpected developments might prove the answer to all my worldly prayers, once more seduced into believing I had any clue whatsoever about what I really wanted and needed.

I'm not going to lie to you. Despite having made healing my mind through practicing forgiveness *A Course in Miracles*-style my primary goal, I could not seem to stop myself from reaching for that remote like the handle on a slot machine just one more time; convinced I had somehow missed a major loophole in my predicted odds. Deliciously intoxicated anew by the far-fetched possibility I might yet tweak the script, adjudicate the conflict, replace a couple of problematic costars; rewrite a few contracts in my favor; thereby securing the happy ending I so deserved. Driven once more, under the influence of the ego's tantalizing story of individuality realized and desired, to change everything I could possibly think of except my mind. Yet, even as the score rose once more in deliciously demented crescendo; a part of me gently smiled and shook its proverbial head. Damn.

In my peripheral vision, I could see my imaginary Jesus draped beside me on the couch, sandals shed, feet stretched out on the coffee table, silently waiting. Enthralled with the images on my imaginary screen, I tried to ignore him, but it's not all that easy to do anymore. At last I slapped the remote down, and turned to face him.

"Long time no see with," I said.

"Ha!"

"I know what you're thinking."

"You always do."

"Step away from the remote," I said. "Well, I mean, as if."

Jesus threw back his head and laughed.

"But what you really meant to say was 'Seek you no further,' right?" I asked, quoting from the beginning of *A Course in Miracles* workbook lesson 200: "There is no peace except the peace of God." The lesson that had, more than once, inspired me to envision, in graphic detail, running back and forth, back and forth, over this big, blue book with my recently purchased albeit subsequently damaged Subaru Impreza.

> You will not find peace except the peace of God. Accept this fact, and save yourself the agony of yet more bitter disappointments, bleak despair, and sense of icy hopelessness and doubt. Seek you no further. There is nothing else for you to find except the peace of God, unless you seek for misery and pain. (Paragraph 1)

The Course does not mince words. If I was honest with myself, I had to admit that *every* road taken in this serial movie of a life so far—despite fleeting pleasures guiltily grabbed along the way—every road taken within the seductively murky memories of all lives past, had never led me anyplace I really wanted to go. Even though I know better, I *had* been looking for the love and peace I craved again on the screen, mistaking dancing, lunging, enticing, terrifying shadows for the content of my life, and then complaining about why I feel so empty. Once more completely forgetting I have no life except the life I share as one with all that is. A "oneness joined as one" I can only remember when I return to the decision-making mind outside seeming time and space and watch the ego's propaganda films with Jesus as my teacher. And yet.

"I still haven't exhausted *every* possibility," I whined. "I mean, there are still places to go, people to meet, books to read and write, mountains to climb." Bold, new horizons to conquer, I thought; final, freaking frontiers.

His brows shot up, the way they do.

Damn. I knew what he was thinking. The Course is not asking us to exhaust *every* possibility; to sample *every* morsel of the world's secular and spiritual smorgasbord. To seek for ourselves in *every* possible special relationship seemingly "out there." That would be the ego's plan for salvation. To look for the love we believe we squandered when we first took the "tiny, mad idea" of individuality seriously only outside the mind where it can never be found. Instead of returning to the mind and looking with Jesus on what never was, within which the insane notion we could divide the eternally indivisible, all-loving Self we share was simply seen for the silly nothingness it remains.

"Come home," I recalled, from lesson 200. "You have not found your happiness in foreign places and in alien forms that have no meaning to you, though you sought to make them meaningful. This world is not where you belong. You are a stranger here. But it is given you to find the means whereby the world no longer seems to be a prison house or jail for anyone." (Paragraph 4)

Even though I had vowed to make my new life's purpose springing myself from the ego thought system's prison of separation through practicing forgiveness, a part of my mind was not yet completely convinced I still had a home to return to. Nowhere near completely sold on Jesus' promise that relinquishing my death grip on this physical and psychological body I still spied in the mirror each morning staring guiltily back at me would deliver the freedom I was really seeking. But I *had* at least learned that trying to rewrite the script left me frightened and stressed. While watching with Jesus offered comfort, completion, and peace, and yet.

A part of me is still too afraid to go home, still not ready to give up forever on this retrospective in which I seem to have invested so much toil and time; blood, sweat, and tears. I sighed and picked up the remote, savoring its icy smoothness with my fingers; the tantalizing texture of all those freaking buttons just waiting to be pushed. I just couldn't seem to help myself.

"I know what you're thinking," I said. "You'll wait with me in hell a while longer. That's just the kind of ever-patient action figure savior you are. Let's have just one more peek, then, shall we? Together this time?"

Jesus just continued to smile.

Forgiveness Slide Show

I sat at my desk, cross-legged in my chair, eyes closed; calling to mind the face of someone I've been struggling to forgive for a long time. Offering a silent apology with as much sincerity as I could find within my slowly unfurling heart for the many ways in which I had used him to embellish my story of seeking and never finding. The tale of ill-fated suffering I was learning I had woven in an effort to keep the fiction of a separate me alive all these years, while denying responsibility for it. The many repetitive accusations I had leveled at this person in my thoughts that seemed impossible to release slowly appeared one by one on the screen in my head beneath his face, like captions anchoring a photograph. And I suddenly understood exactly what the Course means when it asks us to consider, as it does in workbook lesson 134, paragraph 9:

> ... When you feel that you are tempted to accuse some-
> one of sin in any form, do not allow your mind to dwell
> on what you think he did, for that is self-deception. Ask
> instead: 'Would I accuse myself of doing this?'

Because it struck me that I had, in fact, accused myself of doing this ... and this, and this, and this, and this, perhaps not in identical form, but most certainly in content. My blindness lifted for a moment in my longing to share the truth my right mind knows, and I could see clearly in the bright light of forgiveness how every accusation I had made about this person described my own deeply denied faults. The ones I'd carried all my life, never once daring to utter aloud in the confessional of my childhood. How I'd found the perfect canvas seemingly "out there" on which to paint them, that I might convince myself over and over again they were real, but belonged to someone else.

"I'm so sorry," I silently told the image in my mind. Sorry for projecting my inability to forgive myself for these perceived "sins"—but symbols of my belief in separation—on you. Sorry for rigidly portraying you as my antagonist rather than seeing you as but another fragment of the one terrified child of God we remain. Doing your best to survive here as a fugitive from real, eternally whole love, just like me; likewise secretly convinced you will blow your cover if you don't spend every conscious moment picturing the problem "out there," rather than looking within.

I gazed into the eyes of my projection, genuine remorse welling up inside, blinking back welcome tears of recognition that we really were the same. We shared the same repressed belief in what *A Course in Miracles* calls "the tiny, mad idea" that the one child of God (in truth seamlessly fused with our creator) could defect from our eternally unified source. The belief in which gave rise to a guilt so crushing our one mind appeared to split into an ego (the part of our mind that forgot to smile at the preposterous notion), the Holy (Whole) Spirit (the part of our mind that remembered to smile), and the decision maker, the part of our mind that selfishly sided with the ego's version of the myth. Choosing to follow it into an entire universe of projected forms, assuming individual bodies to prove we exist but it's not our fault, and then falling asleep to ensure we never returned to the mind to choose again for our unalterably, all-inclusive, infinitely loving reality.

The dream seems so real, its figures so convincing, its performances so Oscar-worthy. However bizarre its plot, we believe it, and react from our belief. We feel elation and pain, excitement and grief, anger and regret; the cramped and stifling nature of trying to experience love between and within bodies deliberately invented to banish it. Our fortunes deliciously, deliriously, wax and wane. We bond together and bargain to get our needs met and when our contracts are broken, condemn others for breaking them. Triumphantly rejoicing in their greater guilt that at least temporarily relieves that nagging original guilt we sense within that never goes away for long, however gifted at projection we become.

As I sat gazing into the eyes of my seeming nemesis, yearning to see clearly, I suddenly experienced the remorse Ken Wapnick had been talking about in his *Guilt versus Remorse* CD set I'd been listening to that had seemed so puzzling, versus the guilt the ego would have us reinforce in our efforts to foist our self-condemnation on others. A gentle remorse that accuses no one and recognizes only our sameness, as opposed to the guilt that insists on empowering our differences. "I'm sorry," I silently repeated. Sorry for refusing to forgive the badass self I keep insisting on seeing in you. A self that remains innocent of a crime that never occurred, despite my guilty, tortured fantasies. "I'm sorry," I repeated, and really meant it. I was just afraid of losing my mistaken self, just like you.

There was nothing in truth to fear, I could see that now—guilty dreams have no effects upon the truth—only gratitude to you for revealing the mirage of my specialness and the welcome, endless reservoir of light it concealed. A funny thing happened then. The face in my mind, now smiling back at me, faded, replaced by another face, and another, and another. An entire forgiveness slide show of past figures in the long dream of Susan exposed, complete with captions of my former judgments, pausing for reevaluation and release. In each case, I saw our sameness, first in its fearful dream state, and then in its certain, abstract, prevailing innocence. And I gave thanks for this practice, this forgiveness slide show that enabled me to review my mistaken perceptions with the inner teacher of love instead of fear. Allowing me to open my eyes and begin this day anew, realigned with peace.

Do not be afraid to look within. The ego tells you all is black with guilt within you, and bids you not to look. Instead, it bids you look upon your brothers, and see the guilt in them. Yet this you cannot do without remaining blind. For those who see their brothers in the dark, and guilty in the dark in which they shroud them, are too afraid to look upon the light within. Within you is not what you believe is there, and what you put your faith in. Within you is the holy sign of perfect faith your Father has in you. He does not value you as you do. He knows Himself, and knows the truth in you. He knows there is no difference, for He knows not of differences. Can you see guilt where God knows there is perfect innocence? You can deny His knowledge, but you cannot change it. Look, then, upon the light He placed within you, and learn that what you feared was there has been replaced with love. (Chapter 13, IX. The Cloud of Guilt, paragraph 8)

It Is Done

I sat at my desk, cross-legged in my chair; eyes squeezed shut, silently repeating the word "one" in response to a tsunami of other words and images flooding the shore of my scant gray matter, ego-driven directives warning me to act, post-haste, in response to recent dream developments or, you know, suffer the grim consequences. "One," I repeated, "one, one, one," hoping this simple incantation might restore the right-mindedness—that awareness of my real identity seamlessly fused with our creator along with every other seemingly forsaken soul—I had apparently misplaced.

"Seven billion," the ego countered, "and counting," referring to the number of people currently vying for survival on the planet, each capable of destroying said orb and each other in ever more ingenious ways. I *know*. It had been that kind of morning. I'd awakened abruptly less than an hour earlier in the throes of a vivid dream in which I found myself a prisoner escaping from a sprawling, vintage penitentiary; a vision that had hovered just on the periphery of my waking dream, as well. I had somehow made it to the jail yard safely in the middle of the night in my little, striped jumpsuit, had summoned my courage and dashed across it toward the chain link fence only to be suddenly illuminated by an overhead roving light. Exposed like a cockroach on a kitchen floor by the flip of a switch, I froze, fully aware the jig was up.

In my waking dream, too, the jig seemed just about up. I had never been more aware of my allegiance to my special stories of suffering at the hands of imaginary problematic costars and unfair scripts, the anxiety-spiked paralysis that descended whenever I so much as contemplated what my life would look like without the imprisonment of these projections. Abandoning my doomed mantra, I squeezed my eyes shut again and watched the ego's risk-management power point with as much detachment as I could muster while silently begging for truth to weigh in. And then I actually heard the phrase: "Just be kind,"—which surprised me, because I am generally not one to receive these sorts of specific, divine directives—followed by: "It is done."

I inhaled, gratefully, the ego's presentation rewinding, and found myself back in the classroom of the inner teacher of love instead of fear, seated across the desk from my imaginary Jesus (that *symbol* of our mind made sane by truth instead of mad by guilt), the big, blue book open on the desk between us. "I know what you're thinking," I said.

"You always do."

"No, I mean, *really*. See, you're trying to tell me everything my body's eyes report is a lie, based on the lie that the one child of God I remain could separate from eternal wholeness that gave birth to the lie of separate interests and unfair treatment. The lies of my thoughts of specialness, my emotional reactions to passing dream scenes, figures, and plots, my belief in the lie that my waking dreams are more real than my sleeping dreams when both of them are lies. Just one damn lie after another, and another, and another is what you're really saying, isn't it?"

His brows shot up, the way they do.

"The lie the ego keeps pushing and I keep robotically purchasing that I will never find my way home through this Course, never experience more than a passing holy instant, never transform my special relationships into holy ones, never break out of this jailhouse alive. When the truth is, you're trying to remind me that I asked you some time ago to help me change the *purpose* of this relationship from proving I exist separately but it's not my fault to proving our sameness. We share the same ego, the same decision maker, and the same right mind. And we both want to find our way home to the all-inclusive love and innocence we think we destroyed more than we want to hold on to our differences."

"Go on," he said.

"And so what you're really saying is just be kind, and patient, too, because there isn't anything else to do but allow the *undoing* that comes from looking at my dream with you to dissolve my fear and nourish my trust that love will prevail. I have asked, and you have answered, regardless of the time lag I seem to be experiencing and the tantrums it seems to trigger in the guilty self I still hold dear. As you've pointed out many times, there is no time in truth. I need only allow you to use the illusion of time kindly for me, trusting patiently that healing is happening even though I don't yet see or feel the results, or even understand what that means. I may be hard-wired to resist this healing, to accept its comfort, but my resistance has no effects on its power or progress, just like my belief in the 'tiny, mad idea' I could run away from home and experience myself as other than perfectly, infinitely whole and loved had no effects."

"I see," he said, nodding.

"Yes, you do. It's like you said in Chapter 17, V. The Healed Relationship, paragraph 6: 'This is a time for *faith*. You let this goal be set for you. That was an act of faith. Do not abandon faith, now that the rewards of faith are being introduced. If you believed the Holy Spirit was there to accept the relationship, why would you now not still believe that he is there to purify what He has taken under His guidance? ...'

So even though I still feel confused, start listening to the ego again, and reaching for solutions in form, even as the panic rises in my throat at the thought of relinquishing my fantasized special self, you've already corrected the conditions that led to these feelings of sin, guilt, and fear; and I've corrected them, too, because we are one. I just need to remember that if I have joined with you outside time in the eternal present for even a nanosecond and experienced the freedom, all-inclusive innocence, and completeness of our one, true nature—which I have—salvation is certain in this situation, too."

"I see," he repeated.

"You most certainly do. Well, I just have to say, I'm so glad we had this little talk. You were really on quite the holy roll today, weren't you?"

"It was nothing," he said.

Ha! He really is a lot funnier than anybody gives him credit for.

I lifted my palm in the air.

He high-fived me right back, and I found myself back at my desk, in my office, once more happily wrong about, well; that would be everything.

> You and your brother stand together in the holy presence of truth itself. Here is the goal, together with you. Think you not the goal itself will gladly arrange the means for its accomplishment? It is just this same discrepancy between the purpose that has been accepted and the means as they stand now which seems to make you suffer, but which makes Heaven glad. If Heaven were outside you, you could not share in it is gladness. Yet because it is within, the gladness, too, is yours. You are joined in purpose, but remain still separate and divided on the means. Yet the goal is fixed, firm and unalterable and the means will surely fall in place because the goal is sure. (From paragraph 14)

I Want the Peace of God

I had just come through a welcome shift in my perception of a special relationship I had held responsible for the conflict and drama (*A Course in Miracles* teaches us is actually playing out *internally*) in my life for many years and experienced true gratitude to the object of my projection for helping me reclaim and release my own concealed desire to push real love away. Enabling the dawning of true compassion for the secret fear we shared that we truly *had* defected from our one home and could never return.

And yet, predictably, my anxiety over what this Course was *really* saying about the self I still see in the mirror was at an all-time high. I vacillated between elongated holy (whole) instants of clarity and unwavering faith in our true reality and full-blown panic attacks about what that ultimately meant for the body I still think I inhabit, pacing the square footage of my Denver home like something caged. Hobbling on a toe I had broken the night before—while similarly pacing my habitat, my little dog in my arms—when I caught it on the hard edge of a wooden chest.

I had just returned from a limping walk around the park with said dog I hoped would clear my head but instead left me reacting anew to the pollen spewing from the stately old trees bending in the wind. I pressed my fingers to my itchy, leaky eyes, dipped my toes back in the bowl of ice water beneath my desk, and decided to distract myself from my colossal resistance to accepting the comfort of my right mind by tackling various mindless tasks on my ever-lengthening to-do list. But when I went to order tickets to the summer concerts that had gone on sale that very morning, I couldn't find the membership number required to set up an account. Attempting to figure a way around it, I repeatedly timed out of the website. When I finally located the membership number, the required links had mysteriously perished.

I gave up and attempted to convert some audio files to live links on my own website with no success. I tried ordering a cake for my father-in-law's approaching 90th birthday party. A bakery employee answered the phone, put me on hold, and never returned. I called again, was put on hold, and subsequently disconnected. The next time I called, I got a fax tone. When I tried a little later, the phone merely rang and rang. I then attempted to review a DVD for a class I was teaching but a power surge rendered our DVD player incapacitated.

Pacing my cell once more—anxiety seemingly freshly fed by these new frustrations—I had it out with my imaginary Jesus. Had I not committed and recommitted to making this Course the most important thing in my life? Had I not sincerely asked him to help me make learning forgiveness of a separation that never was the true purpose of all my interactions? Why was I still letting such trivial situations in my forgiveness classroom upset me like this? What the hell else did I need to go through to finally heal?

I stopped pacing then, and froze. I had never turned on him like this before. Sure; I'd fantasized taking out the big, blue book many times by a variety of violent methods; argued with my inner teacher, complained and whined, but never; you know, actually raised my voice! I suppose I was waiting for some kind of Biblical retaliation, but there was only silence. There, I thought. I finally scared him away. But before the terror that thought evoked could fully seize me, the silence opened and deepened and beckoned; revealing a certain, complete and completed stillness in which all previous worries and judgments; thoughts and emotions slipped inexplicably away.

"What do you ask for in your heart?" I heard, a familiar line from workbook lesson, 185, "I want the peace of God;" one of my favorites.

And a silent, inner answer arose from a Self beyond this body's brain: "I want to see with you through the eyes of kindness to all; eyes that see everyone and everything as part of eternal kindness. I want to give up this hierarchy of illusions for good. To see the conflict and drama and pain I keep putting 'out there' as merely a reflection of the conflict, drama, and pain in my mind, generated by a false belief that the 'tiny, mad idea' that I could exist as other than infinite, kind, oneness had any real effects."

"What do you ask for in your heart?" The question came again.

"Eyes that can see," I answered, and crawled back in that cradle of silence, closing my body's eyes, and joining with our inner teacher's vision.

> ... Forget the words you use in making your requests. Consider but what you believe will comfort you and bring you happiness. But be you not dismayed by lingering illusions, for their form is not what matters now. Let not some dreams be more acceptable, reserving shame and secrecy for others. They are one. (From paragraph 8)

The lesson's words echoed in my head. And I could see the unkindness—the result of having chosen the inner teacher of unkindness—I had been indulging by making the dream with its twists and turns real, forgetting I was its dreamer, not its heroine. All to preserve the story of a special self imagined to promote a special tale of suffering and defeat that at least proves I exist as an individual but it's not my fault.

"What do you ask for in your heart?" The question came again.

"I ask to see with you," I repeated. "I ask to look through the eyes of kindness on everyone and everything, including the one I see in the mirror."

I don't know how long I sat there in stillness, flooded with gratitude for this Course, this practice, this teacher, the reality of our true, unalterable Self, forever awake in boundless love, merely dreaming of exile. Again certain that choosing the inner teacher of kindness would not cause me to disappear in a flash of obliterating light, only to smile. When I returned to the world, I went back to the tasks on my to-do list and completed them, gently lifted a spider that had wandered inside with a tissue and returned it to the garden, and headed out to Motor Vehicles—where I met the most lovely, helpful, light-hearted people; I swear to God!—to get the license plates I needed for my recently damaged new car.

You want the peace of God. And so do all who seem to seek for dreams. For them as well as for yourself you ask but this when you make this request with deep sincerity. For thus you reach to what they really want, and join your own intent with what they seek above all things, perhaps unknown to them, but sure to you. You have been weak at times, uncertain in your purpose, and unsure of what you wanted, where to look for it, and where to turn for help in the attempt. Help has been given you. And would you not avail yourself of it by sharing it?

No-one who truly seeks the peace of God can fail to find it. For he merely asks that he deceive himself no longer by denying to himself what is God's Will. Who can remain unsatisfied who asks for what he has already? Who could be unanswered who requests an answer which is his to give? The peace of God is yours. (Paragraphs 10 and 11)

Have a Little Faith in Me

"Don't make me go back out there again," I said, resurrecting my "tiny voice." The one I used to use as a kid in the confessional, reciting a rote list of venial sins, the tip of an iceberg I'd kept in the freezer for, well—*ever!* I couldn't tell how long I'd been sitting outside my imaginary Jesus' imaginary office, unable to rise to my feet and enter that ever-open door. I'd been emailing him all week and getting an out-of-office reply but obviously he was in there, grading papers maybe or playing with those finger puppets I gave him a while back that continue to thoroughly crack him up. I'd been hoping to talk with him—to spill my guts, really—and yet. Some kind of invisible force field appeared to glue me to this chair, unable to approach the light spilling out from that threshold.

After a while he came out and sat down beside me, laced his fingers backwards and inverted them, unfurled the pointers and thumbs and pressed them together. "Here's the church, here's the steeple," he said, just like my grandfather used to all those years ago. "Open the doors and see all the people." His thumbs swung open. He wiggled his fingers inside-out at me, threw back his head and laughed; just like my grandfather. But I refused to crack a smile. After all, I was here on serious business, and we were burning daylight.

"Don't make me go back out there again," I repeated, as emphatically as my tiny voice would allow.

He leaned toward me. "Why are we whispering?"

I managed a ragged sigh. I really couldn't say.

"Out there?" he asked. He had lowered his voice, too, ever willing to meet me in the condition I think I'm in here on planet crazy.

"You know," I said. "That 'dry and dusty world, where starved and thirsty creatures come to die?' "

He smiled. "We've talked about this."

"It's just that I really am way over my proverbial head here this semester. I mean, *Jesus*, the forgiveness pop quizzes are coming at warp speed and I can't possibly keep up with all the lab work. You can't blame me for falling behind. I am *so* not ready for this."

"I thought you got an A plus on your last special relationships test?"

"That doesn't mean I'm ready to make it all the same, to look at *everything* with you, to come to *every* situation, *every* encounter with sentient and insentient beings without need. I mean, true, I can now see *that* body I held responsible for the drama and conflict playing out in my head for such a long time was never the cause. But that doesn't mean I'm ready to *give up* the cause. I mean, seeing isn't always believing, you know what I'm saying?"

"I believe I do."

"I don't go down easily, as you may have noticed. And I don't know which scares me more right now. Going out there." I pointed to the door down the hall, portal to the great illusion of my so-called life. "Or going in there." I pointed to his office.

"I see," he said.

"I know you do. I'm just saying I'd like to slow this whole thing down, is that too much to ask?"

"You think I'm in charge of the speed?"

"I am *so* not ready to wake up! I mean, anyone with two eyes can see that. I think I must have missed some prerequisites. Just like that recurring sleeping dream I used to have where I couldn't graduate from college because I forgot to fill that math requirement I kept postponing. Whoa, that was scary! Remember that one?"

"We've talked about this."

"Well, obviously not enough."

Anyway, speaking of dreams, I'd awakened that morning in the throes of a terrifying nightmare in which I found myself adrift in a strange, vast land, unable to speak the language. Bands of armed men who hadn't bathed recently terrorized the countryside, randomly attacking civilians trying to eke out a living from the parched, rocky soil along bald hillsides. I was traveling with my little dog Kayleigh and a group of strangers equally lost, also trying to find a way out while staying under the radar.

In a cloud of dust a bus approached on the steep, dirt road and Kayleigh darted across the road ahead of it, without me. Men waved automatic weapons out the windows and we dropped to our knees and covered our heads the way they used to make us in kindergarten during air raid drills. They passed us by without incident, but Kayleigh was nowhere to be found. I spent the rest of the dream dashing up and down the ravines, frantically calling her name, abandoned by the rest of the group and overwhelmed by the possibility that I had lost her for good.

Jesus reached into his pocket and handed me a tissue from his seemingly endless, invisible supply.

I dabbed at my eyes. "It's just that she's so small," I said. "So sweet and helpless, and loyal, too, you know? You don't run into that very often out there."

Jesus patted my arm.

"I know what you're thinking," I said.

"You always do."

"Have a little faith in me is what you're really saying. I don't have to give up the things I love. I don't have to go around doing everything that scares me just to prove I'm not a body. I just have to go back in there with you. To see things from your perspective, recognize how afraid of love I am; admit I'm not ready to wake up without trying to justify it by defending the reality of my dreams of loss and persecution. That's how they get undone. That's how eyes that cannot see begin to open. It's like it says in the second half of the workbook, number 13. What Is a Miracle?

> … The eyes of Christ deliver them to all they look upon in mercy and in love. Perception stands corrected in His sight, and what was meant to curse has come to bless. … The miracle is taken first on faith, because to ask for it implies the mind has been made ready to conceive of what it cannot see and does not understand. Yet faith will bring its witnesses to show that what it rested on is really

there. And thus the miracle will justify your faith in it, and show it rested on a world more real than what you saw before; a world redeemed from what you thought was there. (From paragraphs 3 and 4)

Jesus nodded. "I couldn't have said it better myself."

"Ha!" I felt better, sort of. I would just have to keep plugging along. Quit worrying about flunking the Course. Trust that "no one can fail who seeks to reach the truth," as he often said. Even when I didn't believe it, even when the thought of losing my dog brought me to my knees, even when I wanted to throttle someone "out there" just for the hell of it. It was all just part of the curriculum.

"Wait, what were my choices again?" I asked.

"We've talked about this."

"Just that one choice, you're saying?"

He nodded.

"Oh man, there has to be another way."

Jesus laughed. I took his hand, rose, and followed him into his office.

Seek for that door and find it. But before you try to open it, remind yourself no one can fail who seeks to reach the truth. And it is this request you make today. Nothing but this has any meaning now; no other goal is valued now nor sought, nothing before this door you really want, and only what lies past it do you seek. (Workbook lesson 131, paragraph 12)

An American in Paris

Standing in line with my family outside the elegant Musee d'Orsay, waiting to be seated for lunch during our recent vacation in Paris, I found myself privy, like everyone else in the general vicinity, to a colossal meltdown on the part of a fellow American standing just behind us with his adolescent daughter.

"Give me that phone," he boomed.

His daughter shook her head, superior smirk intact, dropped the phone into her purse, and hugged it to her chest like a concealed weapon.

"I want the phone. I want to call your mother and tell her I don't want to eat lunch here. Who picked this place anyway? It's just a cafeteria; I want a real sit-down meal."

Never mind that through the adjacent glass walls waiters dressed in formal black-and-white attire scurried back and forth to proper tables, taking orders and delivering delightful platters of food beneath the dappled light of crystal chandeliers I could almost hear chiming. Never mind that outside the restaurant's expansive windows, the City of Light's generous, Left-Bank boulevards fanned out in fairy-tale splendor, beneath trees in full rococo leaf. Having strayed vastly beyond his comfort zone, the unfortunate American found himself under siege by everyone and thing around him, his perception impossibly skewed by the faulty lens of the inner teacher of fear he had no clue he had chosen.

"If you won't give me the phone, call your mother for me right now and tell her I want to go someplace else."

His daughter rolled her eyes and turned away from him.

My daughter rolled her eyes at me.

Up and down the growing line, tourists of various ages, genders, colors, and nationalities, rolled their disgusted eyes.

"Give me the phone," he repeated.

His daughter began to walk away.

He called after her, more than once.

"Who's the parent and who's the child?" my daughter mouthed at me.

His daughter returned, handed him the phone, leveled the look I recall being the recipient of many times when my own daughter attended middle school just a few short years ago, and huffed away.

Our fellow American then dialed his wife and began reporting on his daughter's rude behavior before branching out to repeat the same, sad refrain of complaints he'd delivered earlier. My own eyes itching to roll, I glanced over my shoulder at him, caught his gaze for an instant, and was astounded to see ... myself staring back at me! I am not making this up, well, anymore than usual. I could feel his misery, his terror, the hangover of embarrassment and regret that would surely follow this ego attack, the minor-key regret reverberating throughout the chambers of his heart within my own.

My husband and daughter were shaking their heads, biting back judgment; not their forte really.

But although this was exactly the kind of seemingly random dream figure behavior that used to drive pre-*A-Course-in-Miracles*-student Susan up the proverbial wall, each time he uttered another classically obnoxious line, I reached for the muscle of judgment only to find it happily disabled. We've all been there, I thought, and actually later said. He was probably jet-lagged, sleep-deprived, blood-sugar-challenged, and as bewildered as I by the overwhelming magnificence on display within and without this museum around which I found it almost impossible to wrap my puny little head. He was merely acting out externally an internal condition we shared, I thought, filled with compassion, as a waiter ushered us to our table and we proceeded to lunch in style, later noticing the man and his family seated across the room, sans offensive cell phone and tantrum, sanity seemingly restored.

Although I seemed to have difficulty during our ten-day excursion feeling the presence of the inner teacher of love in the palpable, mystical manner I believed I'd earned as a reward for having completed an intense forgiveness semester, I nonetheless enjoyed several similar experiences that proved the love we share (and our ego tantrums can never scare away) was still there!

Every time I sought to distance myself from certain anti-social behavior seemingly "out there," I found myself gratefully aware of our sameness. The tour groups in the Louvre swarming like a moving hive toward the Mona Lisa and Venus de Milo sweeping anyone in their path aside troubled me not. Although I held on to my daughter, walked briskly, and avoided eye contact with the unsavory seeming characters accosting tourists on the steps to the Sacre Coeur, I felt no impulse to condemn. The disapproving glances leveled at the flip flops I'd donned when my more fashionable walking shoes quickly failed my deformed feet merely amused. Even my husband's inability to refrain from snapping clearly forbidden photos inside various attractions failed to rattle me.

Our sameness shone like the light suddenly igniting a spire of the Notre Dame as we rounded a corner, sunlight breaking through distant thunderheads, illuminating the truth that we shared the same split mind here in this dreamy dream of exile from perfect, all-inclusive love. Whatever the dream's details, the fearful defenses and attacks it inspired, the love was still there, embracing each and every one of us as we wound our halting way home. Even as I found myself sensing the familiar ganged-up-on theme still apparently thriving in the story of my special relationship with my husband and daughter, a part of me remained aware of the one love we share holding us gently in its fond embrace.

I mention this because in the regular weekly *A Course in Miracles* class I teach here in Denver, I am often asked about the benefits of forgiveness, especially by students new to this path who have not yet experienced their own holy instants of release. Who are blundering, as I did, only on blind faith that the content of real love they sense in the big, blue book's pages will help them heal their minds about the condition they think they're in here in a world full of turmoil, drama, and all too fleeting pleasures. Enable them to conquer the deep fear of the finite human condition and the nagging belief they are wandering alone in a strange land, unworthy of love and unlikely to ever find their way back into the loving fold.

I mention this because I want to reassure them, and often still need to reassure myself, that the day-to-day, moment-to-moment *practice* of taking responsibility for our experiences back to our mind whenever we feel victimized or victimizing really does heal in ways beyond our understanding or need to comprehend. Whenever tempted to condemn or distance ourselves from the behavior of others, and willing to ask the inner teacher of forgiveness for help in interpreting what is really happening, we remember the "tiny, mad, idea" of separation from our source had no effects—despite the dream yet playing out in our mind—and re-experience our prevailing innocence that includes everyone.

By focusing on which teacher we are choosing (and have chosen) from moment to moment in the classroom of our lives and choosing again, when needed, our belief in what the Course calls a hierarchy of illusions gradually dissolves. We experience more and more tranquil right-mindedness wherein our rush to judgment is automatically replaced with demonstrations of true compassion, the effortless recognition of our sameness beyond our seeming differences in form.

And so I give thanks again today for this path and offer you and all students of all nationalities my still-fragile, but daily strengthening faith that we *all*—Course students, or not, seeming victims *and* victimizers alike—share the same decision-making mind outside this dream of differences realized ever available to choose again for the part of our mind that knows only our prevailing, shared innocence, unfettered by dreams of love's destruction. An awareness that leads us baby step by step home to the reality of our unwavering, undifferentiated union. The inner teacher of forgiveness' hand (that is really my hand, your hand, and one hand, now and forever) firmly held in my own.

Can You Spell that for Me?

I stood at the whiteboard in front of my forgiveness classroom, Sharpie in hand, finally assuming the teaching role to which I was rightfully born.

Jesus—a jumble of cramped, Picasso-like limbs—had crammed himself into my little desk at my request. I'd asked him to switch places with me today, literally and figuratively, in an effort to raise his awareness (to put it politely since today's lesson had apparently not even entered his airspace) about what it was like to walk in *my* sandals for a change. You know, confined to one of these heavy, high-maintenance contraptions called bodies day in and day out for more years than I wished to count. Schlepping (through the density of time and space and incoming attacks by other high-maintenance contraptions) toward a proverbial Bethlehem to be born; as one poet put it, experiencing with each forward thrust, a pushback that nearly took my breath away.

I mean, with all due respect, what did he know from the weight of physical never mind metaphorical bodies, really; having remembered to smile at the very beginning at the "tiny, mad, idea" of defection from our abstract source? Time for a little walk on the wild side, I reasoned, a character-building, empathy-enhancing, continuing-teacher-education exercise, really. And where better to start than right here, with the basics? I pressed the marker to the white board:

"S U S A N,"

I wrote, in large, clear, block letters, not unlike the ones I had first scratched in chalk on the sidewalk at four years old and gone on to scratch on every surface I could find thereafter, belief in myself strengthening with each stroke of my pen.

I tapped a finger under each special letter, pronouncing it slowly, out loud; over-enunciating as if teaching a non-native English speaker. "Now repeat after me:

S U S A N."

Jesus started laughing, giggling, actually, I am sorry to report—my whole little desk rocking back and forth in mirthful unison around him—and could not seem to get a grip on himself.

Summoning ancient French ancestors on my mother's side, I pursed my lips together, crossed my arms over my chest, narrowed my eyes, and waited for his little chuckle fest to abate, right foot tapping the floor of its own accord the way it does as if hoping to catch a spider in random transit.

After a while, Jesus wiped his eyes, shifted his facial muscles back into neutral, and continued to doodle on his pad.

I sighed.

"S U S A N spells SUSAN," I explained. "Do we know what that means?"Apparently not, because Jesus just continued to doodle in confounding oblivion!

"Ugh. Why can't you just repeat after me for once in your life?" I whined; all too aware my fragile management of this classroom was rapidly slipping away, thanks to *his* authority problem! I walked over to him and glanced down at the pad he was filling with little happy face icons. I hate those little faces. "Sit up straight," I said.

He smiled, but continued to slouch.

"SUSAN," I repeated, struggling to maintain my waning composure. "That's my name. The name I'd prefer you use from now on when addressing me."

"When addressing *you*," he repeated, without looking up, mouth twitching toward hilarity, happy faces procreating like bunnies across the page beneath his pen. "We've talked about this."

Right. I knew this was going to be a tough sell. But I was up for the challenge. "We've also talked about what it says in Chapter 12, III, paragraph 4, of the big, blue book," I countered:

> *Recognize what does not matter*, and if your brothers ask you for something 'outrageous,' do it *because* it does not matter. Refuse and your opposition establishes that it does matter to you. It is only you, therefore, who have made the request outrageous, and every request of a

brother is for you. Why would you insist in denying him? For to do so is to deny yourself and impoverish both. He is asking for salvation, as you are. Poverty is of the ego, and never of God. No "outrageous" requests can be made of one who recognizes what is valuable and wants to accept nothing else.

His brows shot up and down the way they do.

I sighed. I had enjoyed almost an entire right-minded weekend, peacefully observing the trials and tribulations of my costars and the world in general without incident. Kindly responding to the simmering power issues between my husband and daughter (again living at home for the summer after her freshman year away at college) with quiet, helpful, logic. Regardless of the tension smoldering between them I remained sympathetic to (although not always compliant with) her wish to maintain her new-found independence as well as my husband's fear of losing all influence over her, of losing *her*, actually. A fear I clearly recognized as my own.

Even as I popped Ibuprofen, I failed to allow the pain shooting across the middle of my back out of nowhere, or the (in my opinion) untruthful claims of a presidential candidate I did not support—fueled by an infusion of wealthy donor cash that seemed to have hijacked the airwaves—to dissuade me from choosing peace. I completed the work that confined me indoors for hours on a rare, cool and sunny summer Sunday almost effortlessly. And yet, by late Sunday night my annoyance at everyone and everything seemingly "out there" seemed to have reached an all-time high through no fault, let alone *decision,* of mine.

I lay awake most of the night, pondering the way in which my growing right-mindedness seemed to trigger an ego backlash in equal proportion, so that no matter how good I got at forgiving what never was and still wasn't, my right and wrong minds appeared to remain neck and neck in their opposite marathon stampedes toward Heaven and hell. I arose determined to persuade Jesus to experience what I was experiencing right here, right now. To see for once through *my* lens the problem as I saw it here in the condition I still think I'm in, to know and spell and speak *my* name.

"I know what you're thinking," I said. "You already did something outrageous by switching roles with me. Anyway, you would never do something that would set me back on my journey—something like fortifying my belief in a separate, special self by addressing me by name—that's just the kind of ever-helpful imaginary action figure of an awakened Self you are. Besides, as you've pointed out time and time again, you'll wait in hell with me as long as I like, but delay is only hurting me. At some point, I might as well just grow up with this Course and recognize that dragging you into the dream will never work. But looking at the dream of this imaginary body I seem to inhabit with you as my teacher always will."

Jesus just smiled.

I put the cap on my Sharpie and placed it back on the whiteboard ledge. "I think I'm ready to go back to my desk now," I said.

He nodded, and held up his pad: "Well done," it read.

"Well done, *SUSAN,* you mean."

He laughed and laughed, shoulders heaving, desk rocking.

I waited for him to finish.

"Can you spell that for me?" he asked, at last, cracking himself right up all over again.

French heritage aside, I really couldn't take it anymore, and started to laugh, too.

True Empathy

I sat cross-legged in my desk chair early one morning on the cusp of the summer solstice trying to absorb the meaning of real compassion, relinquishing my neediness in my relationships and learning to "make it about them" as Ken Wapnick advises, a correction for our allegiance to an ego thought system hardwired to making it about me. But I'm not going to lie to you. If I am honest with myself, as I am learning I really want to be, I must admit I don't have a clue about what this means, at least not when the characters that populate the imaginary habitat of my dream appear to act in ways that hurt.

I sighed, shut my eyes, began the full-body breathing technique I learned in yoga class, and wiped the screen of my brain clean. Inhaling into the top of my lungs I asked as I do each morning what I needed to learn today to heal my mind of the thought of separation from our source that led to the belief that we are separate from each other. Because I am sorry to report I had dished up a full plate of illusions and didn't know what to do about any of them.

Outside the window the orchestra of distractions beckoning me toward mindlessness was warming up. A lawn mower across the street roared to life. Hammering from a neighborhood construction project resumed with staccato precision. The voices of children on their way to summer camp soared and dove. Please show me, I silently repeated, and started thinking about what to make for dinner. Home from her first year of college for the summer, my daughter had mysteriously transformed into someone who liked to hang out with me, a startling turn of events I could not help but cherish. But with temperatures predicted to climb into the 90s again, I didn't really feel like cooking.

Maybe we should just throw some chicken or fish on the grill again, order in some of that wood-fired, thin-crust pizza with the smoked salmon and goat cheese, or pick up some Dim Sum. Or—considering the mounting, seemingly insurmountable prix-fixe menu of forgiveness opportunities awaiting me—maybe I should, heat wave be damned, opt for comfort and whip up the macaroni and cheese for which I was justly famous with that imported Irish cheddar I just scored on sale.

Mind wandering, I thought; resisting, resisting, resisting. I started wondering what Ken Wapnick sees when he looks out from his podium at the Foundation for *A Course in Miracles*. A sea of incredulous faces, some nodding off, others grimacing, some appearing to have ingested blissfully mind-altering fungi? I mean, that he manages to keep a straight face is a minor miracle in itself!

Resisting, resisting, resisting. I inhaled deeply and exhaled slowly several more times, wiping the white board once more clean. I don't know what to do about anything, I silently repeated, the only honest words I knew, the only prayer I could completely trust. I started thinking about my approaching birthday, reflecting on the birthdays of the close and distant past, markers in the dream of Susan that seemed—like the very body I seemed to inhabit—so heavy and hungry these days whenever I sided with a teacher invested in making me believe they had anything to do with my real Self.

I thought about what I perceived as judgments about my often reclusive nature that had led me to type the question: "Is there something wrong with introverts?" into the Google browser which led me to an article in a scientific journal extolling the brilliance of introverts with "sound research" I had, in true extrovert-wannabe fashion, then emailed to a couple of fellow introverts, temporarily appeasing my ego before plunging me back into self-judgment. I thought about my reaction to discovering that a nonprofit program I had started and written a grant for years ago had been funded and thriving for years although I was never so much as notified.

And then I finally got to the meat of my forgiveness plat du jour: my feelings of betrayal in a special relationship. The "real" seeming issue "out there" in my guilty playpen that had led me once more to the threshold of real learning, the awareness that I do not know what to do, what I want, what's wrong, or what's right. Only that I want to feel light again, forgiven and forgiving, kind and certain and beyond needing to have anything or anyone seemingly external sustain me. I had turned this relationship over to the light of our right mind some time ago. That meant the healing of my mind, my return to unalterable peace, had occurred, even if I chose to dream otherwise a while longer in my secret fear. A fact I could certainly remember now that I'd completed all my mental machinations and was finally ready to see and listen, follow instead of lead.

I turned to Chapter 16, I. True Empathy, paragraph 3 and read:

> Your part is only to remember this: you do not want anything you value to come of a relationship. You choose neither to hurt it nor to heal it in your own way. You do not know what healing is. All you have learned of empathy is from the past. And there is nothing from the past that you would share, for there is nothing from the past that you would keep. Do not use empathy to make the past real, and so perpetuate it. Step gently aside, and let healing be done for you. Keep but one thought in mind and do not lose sight of it, however tempted you may be to judge any situation, and to determine your response *by* judging it. Focus your mind only on this:
> I am not alone, and I would not intrude the past upon my Guest.
> I have invited Him, and He is here.
> I need do nothing except not to interfere.

I sighed. My inner imaginary Jesus smiled and nodded, still as close as my next seeming breath. And I realized I had been trying so hard to suspend my judgment about this person and situation, to feel a compassion I could not while my anger still bubbled beneath the fragile veneer of understanding. Even though I had asked to share my right mind's all-knowing vision, I had been trying to forgive all by myself again, as if there were two bodies involved, forgiver and sinner. Hoping as always to reinforce my secret belief in the "sin" of separation by using another's past transgressions to prove my story of relative innocence, that same old lie that I exist at the expense of infinite union but it's not my fault—it's yours. But I am not alone, even when I pretend to be. No different than you regardless of my apparent "individual experience." Like you, in truth, still one with the part of our mind that knows it and always remembers to smile at all ego efforts to prove otherwise, I remain awake in eternally united love, merely dreaming of exile. Just like every other dream figure, including the ones I love to hold responsible for my pain.

I can only know true empathy for everyone and thing when I am willing to once again stop trying to solve imaginary problems and instead live within the recognition that I know nothing. I must be willing—again and again, from moment to moment, for as long as it seems to take—to own up to the "serious secret" of my anger at this other person that disguises my anger at myself for believing I destroyed the real love of our source. I must bring what I'm feeling in all its gritty badness to the gently amused comfort of the inner teacher of forgiveness. When I do, all anger, anxiety, stress, and worry about how to respond in every situation simply fades into the nothingness from which it came, allowing the one light always shining in our one mind to express its certainty and nourish mine, allowing me to receive and thereby offer the only healing every frightened seeming one of us needs.

... No needs will long be left unmet if you leave them all to Him Whose function is to meet them. That is His function, and not yours. He will not meet them secretly, for He would share everything you give through Him. That is why He gives it. What you give through Him is for the whole Sonship, not for part of it. Leave Him His function, for He will fulfill it if you but ask Him to enter your relationships, and bless them for you. (From paragraph 7)

Unwelcome Guest

I had been up several times during the night frantically trying to locate the perpetrator responsible for a swath of inflamed, itchy bites on my left thigh; seemingly chewed on by an insect of unknown origin (*right*; my leg had *spider* written all over it!) with severe boundary problems that had crept into *my* bed! At dawn I stripped the linens, stuffed them into the washer on the hot cycle, slathered on some more cortisone cream that did nothing to assuage the confounding itch, and fled to the nearest coffee shop to drown my sorrows in a venti-three-quarter decaf, light-room Americano; iced, of course, the better to survive the continuing, record-breaking heat.

After listening at length to what Ken Wapnick had to say about being kind to all seemingly sentient and insentient creatures here in this dream of exile from perfect, undifferentiated wholeness, a correction for the attacks we make to reinforce the illusion of our original attack on God, I'd experienced a change of heart in my long-standing, troubled relationship with spiders. Replacing my previous policy of immediate execution via toilet flush should one stray from its outdoor into my indoor territory with a gentler "capture, relocate, and release" strategy the pillager had obviously taken advantage of. It had gravely underestimated me, however. Game on, I thought, before rushing back to my office and cracking open the big, blue book for a second opinion I was honestly in no mood to entertain, let alone accept.

"I am determined to see things differently," I read, *A Course in Miracles* workbook lesson 21, in which we learn that although anger appears to take many forms and a wide range of degrees, "You will become aware that a slight twinge of annoyance is nothing but a veil drawn over intense fury."

Oh, I was aware, alright. We had just been talking about this very subject in the Thursday night Course class I teach here in Denver while considering Chapter 23, IV. Above the Battleground, paragraph 1:

... What is not love is murder. What is not loving must be an attack. Every illusion is an assault on truth, and every one does violence to the idea of love because it seems to be of equal truth.

"Damn it!" I said, and found myself suddenly transported back to that inner classroom, once more seated across from my imaginary Jesus all decked out at his desk in his colorful summer cloak and sandals; those wacky pink shades sliding down the bridge of his nose.

"Hey," he said, lifting a palm in an attempted high five.

I taught him that, of course, but would have none of it at the moment. I narrowed my eyes at him. "I know what you're thinking," I said.

"You always do."

"We're always choosing between miracles and murder, really. Here in the embodied condition we think we're in, all anger is a projection, an attempt to hold someone or something 'out there' responsible for the unconscious, mistaken inner belief that we destroyed our creator by separating from eternally non-dualistic, all-inclusive love. If I perceive myself attacked by anything, I have chosen an inner teacher invested in keeping me furiously pedaling away on a treadmill of sin, guilt, and fear. An ego thought system intent on proving over and over again that I exist but it's not my fault."

"It's the spider's," Jesus said, mouth twitching in a smile.

"As a matter of fact, it *is*."

His brows shot up the way they do. "Seriously?"

"Well, what I mean is, I can prove it."

I showed him the welts—all red and swollen—looking worse by the minute, actually. I shivered anew at the very thought of that thing creeping around under the covers on its conniving, covert mission ...

He squinted in their general direction, tilting his head, as if considering. But I knew him well enough by now to realize he is extremely farsighted to say the least. Damn.

In truth, it wasn't just the spider that had me throwing a hissy fit. It was the heat, the fires, the unhealthy air burning my eyes, my lungs, the tiny bats mysteriously clattering through the trees in the morning light—one of which had fallen dead on our patio, as if portending Armageddon—as I walked my dog. It was the growing awareness that *nothing* in this world obeyed my rules, respected the most basic of my humble boundaries. Not the weather, not the government, not the wildlife, not the insects, not strangers or acquaintances and—I am sorry to report—perhaps especially *not* the ones I had chosen to hold most near and dear. Who continued to do their own thing with wild, reckless abandon, ever more oblivious to how it might affect *me*. The big, blue book gaped open on J's desk. I sighed and read on in lesson 21, from paragraph 3:

> ... Remember that you do not really recognize what arouses anger in you, and nothing that you believe in this connection means anything. You will probably be tempted to dwell more on some situations or persons than on others, on the fallacious grounds that they are more "obvious." This is not so. It is merely an example of the belief that some forms of attack are more justified than others.

Not so much, I thought, realizing that despite the enormous energy I had thrown its way, my personal "hierarchy of illusions" appeared to be toppling by the minute. Twinge of annoyance, I thought, mind drifting to the spider's dastardly deed? All of it infuriated me, reminiscent of that original belief in murder, a crime that never really happened—ugh!

"OK, so I'm beginning to see how it's all the same," I said. "But there is still this matter of boundaries on the level of form, still this matter of a spider—maybe a whole battalion, perhaps irreversibly poisonous—invading my space. My bed for heaven's sake; my skin! Still this matter of having to deal with fellow dream figures who—how do I put this politely?—do not always have the best interests of my body or its boundaries in mind. What do I do on the level of form when—within the dream—bodies appear to be threatening the self I think I am or other dream figures around me? Is it OK to kill a spider if it's biting the body I still think I am?"

Jesus reached into his desk drawer and—go figure—plucked out a matching pair of shades.

"I get it," I said, slipping them on, even though hot pink is *so* not my color. "I really want to see things differently, which means seeing them with you. I want to see the spider differently, the heat differently, the fires differently, the special relationships differently, because I want to feel better. When I look with you I see all these incoming attacks serve the same purpose: to block my awareness of love's enduring presence in my mind and keep me mindlessly battling an imaginary "out there." I join with your unlimited vision, allowing you to use the very specifics of my life the ego uses to make the dream real to heal my mind of a world of specifics."

Jesus was leaning back in his chair. "Even lawless spiders?"

I nodded. "Sure. But until all my illusions are seen clearly, all the guilt in my mind undone through learning to look at everything and everyone with you, I can take a compromise approach to the world of forms and bodies. That means I can protect myself by washing the linens in hot water to eliminate biting spiders or take a time out from a loved one in the throes of (I am tempted right now to say yet another, but will not) ego attack if necessary without hating them or blaming them, or calling them names. While simultaneously recognizing no one is guilty in truth. We all share the same frightened mind and the same healed mind. There's nothing out to get me after all. I mean, *Christ*, in truth there's no personal me to get."

"Hey," he said, smiling.

I sighed, a sigh of relief this time. "I'm beginning to see that every thought I have that is not kind toward all hides that original thought of murder that hides the thought of all-encompassing love I no longer think I deserve. It's the love I really feel too guilty to face. But it was only a ridiculous thought already laughed at by our one and only real Self. I will awaken to that truth when all my dreams of sin, guilt, and fear have been looked at with you. I mean me. I mean us." I adjusted my glasses. "You know what I'm saying."

Jesus threw back his head and laughed.

I had to laugh, too, in spite of my (little s) self. We laughed and laughed.

It was already getting hot again.

"Time for some frozen yogurt?" Jesus asked.

A little early in the day for me, but it had been a good class.

"Sure," I said, meeting him in the condition he thought he was in. "Let me just go get that wash into the dryer first."

Cloudy with a Chance of Projection

… Think of your mind as a vast circle, surrounded by a layer of heavy, dark clouds. You can see only the clouds because you seem to be standing outside the circle and quite apart from it. … From where you stand, you can see no reason to believe there is a brilliant light hidden by the clouds. The clouds seem to be the only reality. They seem to be all there is to see. Therefore, you do not attempt to go through them and past them, which is the only way in which you would be really convinced of their lack of substance. (*A Course in Miracles* workbook lesson 69, paragraphs 4 and 5)

At five years old, when not trying to dig to China, my friend Linda and I spent many afternoons flat on our backs in tangles of grass and clover studying shifting cloud patterns evidently choreographed from afar by a sorcerer equally possessed by the ridiculous and macabre. A giant's intimidating profile soon morphed into an elaborate, undulating wedding gown that melted into Frankenstein. A hedge of fairy-tale roses grew into a tiered cake, emerging as a wild steed transforming into the ever looming Cold-War threat of a sinister mushroom cloud.

Continued observation of the unpredictable skies above our fledgling suburban landscape combined with surveillance of the unsteady conditions within our homes and the wobbly moods of our fellow inhabitants soon led us to develop an even more dualistic theory. Far beyond what appeared to the naked eye must lie a land of good clouds and a land of bad, each continually launching ambassadors into our atmosphere to strengthen their viewpoint and attract followers. Our fellow earthlings had clearly already chosen one side or the other, although whether or not they could choose again remained a source of constant debate. The Commies and our brothers, for example, seemed far beyond redemption of any kind. But our parents and teachers had good days and bad, bolstering the case for free—however constantly vacillating—will.

In any event, firmly, unalterably aligned with the leaders of the good-cloud tribe as we innately found ourselves, we began to worship them in our own weird way, leaving little gifts of perfume samples and hard candies we pilfered from my Mom in the sandbox and under our pillows in exchange for specific interventions on our behalf. Asking for proof of their presence, protection, and ability to conquer the bad that–despite our vivid imaginations and the elaborate stories we wove to explain their invisible ways—never really came.

I am thinking about clouds and their meaning today because, as I slowly regained consciousness this morning, in that state of not-quite-asleep and not-quite-awake that sometimes produces flashes of welcome and unwelcome insight, I envisioned a special relationship I've used to block my awareness to love's true presence. Splayed across the sky in my mind as a detailed, three-dimensional cloud blocking my field of vision, yet bordered by shimmering light, the guilty residue of just having eclipsed the sun.

I recalled the metaphor the Course uses in workbook lessons 69 and 70 in which Jesus compares our tortured projections of sin, guilt, and fear to clouds that can seem attractive, repulsive, or terrifying, but remain completely unsubstantial and have no effect at all on the light they seem to obscure. A light that continues to shine in the one mind we never really left. A light that envelops all the seeming separated ones we love and hate including the selves we think we are; the one blazing light of our true, eternal, all-loving nature. Instead of choosing sides among illusory clouds, the Course invites us to transcend them by choosing the inner teacher of light always beckoning from our one mind.

... Determine to go past the clouds. Reach out and touch them in your mind. Brush them aside with your hand; feel them resting on your cheeks and forehead and eyelids as you go through them. Go on; clouds cannot stop you. (Lesson 69, paragraph 6)

The meaning I've assigned to the clouds of guilt I prefer to see in an imaginary sky to prove I exist independently but it's not my fault has not changed all that much since I was five. But I now know that trying to coax the light into this dream will only strengthen the thought of being cast into perpetual darkness that sprang from a mistaken belief I could separate from our infinitely indivisible source. Only choosing for the part of my mind that knows *only* light can lead me through the clouds of my projections to the perpetual light of our one being. But walking through the clouds takes courage, and cannot be attempted alone. Only joining—from moment to moment as we examine each cloud we've imagined to obscure love—with the part of our mind certain there is nothing to fear, will lead us back to the light.

Since all illusions of salvation have failed you, surely you do not want to remain in the clouds, looking vainly for idols there, when you could so easily walk on into the light of real salvation. Try to pass the clouds by whatever means appeals to you. If it helps you, think of me holding your hand and leading you. And I assure you this will be no idle fantasy. (Lesson 70, paragraph 9)

Jesus doesn't literally give us a hand, of course, there being no bodies in truth. But if it helps us here in the condition we think we're in to imagine holding the hand of the part of our mind sure we are safe, whole, loved and loving, regardless of shifting cloud patterns, I say, go for it! Because every time I take that hand another cloud vanishes, revealing more light.

As I settled down to work later that morning—gazing out the window at an unusually socked-in cloud cover that had settled over Denver as if with malevolent intent—I had to smile. Even if today is cloudy with a chance of more projection, clouds are but images I make up from moment to moment in my fear, without meaning, but with purpose. A purpose I can use to strengthen the darkness of my secret sin, guilt, and fear, or offer it to the light of forgiveness in our one mind in which all clouds of fear vanish into the healing certainty of our one, forever-beating heart.

Political purpose

Twice last week, while engrossed in friendly, casual conversations with two different acquaintances, I found myself unexpectedly catapulted into unnerving if not downright threatening territory. Steered by these two seemingly benign "others" from the predictable terrain of amiable chitchat into a conversational minefield by what I perceived as their derelict choice to suddenly bring up the Affordable Care Act, or "Obamacare," as those across the aisle not so affectionately call it.

Their previously smiling lips contorted around each syllable in a snarl my mind on ego couldn't help but point out seriously aged them as they continued to wax bitterly on about our president and his moronic followers' (that would be me) horrific attacks on truth, justice, and the American way. Spouting a lengthy litany of astonishing (from my perspective) lies about the new law's stipulations that had me hugging my chest and leaning away as if ducking shrapnel, shielding my ever so innocently beating heart.

I could feel the familiar, welcome sting of saliva gathering in the back of my throat, as if about to consume a long-time-no-tasted favorite meal, the rush of adrenaline coursing through my junkie veins, the hiss of the ego's sweet, triumphant whisper in my ears:

"Go for it! You deserve it. After all, *they* started it. No one can blame you."

Not that the self I still mostly think I am would ever directly, verbally take them on. Open conflict has never been my forte. I felt, rather, that same old call to passively categorize them as people I did not wish to get to know better or spend additional time with. Whose political affiliations—as witnessed by these current tantrums and insensitive assumptions that I could possibly share in their hateful opinions—would forever divide us.

And yet, my surge of moral superiority passed all too quickly, leaving me minutes later with a guilty hangover and the unwelcome recognition that the choice I had once more made to side with the sneaky inner teacher of separation realized hurt like hell. Please help me to choose you instead next time, I silently begged my imaginary Jesus, that *symbol* of uninterrupted, eternally invulnerable wholeness that continues to smile on our tall tales of dividing oneness in which we strut and fret our hours on the stage, signifying nothing but forever fluctuating ratings.

Later that same week, brushing my teeth one morning, I found myself listening to an NPR story about Mitt Romney being booed during a speech to the NAACP while promising to overturn "Obamacare," and experienced the same adrenaline rush followed by the same call to arms on behalf of the inner teacher of sin, guilt, and fear:

"Go for it! You deserve it. After all, *they* started it. No one can blame you."

Although this time I immediately recognized that siding with this voice would hurt too much and chose instead to hear my own call for love disguised in this seeming attack, that same evening I dove right back into the ego's mosh pit, this time while out with friends who share my political views. Over a couple of glasses of wine the conversation exuberantly veered toward media coverage of the upcoming election, with each of us gleefully recounting reports we had heard of the latest blunders committed by those we loved to hate.

After sharing the Romney faux pas broadcast from earlier that day, I wondered aloud how educated people given the same information could possibly arrive at completely opposite—one correct, the other, at best, incomprehensible—conclusions? The tantalizing taste in my mouth, the sting in my veins, and the hiss in my ears was followed, almost immediately, this time, by a sucker punch thud of guilt to my solar plexus.

A despairing sense of helplessness settled over me as I recalled the last presidential campaign four years ago during which I had pretty much thrown practicing forgiveness *A Course in Miracles*-style out the window for several months, at least when it came to this particular illusion within my personal hierarchy. Since then

I'd learned there are no sabbaticals from forgiveness. Attempting to exempt my practice from a specific illusion would only hurt me. And yet here I was again already plunging into the fray, choosing to delay the return to all-inclusive love I claimed to want with all my heart in exchange for the momentary high of believing I was right. We hadn't even made it to the conventions yet, for Christ's sake. How to get through this most divisive of seasons with my right mind intact; strengthened instead of diminished?

> The real world is the state of mind in which the only purpose of the world is seen to be forgiveness. Fear is not its goal, for the escape from guilt becomes its aim. The value of forgiveness is perceived and takes the place of idols, which are sought no longer, for their 'gifts' are not held dear. No rules are idly set, and no demands are made of anyone or anything to twist and fit into the dream of fear. Instead, there is a wish to understand all things created as they really are. And it is recognized that all things must be forgiven first, and *then* understood. (Chapter 30, V. The Only Purpose, paragraph 1)

I realized as I later contemplated these words that I had a long-standing special relationship with my political affiliation. An alliance I had used for decades to further my personal story of victimization (the hidden purpose of *every* dream) and enhance a false sense of self-righteousness whose "gifts" were at best short-lived. If I really wanted to divest myself of the ego's "gift" of guilt—the illusory price I seem to have paid for individuality that appeared to have cost me the everything of my true nature— I would have to relinquish my kneejerk devotion to the inner teacher of differences. Thereby aligning with the inner teacher of equality that sees only our sameness here in the individual condition we find ourselves in. Recognizes only the same split mind at work in the psyches of members of both parties, intent like me, on proving they exist but it's not their fault.

I would have to ask to understand all things created as they really are more than the way I made them up to be, and once more turn to the inner teacher of forgiveness for a different understanding. The complete certainty that "not one note in Heaven's song was missed" as a result of my present decision to believe in the "tiny, mad idea" of separation by seeing it as an outside picture of an inner condition I couldn't bear to own.

This year, as the election approaches, my growing awareness that projection hurts me at the forefront of my mind, I am choosing again with renewed sincerity to really see this season differently. As a welcome classroom in which I learn the gentle lessons of forgiveness and give the loving gift of true compassion. Recognizing that regardless of our beliefs and affiliations, we all share the same split mind made mad by guilt, and heal as we allow our inner teacher to teach us to heal the only thing in real need of healing: our mistaken mind. I will do my best to look no longer to the past to find myself, try from moment to moment to take responsibility for the present I am dreaming up, and choose again to join with the present love of our true nature flowing forever unperturbed in our right mind.

... Be speeded on your way by honesty, and let not your experiences here deceive in retrospect. They were not free from bitter cost and joyless consequence. ... Do not look back except in honesty. And when an idol tempts you, think of this:

> There never was a time an idol brought you anything
> Except the "gift" of guilt. No one was bought except
> At cost of pain, nor was it ever paid by you alone.

(Chapter 30, V. The Only Purpose, from paragraphs 9 and 10)

I Am Not a Body. I Am Free. *Seriously?*

I sat squirming at my desk, unable to find a position that didn't aggravate the persistent pain on the right side of my lower back, scratching a fresh crop of mosquito bites on my arm while struggling to finish an article featuring a person who had endured horrific illness and personal loss. I glanced down at my dog Kayleigh's vacant little bed. She'd been sleeping there earlier, as usual, hadn't she? She was so quiet without her collar on—in "stealth mode," my daughter called it—and must have slipped away to her next favorite spot nestled on top of her yellow satin blanket on the living room couch.

I rose and went to check on her but she wasn't there, either. I hurried to her next likely perch at the bottom of the stairs by the front door, but no Kayleigh. I surveyed the top of the stairs, my daughter's room, the other bedrooms, a sting of fear in my veins. I started yelling her name, opening closets. Downstairs, I could hear a faint barking. I headed to the basement rec room, but no luck. Had she somehow gotten outside? I was running now, out into the yard, shouting her name in the garage and the alley, back inside again and out the front door. The faint intermittent barking continued emanating from somewhere.

I phoned my husband at work as I continued racing around the house and the grounds, hoping to engage him in my hysteria. My mind on ego certain that two terrified people had more power than one. Could she have possibly followed him out that morning without us realizing it? He couldn't recall. Could she have become trapped in a neighbor's garage, fallen into a basement window well, or, you know, worse? We had coyotes in the neighborhood after all, ruthless predators that had wiped out the local cat population including our pet, Daisy. At six pounds, Kayleigh weighed less than our former feline, an easy target. I could hear barking again, thank God, but from where? My husband said he was driving home.

I continued dashing around, near tears, begging for help from my imaginary Jesus, apologizing for requesting assistance in form while explaining I'd been having a tough time in the dream lately, everything so seemingly uncertain. I just couldn't handle the loss of my beloved pet on top of all these other troubling illusions. Could he please make an exception just this once? You know, throw on a cape, swoop down here right now, and find my little dog for me, deliver her safe and sound into my outstretched arms? But he must have been busy meeting some other *A Course in Miracles* student in the condition she thought she was in because he didn't answer.

I raced to the basement again and this time spotted Kayleigh standing on a folding table against the wall filled with listing piles and boxes of papers from my mother-in-law's estate my husband had still not sorted through nearly a year after her death. Amid the surrounding chaos, my little dog emerged like a figure coming into focus in an optical illusion. She had apparently managed to hop up from an adjacent chair–piled with blankets my daughter used when friends slept over—then become afraid to jump down. She hung her head, guiltily. I blinked back tears, scooping her up and holding her to my heart, the place she fit into like a missing puzzle piece when I slept with her at night.

I phoned my husband, carried her to my office, nestled her in her bed on my lap, and opened the big, blue book to Lesson 199, "I am not a body. I am free."

Seriously? After all, not once in the half hour in which I frantically sought for my dog had it so much as entered my fictional brain that I was anything other than a body having a hell of a time, seeking another body I believed delivered the love I found so hard to hold onto in this world, a love that could be cruelly snatched away by circumstances beyond my control at any moment. And yet *A Course in Miracles* calmly insists, over and over, that we are one mind not many bodies hiding out in a world we dreamed up in which to seek refuge from an imaginary God intent on punishing us for the imaginary crime of separation.

It is essential to your progress in this course that you accept today's idea, and hold it very dear. Be not concerned that to the ego it is quite insane. The ego holds the body dear because it dwells in it, and lives united with the home that it has made. It is a part of the illusion that has sheltered it from being found illusory itself. (Paragraph 3)

I glanced down at my dog now sleeping in my lap, at my sun-damaged hand resting on her soft fur. I thought of my daughter away in Boston, flying home tomorrow in another storm, no doubt. My back ached, my bites itched, the world wound wearily on. There was just no way the person I thought I was reading the big, blue book could grasp her true identity as spirit except in the holy instant in which I was willing to look with my inner imaginary Jesus at the body's purpose as a finite limit on boundless love. Preprogrammed to endure abandonment by other bodies and eventually self-destruct.

I sighed and asked at last for help from our inner teacher, whose vision always offers the real, enduring, invulnerable comfort of prevailing life as one beyond ever-vulnerable bodies.

Here does it hide, and here it can be seen as what it is. Declare your innocence and you are free. The body disappears because you have no need for it except the need the Holy Spirit sees. For this, the body will appear as useful form for what the mind must do. It thus becomes a vehicle which helps forgiveness be extended to the all-inclusive goal that it must reach, according to God's plan. (Paragraph 4)

Only when I join our inner teacher in the one mind outside the illusion of time and space can I *experience* the truth of these words and know I am safe and whole, innocent, loved, and loving. The Course does not ask us to deny our very real seeming experience within bodies—not the bodies we think we inhabit or the bodies we think bring us happiness or cause us pain—but it does ask us to bring our obsessions with them, again and again, for however long it takes for our guilt and fear to subside, to the light always shining in the classroom of our right mind. We *are* asked to allow Jesus–that *symbol* of our invulnerable wholeness–to use them to teach us the impossibility of containing or limiting real love, observing with him our robotic identification with many bodies over one mind at the root of all suffering; that it may be healed. We *are* asked to choose again and again for the inner teacher of truth over lies.

Be free today. And carry freedom as your gift to those who still believe they are enslaved within a body. Be you free, so that the Holy Spirit can make use of your escape from bondage, to set free the many who perceive themselves as bound and helpless and afraid. Let love replace their fears through you. Accept salvation now, and give your mind to Him Who calls to you to make this gift to Him. For He would give you perfect freedom, perfect joy, and hope that finds its full accomplishment in God. (Paragraph 7)

Seriously!

What Does it Mean to Heal?

I sat once more in lotus position on a Monday morning, eyes shut, unsuccessfully attempting to connect with my seemingly missing right mind.

"Server down," the ego said.

"I'm not listening," I told him.

"Then why did you answer me?"

He had a point, despite the snide tone. For more than a week I'd been grappling with a series of scenes in my dream secretly crafted by moi to keep the character of Susan within the fantasy I'd cooked up on her wounded-warrior-woman toes, battling dragons first in the form of seemingly attacking "other" bodies, and then in the form of the body I think I am, attacking itself. So that before I could fully forgive the excruciating drama I made up in a special relationship (and then forgot I made it up) I needed to dash off to attend to the excruciating drama I made up (and then forgot I made it up) within my own body involving a misplaced sacroiliac joint and several misaligned vertebrae in my lower back. Rendering me effectively minus a mind!

The first trip to the chiropractor only served to increase the pain keeping me awake at night, causing me to return two days later for additional, more invasive adjustments that ended up wreaking havoc with my digestive system, causing me to back out of an idyllic hike in the mountains during a weekend getaway to Rocky Mountain National Park with family and friends. When I returned home last night, I called my Traditional Chinese Medicine doctor and secured the first available appointment for tomorrow morning, leaving me with more than 24 hours to go before the possibility of some relief.

I drew a deep, full body breath—inhaling into my upper chest, my stomach, and then abdomen, and slowly exhaling in the opposite direction—designed to calm the body's central nervous system. I asked to see my situation differently—the way it really is instead of the way I set it up, to paraphrase the Course—through the eyes of the inner teacher of love instead of fear. It was difficult to keep my back straight, my shoulders back, the illusion of benevolent chi flowing.

"What the hell *is* chi, anyway?" the ego asked. "Sounds like some kind of energy drink, to me. Those can really wreak havoc with your system."

I ignored him. I ached all over, really, on every level. Suffice it to say I did not feel the peace of God shining in me now.

"Chi whiz," the ego said, smiling his Cheshire-Cat smile. "Connectivity error."

"You're a connectivity error," I countered, opening one eye, as if there was actually something out there speaking.

I thought about what *A Course in Miracles* refers to as "magic," the attempt to solve the internal problem of our unconscious guilt over the belief that we separated from our infinitely united source by external means. The body's physical and emotional noisy, frequent distress to the contrary, the one problem of separation from our source that never really was remains in the one mind, just like the world of bodies that have never left their source. I sighed. I had never been more aware of my resistance to accepting the Course's insistence that we are really just one mind, not many bodies, or my attraction to defending the special self I still think I am that led to my addiction to suffering.

My mind drifted back to the past week. Although hugely distracted by pain, I'd experienced lucid moments in which I could clearly observe how I was using the lack of control I felt in a special relationship—my inability to change the "other" or fix the situation—to reinforce the story of this personal self. To prove the ego's propaganda that I autonomously exist but it's not my fault. I recognized briefly that the problem was not the other person but my choice to side with the inner teacher of fear over love and return to peaceful right-mindedness. But secretly terrified of disappearing into the arms of real, eternally unified love, I quickly detoured once more into fear, attacking my body to make it all the more real and, in so doing, attacking the other person for failing to meet my perceived personal needs. "Look what you did to me!" my body silently screamed. Not that anyone appeared to be listening.

The Course quote "… Behold me brother, at your hand I die" came back to me. I had never completely *experienced* its meaning, but I did so now. In an effort to make the "attacks" I perceived coming from this other person real, my sense that they remained hopelessly unresolved to my mind on ego's satisfaction, I had attacked the body I think I inhabit to punish this imaginary special relationship for my pain, to prove him guiltier in God's eyes than I secretly believe I am. (As if *that* were possible!)

> Whenever you consent to suffer pain, to be deprived, unfairly treated or in need of anything, you but accuse your brother of attack upon God's Son. You hold a picture of your crucifixion before his eyes, that he may see his sins are writ in Heaven in your blood and death, and go before him, closing off the gate and damning him to hell. (*A Course in Miracles* text, Chapter 27, The Healing of the Dream, I. The Picture of Crucifixion, from paragraph 3.)

The Course does not mince words about the ego's intentions, but merely exposes its lies. In truth the ego's hallucination that the "tiny, mad, idea" of separation from our non-dualistic, all-loving Self had, and continues to have, no real effects on anyone or anything. We never sinned against God, don't need to feel guilty about it, and don't need to fear retribution for a "crime" that never happened. We remain awake within the embrace of eternally abstract loving wholeness merely dreaming of exile. We just don't know it.

We awake from the mad dream from moment to moment through our willingness to change our minds about our belief in bodies competing for survival, constantly in need of defending themselves from external and internal assaults. By choosing again and again to look at each specific fear our mind on ego cooked up to keep us from realizing there is nothing to fear with the inner teacher of forgiveness of what never was, we rise above the linear, ego-invented world of time and space, and allow our split mind to heal. The robust health of innocence I am really always seeking lies in changing my mind about my belief that you have caused me real pain, the belief that anything a body experiences could compromise the comforting memory of our one, eternal nature always waiting in our one, real mind.

Attest his innocence and not his guilt. Your healing is his comfort and his health because it proves illusions are not true. It is not will for life but wish for death that is the motivation for this world. Its only purpose is to prove guilt real. No worldy thought or act or feeling has a motivation other than this one. (From paragraph 6)

Healing my mind of the belief that my body, or any body, ever lived apart from the only child of God seamlessly fused with its creator is always a present decision I can make when I have once more strayed away from the mind, a decision to side with mind over bodies, with the inner teacher of love over fear. When I do, healing my mind's sick belief has happened and wholeness abides regardless of what seems to be transpiring in my relationships with other imaginary bodies or my relationship with the imaginary body I appear to inhabit. Even the pain in my own body has no power whatsoever to rob my mind of sustainable peace.

The ego's triumphant smile slowly faded into the spurious ether from which it sprang. Having joined with our right mind, I was still remotely aware of the afterimage of pain but could no longer take the illusion of it seriously or attempt to hold any other illusion responsible for it. No longer identified with it, it no longer appeared to threaten my inner peace or disrupt the true mind-healing purpose of my day. One of these days, when I had looked at all my illusions through the eyes of real love outside the dream, I would come to the joyful realization that I could never die apart from oneness because I had never so lived. I made some more chamomile tea and got down to tackle the work on my desk.

What Is a Miracle?

Déjà vu, I thought, back at my desk in pain writing a post about the true meaning of healing. Trying, as always, to connect with my right mind, thereby allowing all I really wanted to learn to flow through the little seeming self I still mostly think I am but have at least begun to doubt or—perhaps more accurately—withdraw a portion of my faith in. My lower back throbbed. My stomach ached. A situation in my personal life continued to confound. And yet the problems du jour began to disappear into the imagination from which they had wandered as my fingers raced across the keyboard, delivering comforting words I needed to hear. Reminding me I am not a body but a decision-making mind beyond this dream of exile from authentic, all-inclusive, eternal love. A mind that became confused about what it was and what it wanted and seemed to choose against itself but could, at any moment, choose *for* its real Self and heal.

The many seeming problems merged into the one problem and then into the welcome recognition of no problem. Our childish wishes to the contrary, the "tiny, mad idea" that we could fragment our one Self into a gazillion needy, competing pieces, had no effects. We remain seamlessly fused with our creator, endlessly extending the infinite kindness of our true nature, merely dreaming otherwise. La-di-da-da!

I read the words I wrote for the next hour-and-a-half with wonder and gratitude for the grace of forgiven perception flowing happily beyond the comprehension of the body I seem to inhabit. And then, nearing the essay's finish, my Word program inexplicably shut down. When I went to open the document representing the morning's work, only the first paragraph appeared on the screen. I searched for it in all my files. I googled how to retrieve a Word document, followed the instructions written in teeny-weenie type apparently to be read only by teeny-weenie boppers, and came up with nothing. I checked my computer's settings and discovered that the backup file function I thought I had turned on was off. That's when the swearing started.

Now completely identified with *my* work (as if) I am sorry to report, I frantically continued in this vein for nearly an hour, unwilling to accept the loss of *my* document, unwilling to begin again. Certain a miracle in form would arrive at any moment if I just willed it strongly enough. I'd hardly slept for the past two nights for crying out loud. I was too tired to start all over again. The pain in my back raged. My stomach knotted. I deserved a break, didn't I? I tried another document retrieval method. It, too—like everything here on planet crazy—failed. "Damn," I said. Out loud. Again.

My little dog stared up at me, brows knit in concern. I decided to take her for a walk. I walked and walked, swinging my arms as though with real purpose, Kayleigh scurrying to keep up with me. Asking for help from our right mind to see this situation differently but resisting the realization that the words had come through me but not of me and would come again if I would simply choose for the inner teacher of truth patiently waiting to help me remember what I *really* wanted to learn.

I thought about the Course's challenging contention that we do not perceive our own best interests. I thought about the way in which pre-*A Course in Miracles* student Susan had labored to coax physical miracles from a hallucinated benevolent universe, the exhausting practice of attempting to deny the cruelty of this world made as a defense against real love in order to maintain the blissful outlook required to attract what my ego thought it wanted. And I recalled the disillusionment that had brought me to this path in the first place. The recognition that nothing I sought (and occasionally actually even found) in the world had ever delivered the comfort I was really seeking, the all-inclusive innocence and reassuring awareness that despite my secret fears, I remained infinitely loved and loving, along with everyone else seeking for themselves where they could never be found. There has to be a better way, I thought, echoing the certain sentiment that had invited the Course's scribing in the first place. And there is.

> Forgiveness is the home of miracles. The eyes of Christ deliver them to all they look upon in mercy and in love. Perception stands corrected in His sight, and what was meant to curse has come to bless. (*A Course in Miracles* workbook, 13. What Is a Miracle?, from paragraph 3)

The "eyes of Christ" is simply a metaphor for the real vision available when I am willing to choose against my misperception of personal need, thereby shifting my awareness to the perspective of no needs, the memory of our one true Self, within which all needs are endlessly met. I smiled. The dog curled up in her bed at my feet. And I rewrote the post, easily and effortlessly, once more reassured by all I had forgotten but really wanted and needed to hear.

> The miracle is taken first on faith, because to ask for it implies the mind has been made ready to conceive of what it cannot see and does not understand. Yet faith will bring its witnesses to show that what it rested on is really there. And thus the miracle will justify your faith in it, and show it rested on a world more real than what you saw before; a world redeemed from what you thought was there. (Paragraph 4)

Without Forgiveness I Will Still Be Blind

I lay awake in the middle of the night as I sometimes do, adrift in that yawning chasm of lonesome silence in which my ego thoughts spring to life like taunting little toys, raucously reviewing problems large and small, worldly and intimate. Helplessly, hopelessly, pondering the state of the union and the state of my sun-damaged skin. The status of my little dog's hurt leg and the safest place to sit in a movie theatre to avoid death by insane gunman, the escalating rhetoric in the presidential campaigns, and the possible infection of my recently scraped toes. Looming work deadlines, the bitter sweetness of my daughter's impending return to college, and what to do with the tiny golden beets I'd scored at the Farmers' Market.

I asked to see things differently—through the eyes of the inner teacher of love instead of fear—over and over again, but nothing happened. I popped another magic herbal supplement and breathed deeply, tensing and then relaxing my muscles, head to toe. I squeezed the insomnia acupressure points on my ears and visualized the waves on my favorite beach rhythmically lapping the idyllic shore. I envisioned my chakras spinning in synchronized harmony. Still, I remained awake, increasingly concerned about the encroaching busyness of my Monday versus the guaranteed fatigue of my body if I couldn't fall back to sleep for at least a couple hours.

I thought about the way I had often lay awake like this as a child, focused on every little creak in the house, the lights of an occasional, passing vehicle lunging wolf-like across the walls, the menacing rumble of the refrigerator, the hiss and tick of the hot-water heater, the roar of a distant jet perhaps launched by the Commies to bomb Manhattan a ways down the river. The possibility—however remote—that the flying monkeys from *The Wizard of Oz* had escaped the castle once and for all and were, at this very moment, winging their way up the Hudson toward a target with my name on it. In more ways than I cared to consider,

I was still that frightened child, stranger in a strange land just waiting for the punishment I secretly knew I deserved for running away from home, like every other frightened child here on planet crazy.

Eventually I drifted off to troubled dreams, the last of which found me alone in a pitch-black forest, immobilized with terror that any forward movement might mean stepping into a trap or a land mine. Breath held, seemingly paralyzed, willing myself invisible to nocturnal predators, I suddenly became aware of my hand nestled inside the perfect-fitting glove of a larger one. Embraced by the abrupt certainty that I would see my way through, if I could simply dare to place one foot in front of the other, and continue to hold that hand.

And so I did. Despite my crushing fear, I drew a deep breath, raised my right foot and set it down, followed by the left. Each time I did so, the path suddenly revealed itself in the light at my feet as if an invisible someone were flipping on an invisible flashlight. I walked faster and more certainly then, and as I did, the light grew steady, revealing just enough of the path before me to prevent me from stumbling.

I awoke thinking about *A Course in Miracles* workbook lesson 247: "Without forgiveness I will still be blind."

> … For forgiveness is the only means whereby Christ's vision comes to me. Let me accept what His sight shows me as the simple truth, and I am healed completely. (Lines 3 and 4).

And I realized that although I'd been begging to see things differently, I hadn't been willing to get Susan out of the way. I was still standing guard—wedded to the ego's deliberate blindness and dubious security—trying to puzzle out solutions to non-existent problems while unwilling to take the hand of my right mind that would lead me toward the light of perfect oneness I really craved. I was still unwilling to *fully* acknowledge the pervasive darkness of the shameful, bereft belief in separation and *fully* trust in the inner teacher of forgiveness. Whose X-Ray vision penetrates the illusory facade of our many problems to the "tiny, mad, idea" of the one problem that never really occurred, our impossible, devastating dreams notwithstanding.

Now illuminated by the light of our right mind, I saw that I didn't need to do anything about my perceived sleeplessness because I was never really awake here in this dream of exile from all-inclusive, non-differentiated love in the first place. I didn't need to do anything about the problems and distractions that seemed to be keeping me awake either. I only needed to stop attributing my distress to outside causes and deliver the darkness of my illusions back to the light of one mind. Where Jesus—that *symbol* of our unalterable oneness—waits patiently to lead each and every seeming one of us through the dense clouds of our tortured dreams to the one real home we never really left.

It all comes down to trust. To my still intermittent but gradually growing willingness to grasp that hand in the darkness and put one foot in front of the other, allowing the part of my mind that can truly see to light my way. Although my body is tired this morning as I write these words it no longer concerns me. And I am a little more willing to embrace the possibility that I am not a singular body but a unified mind. Capable of choosing the guide that will lead me to the awareness that I have never left our one and only, blessedly formless, infinitely integrated home.

So would I look on everyone today. My brothers are Your Sons. Your Fatherhood created them, and gave them all to me as part of You, and my own Self as well. Today I honor You through them, and thus I hope this day to recognize my Self. (Paragraph 2).

I Want to Hold Your Hand

... Whenever fear intrudes anywhere along the road to peace, it is because the ego has attempted to join the journey with us and cannot do so. Sensing defeat and angered by it, the ego regards itself as rejected and becomes retaliative. You are invulnerable to its retaliation because I am with you. On this journey you have chosen me as your companion *instead* of the ego. Do not attempt to hold on to both or you will try to go in different directions and will lose the way. (*A Course in Miracles* Chapter 8, section V., paragraph 5)

While attending Ken Wapnick's weeklong August 2012 Academy class at the Foundation for *A Course in Miracles* in Temecula, California, I experienced a sense of profound and enduring comfort and renewed faith in this journey home to the place in the one mind we never really left. A kind of elongated "holy instant" outside the imaginary realm of time and space wherein, with rare exceptions, I remained largely right-minded, happily aligned with the inner teacher of love over fear. More certain than ever that learning to see everyone and everything seemingly "out there" innocent through forgiving eyes truly offered everything I could possibly want. Able to easily welcome the awareness of the healing of my one split mind as the only real purpose of my days, the transformation of my life from a prison of individuality and special interests to a classroom of all-inclusive forgiveness as my only goal.

Toward the end of the week I had a dream that continues to haunt me—in a mostly good way—revealing as it does the two inner voices always available for us to check in with, the two hands always available for us to hold. One extended to lead us back to wholeness, the other to escort us more deeply into this dream of exile from our true, undifferentiated, eternally loving nature.

I'd been climbing in mountainous terrain, non-stop, for a long time, navigating seemingly endless switchbacks that grew steeper and rockier with each step. Drawing deeper and deeper breaths as the air and trees began to thin, wildlife and vegetation shrinking in self-defense. Just above tree-line the wind came unhinged, ravaging the granite walls, howling triumphant down the hollow canyon.

Pausing to catch my breath at a jagged outcropping, I shivered and strained to hear a voice over the gale, a warning I knew I must heed, sternly explaining that the journey would grow much more difficult now. I would need additional protection to go on from here, special clothes to shield me from the obviously harsh elements, special boots, and special gear for—you know—a special me. I might not survive without them. Obviously I had neglected to do my homework, had failed to adequately prepare. I had seriously underestimated the difficulty of this journey. I would need to turn back, the voice insisted, descend and re-provision before once more ascending my special path with my special props to my special home, with my special friend, and yet …

In my peripheral vision, my imaginary Jesus leaned back against the sheer wall in his flimsy robes and worn sandals, smiling his perennially amused smile, hand, as always, patiently extended.

"I know what you're thinking," I said.

His eyes widened.

"I already have all I need to be safe. All I need to go home." I knew what he would say, at least, in every circumstance. I just didn't really believe it.

"You think?"

"I just need to trust is what you're trying to say."

He smiled some more; hand outstretched.

I wanted to take it, I really did. But that voice continued its concerned, sober warning. I could even perceive the official presence just behind me from which it apparently emanated—not unlike a ski patrol or rescue party leader—the palpable gravitational pull of another, strong, outstretched hand. The cautionary litany persisted. Jesus just shook his head and continued to smile as gothic clouds swirled and thickened overhead, the hail moved in, and darkness fell hard and sudden around us.

Blinded now, unable to move, I found it increasingly hard to breathe and awoke more conscious than ever of the ego's noisy conviction that reaching for the hand that would lead me out of this dream we call life would prove certain death. Aware that my recent willingness to make inner peace my life's only goal (despite ebbing and flowing external "evidence" to the contrary) had once more rallied the ego to make it perfectly clear that my current trajectory spelled curtains for Susan.

But I am learning the ego lies, that the voice I listen to, the hand I hold; is an ongoing *choice*. Even though (and perhaps especially because) I have experienced more and more the comfort, completion, and certainty of my right mind, the fear continues to beckon. Until *all* guilt in the mind over taking what the Course rightly refers to as "the tiny, mad idea" of separation seriously is undone through forgiveness of what never was, the fear will return, often in a more compelling, convincing package than ever. But when I am willing to take Jesus' hand despite the fear, my belief in the ego's voice weakens a little more while my ability to recognize its many clever impersonations continues to strengthen.

I recalled another recent dream in which I stood atop a cliff beside the draped marvel complaining that I didn't know what to do about anything in this world. Enumerating and bemoaning the many specific ways in which life had fallen short of my mind on ego's increasingly meager expectations. Jesus patiently ignored the details of my little hissy fit while continuing to telegraph the silent message that I just needed to jump. I stared down into the perilous pit below and wondered what he might be smoking but he just kept silently encouraging me to take his outstretched hand. The ego's warnings thundered in my ears. Still, at some point, the terror of continued paralysis exceeded the terror of forward momentum. Suddenly, without thinking, I grabbed his hand and held tight. He returned the pressure and ... we jumped!

To my amazement, instead of disappearing into the void, we landed in cool, clear, pure, healing water, laughing our heads off. For weeks afterwards, whenever something seemingly "out there" tempted me to throw away my peace, I pictured me and my imaginary Jesus cannon-balling, swan diving, or somersaulting off that cliff, cracking ourselves up. And eventually went on to deal with problems that no longer seemed pressing, decisions that no longer seemed weighty, blessedly oblivious to my former need to have them work out to my "special" satisfaction.

... Never accord the ego the power to interfere with the journey. It has none, because the journey is the way to what is true. Leave all illusions behind, and reach beyond all attempts of the ego to hold you back. I go before you because I am beyond the ego. Reach, therefore, for my hand because you want to transcend the ego. My strength will never be wanting, and if you choose to share it you will do so. (From paragraph 6)

I Am Entitled to Miracles

Suffice it to say the day had not gotten off to an auspicious start. I'd arisen consumed with repetitive judgments of imaginary external events no amount of vowing to make peace of mind my only goal seemed to dispel. Then, too, while brushing my teeth, the mere mention of the recent movie *Rock of Ages* on NPR had triggered the song *We Built this City* to lodge itself unbidden in my head, replaying over and over again! As the tune echoed on in those empty chambers, I mentally complained about having to make myself presentable on a weekend to attend an event I'd really rather not. Indoors, no less, just when the temperature outdoors had begun to cool enough to dare to once more venture there.

Driving to the event annoyingly consumed with rocking memories of the 1980s I'd rather not revisit, the confounding song abruptly ceased, replaced by a sense of deep stillness in which time dropped away and the presence of my imaginary forgiveness companion revealed itself in a welcome wave of spacious gentleness. Enabling me to look, without self-condemnation, at the way I reenacted my original fear of love by pushing its reflection away right here in this dream I called life. More often than I cared to admit, withholding unqualified support and approval of others, particularly those "special" ones I professed to hold most dear.

In my mind's eye, my 19-year-old daughter's beautiful face emerged. I gazed at her directly, looking more deeply into her eyes than I had perhaps ever dared to look since she first began to speak and—suddenly willing to risk everything, as if there were anything real to risk—silently told her how much I loved her. How proud I was of her. What a wonderful person she was—so kind and strong, so smart, independent, and funny. All worries about her dissolved. There were no spoken or unspoken "buts" in this conversation. No exceptions. No tacit advice about what she might want to "work on"—just truth.

Eyes brimming with gratitude, still aware of the presence of my imaginary Jesus; that *symbol* of our invulnerable eternally united nature, I realized she was absolutely perfect and always had been. And with that realization flashed a sudden awareness that I was, too. We shared the same fear of disappointing each other and ourselves here in the dream. The same fear that we were never enough, the same wish for reassurance that we would always be loved and loving despite our secret belief that we separated from our source and could never return home again. But we shared the same fearlessness available in our right mind, too, a bravery based on the certainty that our self-worth comes from what we still really are within our creator, not from the parts we so skillfully play in our dreams.

My heart blown wide open, I arrived at the event and settled in to listen to speakers I often disagreed with and too often found myself struggling not to judge. This time, however, I heard only our shared truth in their words. The occasional points of disagreement that had seemed so glaringly essential in the past, no longer seemed important. Only our common interest—the fundamental, common yearning to find our way home to our unified being—prevailed. Afterwards, I lingered to chat with people I hadn't always found it pleasant to chat with.

Later that day, still in a welcome haze of healed awareness and profound appreciation for the unexpected shift to right-mindedness, I revisited *A Course in Miracles* workbook lesson 77: "I am entitled to miracles."

> You are entitled to miracles because of what you are. You will receive miracles because of what God is. And you will offer miracles because you are one with God. Again, how simple is salvation! It is merely a statement of your true Identity. It is this that we will celebrate today. (Paragraph 1)

When I first read these words eight years ago, I had no idea what they really meant, still relating the word "miracle" to

Biblical references to converting water into wine and healing broken bodies or New Age references to manipulating the form of our perceived reality to support and enhance our egos. But I soon enough realized that the Course's miracle meant shifting our goal from the insatiable neediness of our illusory bodies to the abstract mind outside this dream of exile from our true, all-inclusive Self.

Your claim to miracles does not lie in your illusions about yourself. It does not depend on any magical powers you have ascribed to yourself, nor on any of the rituals you have devised. It is inherent in the truth of what you are. It is implicit in what God your Father is. It was insured in your creation, and guaranteed by the laws of God.

Today we will claim the miracles which are your right, since they belong to you. You have been promised full release from the world you made. You have been assured that the Kingdom of God is within you, and can never be lost. We ask no more than what belongs to us in truth. (From paragraphs 2 and 3)

Our self-worth comes from God, with whom we remain seamlessly fused, not from anything our imaginary personal selves achieve or fail to here in a dream of individuals vying for survival in a hallucinated world. The miracle results from making forgiveness ACIM-style our primary goal. Beginning to see our lives as a classroom in which we learn to look on everything we perceive outside ourselves through the lens of the inner teacher of love instead of fear.

When we look with the inner teacher of enduring love we experience healed perception. We "see the problem as it is and not the way we set it up." We realize the defection from perfect oneness that haunts us day and night like an unwelcome song stuck in our head, the city apart from God we think we built, is a false memory. There never was a problem, not then and not now. We remain awake in eternal wholeness only dreaming of exile, simply acting out the imaginary, conflicted consequences of the underlying belief that something altered our enduring, undifferentiated union.

The practice of looking at our painful misperceptions about each other and ourselves with the part of our mind that sees only our frightened sameness and, just beyond it, our certain, invulnerable reality, is not of us. Our job is only to recognize we are wrong, ask for corrected vision, and then wait for its certain arrival. The Course's miracle—a shift to right-mindedness in which we truly see *through* our illusions without judgment—will reveal itself when our unconscious fear of losing our false self allows it to. Sometimes that happens immediately, sometimes in a seemingly delayed fashion, and sometimes randomly as it seemed to for me in this instance. But it will always replace *all* grievances toward others (and ourselves), as our one heart opens to embrace the reality of unconditional love for all.

I Will Step Back and Let Him Lead the Way

I don't often hear voices—well, I mean, except for the imaginary cast of characters with whom I appear to interact on a daily basis here on hallucinated planet crazy—but this morning I awoke with a clear directive that, trust me, was not the kind of thing the self I still mostly think I am would ever in a gazillion years make up.

"Give up control," the voice said, "and let one who knows the way guide you."

"Seriously?" the ego asked.

But I ignored him. A wave of joyful relief and renewed hope washed over me as I recognized the words as the answer to a prayer I'd been silently repeating for as long as I can remember; whenever the going got rough here in dreamland as it inevitably does. Whenever the part of me I am not really in touch with—that fugitive within who's terrified of returning to eternally all-inclusive love—became once more convinced that my allegiance to awakening through forgiveness *A Course in Miracles*-style would result in certain annihilation. Again intent on coaxing me toward yet another roadside attraction designed to lure me off track, prevent me from ever finding my real identity within the one and only abstract Self I really want to remember I am.

"Give up control and let one who knows the way guide you," the voice came again.

Although the words spelled kryptonite to my control freak special self I felt nonetheless as filled with gleeful gratitude as Ebenezer Scrooge on Christmas morning. After all, I'd spent the prior day in a complete ego funk in which I felt as hopeless as I can remember feeling since I first cracked open this big, blue book and embarked on this journey away from personal interests toward enduring wholeness for all. Once more convinced, under the ego's influence, that I would never be worthy of redemption, could not possibly deliver the necessary goods. I would never overcome my guilty little habits and judgments designed to prove my fundamental unsuitability to assume the role of the redeemed.

I remained an imposter, let's face it, the ego sadly reminded me, recounting in lurid detail the many foibles I thought I had hidden so well that nevertheless remained glaringly obvious to our creator.

Predictably enough the previous day's angst had followed increasing time spent in a state of inner peace driven not by past regrets, future possibilities, or current dream developments, but simply my burning desire to quit siding with the inner teacher of fear. My growing willingness to simply follow in what the Course calls "the way appointed me," the way appointed each and every seeming one of us. That moment-to-moment path of the willing student, in which my job was simply to remember my goal of finding the light, even in utter darkness, by taking the figurative hand of the inner teacher of love and stepping softly, trusting his light to illuminate where to touch each foot back down. Counting on my inner strength as one with him instead of my weakness as something sinfully apart.

And yet, and yet, I had once more veered off course toward the gleaming buried treasure of my "secret sins and hidden hates." Once more become intoxicated by self-judgment, mesmerized by the part of my mind so adept at graphically recounting and reviewing the fantasized crime of separation from our source we all cherish in our blindness and robotically reinforce through our projections. Believing, as we unconsciously do, that they allow us to prove we exist at God's expense while continuing to assert that it's not our fault by blaming it on the bodies we think we interact with or the body we think we inhabit. In this case, the ego had me almost completely convinced I would never write again if I kept this up, would have nothing left to do in this world but blissfully stare into space, drooling, no longer able to act, plan, cope, or navigate the twists and turns of this dream's rugged terrain.

I was not born yesterday to this Course. I knew what the ego was up to, and that I must have given it my secret blessing. And yet, I could not seem to access the part of my mind that had chosen to protect its imaginary private interests at the expense of all I really wanted, and remained painfully paralyzed, aware I could choose for unwavering peace, but seemingly unable to. Although conscious of my deep ambivalence toward following the part of my mind that could lead me out of this nightmare, I still judged myself harshly for this apparent unwillingness to choose again. I knew a part of me was simply too afraid, but could not muster any sympathy for that part, and so the pain and guilt festered. I went to bed disgusted with myself, again appealing to a part of my mind I had forsaken for a better way. Although I tossed and turned all night, I awoke this morning to find the answer floating in my mind like a welcome fortune wrested from a cookie:

"Give up control and let one who knows the way guide you."

Although in truth there is really only one child of God, until all ambivalence vanishes and we completely accept that slowly dawning certainty the journey home is a voyage in learning to follow instead of lead. Learning to grasp the stronger, certain hand of the part of our mind that has gone before us, the part of our mind outside the body's brain (and the world it thinks it inhabits) that remembered to smile at the "tiny, mad idea" of separation from the seeming get go. We have nothing to lose and everything to gain by relinquishing all delusions of control, stepping back, and letting one who knows the way guide us.

> The world is an illusion. Those who choose to come to it are seeking for a place where they can be illusions, and avoid their own reality. Yet when they find their own reality is even here, then they step back and let it lead the way. What other choice is really theirs to make? To let illusions walk ahead of truth is madness. But to let illusion sink behind the truth and let the truth stand forth as what it is is merely sanity. (*A Course in Miracles* workbook lesson 155: "I will step back and let Him lead the way," paragraph 2)

Hell No, I Won't Go!

"I'm not going anywhere with *you*," he repeated, stomping his little, bare foot.

I ignored him. "I told you to get dressed."

He stuck out his tongue.

"Now," I said.

He was wearing what appeared to be a cheap Halloween costume, my little e ego, impersonating some kind of wizard or superhero in his puny, wanna make-something-out-of-it way. He'd been storming around all morning in my head as I sat at my desk trying to write. Telling tall, mean, nonsensical tales about mutual friends and family members, whispering past secrets and grudges, doing his damnedest to get a rise out of me as I tried my best to get through one lousy morning in dreamland without blaming my lack of something I couldn't quite name on an external source. When he failed to get a reaction he upped the ante, roaring around, arms flailing, conjuring imaginary disasters and predators, thunder and lightning, zombies and goblins, in graphic detail. I couldn't take it anymore.

"I've had it with you, buster," I told him, as he raced around and around in circles, screeching.

"I want the peace of God," I whispered, pressing my palms together at the altar of my heart as earnestly as someone currently fantasizing about grabbing a small child by the scruff of his neck and wringing it possibly could. "I don't want this anymore," I told my imaginary Jesus. "Please help me find my way home." But he must have been busy with some other *A Course in Miracles* student again because nothing happened. I still had nothing but murder on my mind.

"Enough." I said, deciding to literally take matters into my own hands—never, I remembered in retrospect, the best idea—charging out of my chair and grabbing the ego by his bony wrist. "Get dressed and put on some shoes, mister—we're going home!" I didn't have to take this. After all, I was in charge. I was the decision maker who had chosen to believe this pathetic one's preposterous story of defection from our one loving parent in the first place. I did not have to listen to this.

"Stop it, you're hurting me!" he screamed at the top of his surprisingly cavernous lungs. "Help, police, help!" he yelled. "There's a maniac trying to kill me!"

"Knock it off and get dressed you little vermin," I hissed.

He squirmed away, threw himself on the ground kicking and screaming; dissolving at last in hysterical tears.

Jesus, I thought.

Overcome with guilt, I knelt beside him, my hand now and then inching toward a comforting pat on the back, only to get slapped away, with a snarl. At my wits end, I sat cross-legged, spine erect, assuming the yoga posture I found so comforting. I closed my eyes, drew deep breaths, and asked again for help from you know who to see things differently. To view this spoiled brat through the eyes of the teacher of love instead of fear.

After a while, sobs giving way to hiccups, the ego stood up, marched across the room, flung himself on the couch, and curled up on his side, thumb in mouth.

I continued to sit in lotus position, rhythmically inhaling and exhaling, in silent prayer. Eyes open, now, watching him.

He sat upright again, cheeks tear-smeared, nose running, sucking away on his thumb. "I won't do it," he said, extracting the thumb. "You can't make me." He plugged it back in his pie hole.

"Won't do what?" I asked.

He glared. The thumb came back out, with a little smack. "Go home, you nincompoop!" he shouted, before plugging it back in.

I opened my mouth to respond, but no words came. I breathed some more, asking for help from our right mind, still watching him.

He sucked away, stroking his nose with his index finger, curled inside the edge of his cape; eyes darting around the room like a tiny, trapped rat. He yanked the thumb back out. "You're a sneaky one."

He had a bit of a lisp—*thneaky* one. I bit my tongue, waited for him to go on.

"You said you would never go there," he continued, voice rising. "Never, never, never, ever!"

"I never said."

"Liar, liar, pants on fire!"

I opened my mouth, and shut it again. After all, he was the one who said we could never go back. But I figured pointing that out right now wouldn't do much good.

"Pinky sweared and everything," he continued. Pinky *thweared.* The memory of the alleged betrayal seemed to energize him. He leapt off the couch, flung off his cape, wiggled out of his shirt. He was wearing flannel pajamas with dinosaurs on them. Way too big for him, like everything else in this imaginary world, practically falling down. Something about those PJs, the thumb, the lisp, the little whorl of a cowlick at his hairline. Those chicken ribs poking out his scrawny chest. He was no wizard, no superhero, just a scared little boy. I asked him what might make him feel better.

He sucked away, thought on it a while. "A grill-cheese sandwich," he said, finally. "Tomato soup." Grill-cheese *thamwich.* Tomato *thoup.*

"You got it, buddy." I said.

"The orange melty kind." He climbed back up on the couch. "White bread cut up in triangles."

I nodded. "I can do that." I collected the ingredients, buttered slices of bread, and unwrapped squares of cheese. I opened a can of tomato soup, added the milk, and stood stirring it over the heat until the little pinkish clots dissolved. I set the food down on the coffee table in front of him, poured him a glass of milk. "Anything else I can get you?"

He extracted his thumb. "You could tell me a story."

I smiled. In my peripheral vision, Jesus was smiling, too, go figure. I hadn't noticed him come in. Talk about *thneaky* ones.

"Once upon a time there was a little boy," I began. "He lived with his father who loved him more than anything in the whole wide world and the little boy loved him right back. They were always together—inseparable, really—playing and laughing all day and all night.

"Finger painting," he said.

"Yup. And coloring."

"Building things."

Just keep humoring him, I thought. "Sure. Playing with Legos. Eating grill-cheese."

"And tomato soup."

"Exactly. Then one day the little boy, who had a wonderful, wild imagination, wondered what it would be like to run away from home? It was a ridiculous idea, of course, because he loved his father and would *never* really want to leave him. But instead of laughing at the silly thought of it the little boy believed it! As soon as he did, his imagination ran away with him as imaginations will, creating a whole universe—planets and stars and mountains and oceans and people and you name it."

"Horses and cows," he said, slurping his soup. "Dogs and cats and giants and Cyclops." *Thyclopths.*

"That's right. Only now the little boy thought his father was really mad at him and so he could never come home. But it was all only a bad dream, really, just a figment of his vivid imagination."

He had fallen asleep by the time I finished. The crusts of his sandwich abandoned on the plate, the white soup bowl empty save for a faint pinkish film. We were nestled on the couch together by then.

"And so his big sister came and told him he was just having a bad dream and she would take him home but he was too afraid and hungry so she made him some lunch first," I concluded, yawning. This kid was contagious. I could barely keep my eyes open.

Jesus just shook his head and smiled, covering us with the fleece throw.

"Thanks," I said.

"No worries. I'll wait right here until you're ready to go on," I thought I heard him say, right before I slipped away into another dream.

Identify with What Will Make You Truly Safe

I sat once more reflecting on the sense of paralysis I'd been feeling around my awareness that I always had a choice about which inner teacher I was listening to but did not always feel capable of choosing. Despite my best efforts to apply the Course's message of seeing everything that seemed to upset me as a call for love, I still did not always feel loving toward others or myself, not by a long shot. Although my ego attacks passed much more quickly than they used to, the awareness that I had a choice but couldn't seem to choose rendered them much more painful. I knew the part of me that seemed to act completely independent from my decision-making mind—defending the bogus reality of its individual body at all costs—was merely afraid that returning to the loving, abstract oneness of our true nature would destroy me, but still found it difficult to suspend self-judgment.

The previous week's forgiveness curriculum had involved my ego's typical struggle to wrest control of seeming conflicting external demands and revise them to its liking. To somehow arrange my imaginary schedule to maximize "valuable" experiences and minimize the "valueless" (as if I could tell the difference), defending myself from imaginary assaults on my precious time, Don Quixote-like, while attempting to manipulate characters in the dream to perform and conform to my wishes.

Although I attempted to observe my initial negative reactions to a flurry of apparently outrageous demands from my costars without judgment, I often failed to do so, remembering only intermittently that "all things are lessons God would have me learn," as *A Course in Miracles* workbook lesson 193 so poetically puts it. Meaning not that God has a clue about our imaginary flight from our seamless union with all-inclusive love but that, if I have made awakening through forgiveness my primary goal, then everything that appears to occur must ultimately help serve the purpose of releasing me from the ego's exhausting, unconscious cycle of sin, guilt, and fear.

I knew everything that appears to occur "out there" in the classroom of my life—all that seems to happen to derail my day and destroy my peace—was a disguised opportunity to expose the ego's ongoing campaign to make the error of separation real by viewing it through the lens of the inner teacher of forgiveness. The part of our mind that remembered to smile at the "tiny, mad idea" that we could fragment ourselves, the insane belief that we are many finite bodies vying for survival in an unpredictable, dangerous world rather than one whole, eternally loving mind. The spiritually mature part of us that supports us in looking at the details of our individual experience the ego dreamed up to reinforce the guilty thought of separation to heal our mind of it.

Still, sitting at my desk, feeling less than enthusiastic about the start of another week here in dreamland, pondering my forgiveness lessons du jour and attempting to communicate what I was learning, I found it impossible to concentrate, to allow my right mind to do the looking and the listening, the teaching and reporting. And so I declared a field trip, leashing up my little dog and charging out into the blessedly cool and uncharacteristically misty morning to clear my head beneath towering ash, elm, and locust trees in full autumn blaze. We headed west through our residential neighborhood toward the University of Denver but five or six blocks away where the fitness center where I normally work out had been closed for the past few days in preparation for hosting the first presidential debate of 2012.

A six-foot fence had been constructed around the area over the course of the past few weeks. Barricades had appeared at major intersections along with flashing warning signs predicting traffic delays over the next few days. The nearby interstate was scheduled to close for five hours during rush hour the day of the debate along with the light rail stop. Neighbors, shop owners, students, and professors were anticipating the event with varying degrees of elation, exhilaration, nervousness, and annoyance at almost a week of daily inconvenience.

Along the fencing, security had constructed higher, stronger, metal riot barriers to allow authorities to defend against potentially violent protesters, or worse. Drawing near, I stopped abruptly to process the thought at work behind the heightened security—the barricades and double-fencing, detours and traffic re-routing—all designed to protect two people each representing roughly half of a split-minded American electorate about to square off to reinforce opposing viewpoints. Kayleigh sat quietly at my feet, cocking her head and gazing up at the fortress, as if equally puzzled by it all.

Words from the second half of *A Course in Miracles* workbook, section 5, What is the Body? came back to me.

> The body is a fence the Son of God imagines he has built to separate parts of his Self from other parts. It is within this fence he thinks he lives, to die as it decays and crumbles. For within this fence he thinks that he is safe from love. Identifying with his safety, he regards himself as what his safety is. How else could he be certain he remains within the body, keeping love outside? (Paragraph 1)

I thought about how terribly important it all used to seem, this business of opposing political bodies, the self-righteousness with which I uttered my convictions, the vehemence with which I defended the correctness of my positions and fought for their representatives. While I still had strong opinions about the state of our world and how to solve its problems—opinions that seemed diametrically opposed to the solutions advocated by the "other side"—I could no longer sustain my belief in our fundamental differences for long. No longer muster the hatred necessary to keep them going, at least in this macro level of the seeming dream.

And yet, on the micro level, I still identified with the body's fences, confusing them with love. The closer the relationship to the personal self, the "fence" I believe I inhabit, the more unstable and unreliable my neutrality, the more likely I was to forfeit it completely in favor of false fences that can never keep us truly safe. I believed I must constantly protect (as if it were really ultimately possible) the unique body I seem to inhabit and the special body of my daughter, for example, to maintain an illusion of safety and sanity, as if our true being were at stake when it is not. In short, although still intact, my "hierarchy of illusions" was crumbling from the outside in.

Above us a peregrine falcon circled, scanning the earth inside and outside the fences for prey. Kayleigh's tiny ears lifted. She drew a little closer to my feet. I walked home with renewed appreciation for the part of my mind that was learning to see beyond fences to the undifferentiated, loving union we remain. Beyond the thought of separation realized that conjured the need for boundaries, the unconscious fear that something real had or could be threatened, that something unreal required protection. Feeling a little more compassion for the part of me that just wasn't ready yet to see beyond the fences I still held most near and dear, and a little more faith that the seeming time to do so and know our true and only unbridled Self would come.

You will identify with what you think will make you safe. Whatever it may be, you will believe that it is one with you. Your safety lies in truth and not in lies. Love is your safety. Fear does not exist. Identify with love, and you are safe. Identify with love, and you are home. Identity with love, and find your Self. (Paragraph 5)

Diamonds and Rust

Last weekend I taught an *A Course in Miracles* forgiveness workshop in which I shared my ever-strengthening conviction that learning to follow the inner teacher of love instead of fear is leading me home, however convoluted the journey sometimes seems. Home to a peace beyond its shackled version in this dualistic world where even its shabby imitation is always purchased at a steep price, experienced by the buyer as a loss of personal identity filled with remorse.

During the workshop, though—using the body I think I inhabit merely as a communication device for our right mind—I experienced the enormous freedom that lies in the *absence* of personal identity. A renewed and renewing sense of connectedness to all beings and things, a sense of no need for anything or anyone in my personal world—including the workshop—to go, or be, a certain way. A boundless sense of support and nourishment that sated and quenched the insatiable hunger and thirst for something more to fill the gaping absence of love we feel within. Relief from the voracious appetite that drives the ego's ongoing flight from the real, all-inclusive love we no longer believe we deserve. The seeking for ourselves where we can never be found hard-wired in bodies by a mind made mad over the false belief that we could experience ourselves as other than harmoniously, gratefully, joyfully, seamlessly united with our creator.

And then the workshop ended. Back in my body again, feeling the weight of it, I cleaned up, packed up, and headed home in the freezing rain, stopping to pick up flowers and a bottle of wine to take to a friend's house that evening. My husband lay on the couch lost in an old movie on TV, nursing a cold. I went about folding laundry, bathing the dog, and answering emails, empty inside, harboring a confounding sense of severed connection. The wrenching awareness that I must have become afraid of love again because my bodily needs—the sharp, mysterious pain in my toe and sinus headache I had awakened with that morning—had returned. Worse, my heart hung heavy in my chest, straining beneath the imaginary burdens and limitations of the finite being I see when I look in the mirror.

The next morning, the nagging sense of lack still lobbying for my full attention, my husband having left before dawn for a business trip, I showered and headed out with the dog to my favorite Farmer's Market beneath an optimistic sun once more bright overhead in a blue sky reminiscent of the Italian painter Giotto's translucent work. As I walked down the cracked sidewalks toward the market stalls bearing the season's final gifts, the dog prancing at my ankles, past glistening brick bungalows and Denver squares, leaves still clinging to their tree branches in a last gasp of glory, the door to my heart unexpectedly swung wide open.

The multi-colored squash and pumpkins, fingerling potatoes, and misshapen, delectable heirloom tomatoes, plump wild mushrooms, and jars of amber honey had never seemed so promising. People strolled calmly by, smiling, children and dogs in tidy tow, holding paper cups of strong coffee, munching tamales or pastries to the strains of a folk band playing on a patio outside the neighborhood auto garage.

I sat down at one of the small, round, metal tables to listen with Kayleigh on my lap, luxuriating in the music and continuing to watch the stream of benevolent passersby. A woman approached us and asked if she could take our picture. Kayleigh and I smiled up at her as she snapped our photograph and then moved on. As mysteriously as it seemed to have vanished, the sense of connection with spirit that included a sense of union with everyone and everything had returned. I lingered over my coffee, misty-eyed behind my sunglasses, eventually rising to go purchase the greens and onions and tomatoes I needed, drawn back to the patio minutes later by the chiming of a woman's voice singing the Joan Baez tune *Diamonds and Rust*; a personal favorite written years ago about her ill-fated relationship with Bob Dylan.

Coaxed by the strains of the music, I sat at another empty table, surprised to see the woman who had taken our picture earlier breathing into the microphone. Transported, I recalled the addicted-to-her-suffering young woman I had been on first hearing these haunting lyrics many years ago when I lived in San Francisco, a city intimately acquainted and well suited to broken hearts and ill-fated affairs. And I thought about how the story of our lives, the story of this wearily spinning world, is a story of diamonds and rust. A tale of love pledged and forsaken, sought where it can never be found and eventually mourned.

> What is the real meaning of sacrifice? It is the cost of believing in illusions. It is the price that must be paid for the denial of truth. There is no pleasure of the world that does not demand this, for otherwise the pleasure would be seen as pain, and no one asks for pain if he recognizes it. It is the idea of sacrifice that makes him blind. He does not see what he is asking for. And so he seeks in a thousand ways and in a thousand places, each time believing it is there, and each time disappointed in the end. 'Seek but do not find' remains the world's stern decree, and no one who pursues the world's goals can do otherwise. (*A Course in Miracles*, Manual for Teachers, 13. WHAT IS THE REAL MEANING OF SACRIFICE?, paragraph 5)

Robotically hooked on the duality of the ego's thought system we're unaware we crave the rust as much as the diamonds. Guilt's gleam sparkles more brightly than any jewel. Our stories of suffering at the hands of those we love sustain us in ways beyond our awareness; inspire us to write exquisitely poignant songs that attest to the universal "human condition." Our seeming plight here in bodies secretly aware they can never truly unite but nonetheless intent on proving they can.

And yet, sitting here with my dog, ears cupped to receive an excruciatingly seductive tale of love and loss, I heard only the space between the form of the notes and words, the forgotten song always calling to us from within and without the sound barriers we erected to silence it. The score beyond a story of sacrificing ourselves for each other in a futile attempt to fill the gaping hole blown open in our heart the moment we believed we had crafted a separate reality from the only one we know could ever make us truly happy.

As I continued to listen, I couldn't help but notice that the attraction of pain expressed in the story's form that had seemed so profoundly compelling to my younger self appeared to have vanished. While the attraction to the song of a love that has no opposites, entertains no sense of specialness and thereby no sense of lack—rang free. Time seemed to slow even more—to pause, really—as I continued to listen, aware of our eternally uninterrupted bond.

Men and women, children and pets, vegetables, fruits, birds, trees, and sky merged into an Impressionist blur that had nothing to do with the tears standing in my eyes. But everything to do with the only thing I could ever really want: a self and a love that could never go missing. That grew more and more accessible moment to moment, day by day, through my willingness again and again to resign as my own teacher, choose for the inner teacher of wholeness, and through that healed awareness, experience the dissolution, however gradual, of the crazy idea of sacrifice that, in truth, has had and continues to have no consequences, our ongoing dreams to the contrary notwithstanding.

> ... Decide for God and everything is given you at no cost at all. Decide against Him, and you choose nothing, at the expense of the awareness of everything. What would you teach? Remember only what you would learn. For it is here that your concern should be. Atonement is for you. Your learning claims it and your learning gives it. The world contains it not. But learn this course and it is yours. (From paragraph 8).

Forgiveness is the Key to Happiness

My weekend had been humming along rather nicely here in dreamland. I had finally gotten moving on a writing project I'd been fussing with and, OK; procrastinating about, as I am wont to do. Clinging mother-like to my creations; afraid to see them off into a cruel and bitter world; longing to hold them to the dubious safety of my throbbing heart just a little longer.

Crossing the final t and dotting the final i without further flirting with form or content, I'd sent the manuscript off to the designer at last. A flood of new ideas rushed into the void. I spent all day Saturday tackling long overdue projects around the house, cooking and running errands, cleaning the refrigerator and emptying cupboards and closets of their expired, occasionally mysterious and even terrifying contents as brainstorms for classes, essays, and stories percolated along the horizon of my adrenaline-powered little head.

Toward the end of the day, I rushed home from the giant warehouse store having completed my final tasks and headed downtown with my husband to catch dinner at a favorite French restaurant followed by a deft performance of Sleeping Beauty with the Colorado Ballet. Awaking the next morning with a sore throat and stuffy nose, I lingered in bed with my little dog, weakly attempting to connect with the inner teacher of kindness for all as I do every morning before surveying the day's upcoming activities. My husband had flown out before dawn to attend to putting his parents' newly renovated home back East on the market. I had scheduled lunch with a friend and a late afternoon movie with another. Despite feeling the onset of the bug that seemed to be going around, I rallied and rose, looking forward to a day of leisure, my just reward for a day of productive toil.

After feeding Kayleigh the dog and Victor the fish and downing a fistful of magic in the form of vitamin and mineral supplements, I grabbed the big, blue book and my jacket, intending to head to the gym for a workout on the stationery bike while reviewing a text selection for the weekly *A Course in Miracles* class I teach, only to discover that my keys had gone missing. Thinking I'd probably grabbed them while getting ready to leave, I retraced my steps in the kitchen and bathroom to no avail, rummaged in my pockets and purse, and paused. OK, when had I last used them?

I recalled returning from Costco after being unexpectedly caught in a construction-induced bottleneck of traffic that sent me crisscrossing around back streets in an effort to make it home in time. As I was unloading the car, my neighbor had pulled up and—citing our impending engagement—I'd excused myself from our usual conversation as I lugged a case of Vitamin Water Zero and a few other groceries into the house. I thought I remembered heading back out to lock the car with the remote on my keys. I checked outside and found the doors to my car indeed locked. I checked the refrigerated items thinking I might have set the keys on top of something in my distracted state, the pants pockets I'd been wearing and the jacket I'd donned for the ballet.

Before going any further, let me just state for the record that—unlike some other people with whom I cohabitate, for example—I am not a chronic or even an occasional loser of keys. I am a creature of devoted habit who returns her belongings to their proper places the moment she walks in the door. Jackets are hung on the same hanger from which they were removed. Shoes are placed on the special shelves precisely designed for that purpose (apparently invisible to said cohabitants), conveniently situated by the doors. Mail is immediately sorted and dealt with. Shopping bags are stored in their containers in the closet. Keys go back in the same pocket in my purse. Not knowing where something I need could be is clearly unacceptable to the person I still think I am when I look in the mirror; unacceptable and—apparently—terrifying.

I began ransacking the house like a forensic scientist, flinging kitchen and bathroom cabinet drawers and doors open. Peering under the bed with a flashlight, scanning the floor of my office, donning dishwashing gloves and sorting through trash cans, questioning the dog staring up at me with her ancient-looking eyes, seized by a growing sense of panic I couldn't really explain. I called my husband who sagely advised me to look in all the places I already had.

My throat and eyes burned, my neck ached, and my heart seemed to contract, gripped by a wild, reckless, dangerous sense of lost control. Suddenly nothing in the world seemed more important than finding those freaking keys! My entire well being and future safety illogically appeared to hinge on it, even though I had another set of car keys and my house keys were not on the key ring.

I knew from studying, practicing, and teaching *A Course in Miracles* that the missing keys were not responsible for my panic attack. I knew I could see peace instead of this by choosing the inner teacher of unalterable peace instead of the inner teacher of constant chaos. But quite honestly, in that moment, I wanted to find those keys more than I wanted to learn that lesson. Still, I couldn't quite dodge a vague awareness of Jesus—that *symbol* of our awakened mind the Course uses to teach us we are not many demented bodies but one sane mind—hovering in the background of my awareness.

I spun around and—just as I suspected—there he was, our robed wonder, smiling his signature smile.

"I know what you're thinking," I said.

"You always do."

"Well, don't worry; I'm not going to ask you to find the freaking keys for me."

His brows shot up the way they do.

"No, really," I said. "I wouldn't think of dragging you into this. I mean, it's not like you're a valet or something. Anyway, bringing you into the world to help me out just makes me want to stay here and we know only too well the thing to do in a desert is leave."

"I couldn't have said it better myself."

"It's just that I need my keys for that," I said.

"Funny."

I sighed. "That's why I'm calling in Saint Anthony."

"Saint Anthony?"

"Patron saint of all things lost."

"I see."

"Even though I know what you're thinking. If I do that I'm really pushing your love, I mean my love, I mean our love, away, and I know that's not what I really want. And you probably can't leave the Catholic Church and still feel free to dial up a saint when the going gets tough, right? I'm just saying it's worth a try. Who knows what rules might have changed in the last forty years."

"We've talked about this."

I sighed. "OK, I want to have my Course and my keys, too, is what you're really saying. I mean, if I ask for your help in looking at this I might not get my keys back, right?"

"True. But you might not get them back anyway."

"You don't believe in Saint Anthony, do you?"

He just kept smiling.

And, go figure, I started to smile, too. My breath slowed. My shoulders relaxed. My chest expanded to embrace the possibility that I was once more wrong about, well, everything. "It's like it says in workbook lesson 121, 'Forgiveness is the key to happiness,'" I said, after a while.

> Here is the answer to your search for peace. Here is the key to meaning in a world that seems to make no sense. Here is the way to safety in apparent dangers that appear to threaten you at every turn, and bring uncertainty to all your hopes of ever finding quietness and peace. Here are all questions answered; here the end of all uncertainty ensured at last. (Paragraph 1)

"Well stated," he said.

"Ha! And all that means is choosing your viewpoint, your awareness—but *only* yours. The teacher of love and fear can't speak over each other. And peace is never found or lost in form."

"A+," he said, with a little thumbs up.

I returned the gesture, heart full. "How about that coffee?" I asked.

But he was already gone. I grabbed my spare set of keys and headed to the gym.

A Forgiveness Prayer

The day began with news that the super storm creeping toward the East Coast dubbed Frankenstorm by the media due to its proximity to Halloween and coincidence with a full moon was already wreaking havoc, unleashing damage, and threatening lives, even though it had not yet fully zeroed in on its massive, densely populated target. As they had the night before while listening to news coverage, my thoughts raced to embrace the welfare of family members in New York where I grew up, my friends in Washington, DC where I once lived and worked, and the fate of my husband's parents' newly renovated and just-put-on-the-market home in Maryland.

Brushing my teeth as the radio coverage continued, I found myself wishing there were someone to blame—the naysayers of climate change, for example—reaching for the muscle of judgment only to find it annoyingly disabled. In truth I had come too far with this Course to deny responsibility for my reactions to this nightmare scenario, to refrain from recognizing within it my wish to perceive a cruel and dangerous world in an effort to prove that I exist but it's not my fault.

I knew that despite the personal and collective consequences of this seemingly random act of nature I could nonetheless experience inner peace, as the Course assures us we always can when we're willing to choose the inner teacher of peace over the inner teacher of fear. But a part of me I am not in touch with was just too afraid of what that would mean for the story of victims and victimizers I keep siding with to protect the story of this individual identity always at risk here in the year 2012. A year in which I had allowed challenges in a special relationship to nearly break me before finally remembering I had the power to choose a better way that had nothing to do with what happens in form. A year in which the outcome of the approaching presidential election sometimes seemed as potentially threatening as an approaching super storm, in which my very survival often appeared to hinge on other bodies behaving according to my wishes and my own seeming body behaving according to my wishes. (I *know*.)

An image of me as a young girl kneeling beside my bed next to my grandmother sprang to mind along with the scent of her talcum powder, the softness of her pastel, flannel, bluebell-dotted nightgown, gnarled fingers working the smooth, cool beads of her rosary. I would bend my head just like she did, trying to keep my eyes closed, likewise whispering Our Fathers and Hail Mary's but always succumbing to the temptation to sneak a peek at her face. She seemed so much younger in prayer, glowing and beatific, on the verge of morphing into sainthood before my unworthy eyes.

Try as I might, I never experienced that transformation by repeating rote prayers, never stopped wanting to spill my guts instead, to tell someone bigger and stronger and kinder and more powerful how hard I found it to be good. How much this world filled with bombs and broken promises worried me. But those thoughts seemed so sinful, so selfish. After all, I wasn't hungry all the time like the starving children with distended bellies that appeared with alarming regularity in TV commercials. And unlike Commie kids, I lived in America, land of opportunity, home of the free and the brave. And so I kept my real thoughts to myself, uttering prayers I didn't really understand or believe in hopes I would grow into understanding and belief—perhaps even achieve the state of grace my grandmother seemed to so effortlessly embody.

For reasons still beyond my understanding here in the condition I still mostly believe I'm in, I longed to pray now, to offer my doubts to someone bigger and stronger and kinder and more powerful. But who would I be praying to and who would be doing the praying? When I knew that, despite appearances, the problem, regardless of how it presented, was an inside rather than an outside job. And that meant the solution lay within, too. There was no one "out there" to pray to and no one real doing the praying. The problem and solution lay side by side in a mind I couldn't remember outside the dream that made them up, choosing from moment to moment to believe that its imaginary experiment in duality had any real consequences.

And so I sat at my desk and shut my eyes and prayed to withdraw my belief that anything real could be threatened, to join with the part of my mind that knows that nothing unreal "out there" exists. I prayed as I've been praying ever since I first cracked open this big, blue book to experience true forgiveness of what never was in all its menacing guises, to forgive myself for my wish to make this risky venture in individuality real. I prayed to remove the many forms blocking my awareness of our one, invulnerable reality within God, to side once again with the inner teacher of endless, all-inclusive love over temporary, exclusive fear. And for a while, at least, until I became afraid again, I experienced peace not of this world, a certainty of safety and comfort for all, the only real answer to every sincere prayer.

God is the goal of every prayer, giving it timelessness instead of end. Nor has it a beginning, because the goal has never changed. Prayer in its earlier forms is an illusion, because there is no need for a ladder to reach what one has never left. Yet prayer is part of forgiveness as long as forgiveness, itself an illusion, remains unattained. Prayer is tied up with learning until the goal of learning has been reached. And then all things will be transformed together, and returned unblemished into the Mind of God. Being beyond learning, this state cannot be described. The stages necessary to its attainment, however, need to be understood, if peace is to be restored to God's Son, who lives now with the illusion of death and the fear of God. (*A Course in Miracles, The Song of Prayer*, II. The Ladder of Prayer, paragraph 8.)

Seeing Purple

You do not offer God your gratitude because your bother is more slave than you, nor could you sanely be enraged if he seems freer. Love makes no comparisons. And gratitude can only be sincere if it be joined to love. We offer thanks to God our Father that in us all things will find their freedom. It will never be that some are loosed while others still are bound. For who can bargain in the name of love? (*A Course in Miracles* workbook lesson 195, paragraph 4)

I stood at the base of a stranger's sloping driveway in an unfamiliar, outlying Denver neighborhood dotted with ranch homes and undulating lawns reminiscent of the community I grew up in, long ago and far away. Another place and time altogether and yet, I had been walking precincts like this—earnestly, at times fervently, defiantly, even—knocking on doors in the name of one just cause or another for most of my life. But this presidential election felt different somehow and not just because I'd been deployed to a part of town with a much more suburban, circa 1960s vibe.

Juggling the clipboard, pen, and a stack of long, bulky campaign door-hangers brandishing a compelling close-up of President Obama and information on the nearest polling center, I struggled to organize pages of addresses fluttering in the light breeze. A sun still high and hopeful in the sky, trees still clinging to the last of their burnished cargo, and temperatures in the low 70s propelled me back four years to another presidential election day, walking another precinct in my own University Park neighborhood.

Back then I'd been captivated by the possibility of the democrats claiming back the White House after eight bitter years of "enemy" rule, as well as the tantalizing prospect that a brilliant, compassionate, articulate man who happened to be African American might rescue our nation from its downward spiral.

Miraculously mending divides at the same time, as if that could happen while I still harbored the thought of enemies in my heart, still cherished the illusion of my obvious rightness at the expense of their confounding wrong. There had been college students waving signs and singing that day, instilling faith in yet another generation, arousing in me the long dormant hippie child I once had been, traipsing after adults in her life to civil rights and anti-war rallies. I had come full circle, I mused, strains of *We shall Overcome* playing out in my head. Finally, after all this time, peace and justice would prevail.

I *know*. Although four years into practicing *A Course in Miracles* at the time during the previous presidential election, I had exempted my political life from my right mind's review. While I continued practicing forgiveness of what never was in my personal relationships, at least learning to entertain the possibility that my happiness did not depend on other people in my life behaving according to my wishes, I had completely disassociated the Course's forgiveness of the belief in separate interests in this particular venue.

A part of me realized I had a choice about whether or not to side with the ego's story of separation realized played out so convincingly in the guise of an American electorate split down the middle over the nature, role, and direction of government. But I was still too invested in keeping what had been a huge part of my special identity for such a long time intact, convinced that withdrawing my dependence on this defense against truth would bring down the whole charade. Unconvinced I could live within its demolished remains.

But things had changed. This time around I at least recognized in my need to see the voice of "my people" prevail over "theirs" the same old problem. The same old preposterous assertion that our failure to laugh at the "tiny, mad idea" of fragmenting a oneness eternally joined as one had any real effects. This time around, the price I knew I would have to pay for siding with the belief of "our" rightness versus "their" wrongness was just too great.

Sure, I had slipped into gluttonous frenzies—especially in social situations—of reveling in our differences. But the hangover was swift and painful enough to keep me largely focused on my real goal of experiencing an innocence not of this world by raising the real cause of my reactions to doubt, allowing the healing of my one split mind.

Then, too, this time around, I couldn't help but claim the same fear, the same underlying yearning, the same earnest conviction driving the viewpoints and behaviors of those on the "other side" as my own. Couldn't help but recognize the same call for love shared by everyone who walks this earth tired and alone, desperately trying to find their way home to a certain, loving safety they secretly believe they permanently squandered and no longer deserve. Foisting their guilt on chosen enemies in a futile effort to prove they exist at all-inclusive love's expense but it's not their fault. It's the blue ones. It's the red ones. It's that "other" forty-seven percent responsible for the sorry state of this union—the mess of my life—that just refuses to see the light.

It's really important that we begin to acknowledge with our right mind beside us how deeply invested we are in siding with our candidate, cause, viewpoint, and observe the many compelling reasons we use to justify our investment. It's really important to recognize without judgment that even though the many reasons that led to our decision to support one or the other position appear perfectly logical and certainly, undeniably convincing from our frame of reference within the dream, outside the dream, where non-duality continues to reign, they make no sense whatsoever. And all we really want; have ever wanted, or could ever really want lies *outside* the dream.

As I walked up and down a maze of convoluted cul de sacs in search of often elusive seeming addresses and fellow citizens (aware that every vote counted in this widely and loudly predicted-to-be historically close race) a funny thing happened. Jesus (that *symbol* of our one awakened mind) appeared in stealth mode, apparently enveloped in his invisibility cloak again. Nonetheless his presence was clear. And for reasons beyond my understanding, the colors and names on the lawn signs ceased to have any real meaning for me. As I rang doorbells and talked with voters and scribbled on my clipboard I found myself astonished (dare I say flabbergasted) to discover all investment in the election's outcome had abruptly vanished, replaced by a deep sense of tranquility and empathy for all.

The televised digital map of the United States imprinted from repeated exposure in my head complete with its blue-and-red coloring shaded to indicate democrat versus republican identification spontaneously transformed, the colors somehow blended into a stunning shade of purple; no longer mine or theirs, but *ours*. In slow motion the color bled into the entire map, gently obliterating and uniting, city, county, and finally state boundaries as if—you know—we really *were* all on the same side!

We thank our Father for one thing alone, that we are separate from no living thing, and therefore one with Him. And we rejoice that no exceptions can ever be made which would reduce our wholeness, nor impair or change our function to complete the One Who is Himself completion. We give thanks for every living thing, for otherwise we offer thanks for nothing, and we fail to recognize the gifts of God to us. (Paragraph 6)

My Salvation Comes from Me

I crouched on the floor near the side door to our home trying to convince my tiny distressed maltipoo that her salvation did not rest on my husband's absence but on her one true Dog. I held her up to my face, explaining that, in truth, love could never leave as we have secretly convinced ourselves it can, projecting the guilty thought of it onto objects of our affection that come and go like everything else in this mortal dream. But despite the fact that she had listened to almost as many hours of Ken Wapnick's workshops as I had, Kayleigh wasn't buying it, and what self-respecting canine could blame her? After all, in her book, she sacrificed her beloved to the work routine that kept her kibbles coming during the week without complaint. Dutifully coiling at her human Mama's feet as I sat for hours in my office watching a mysterious screen and banging away at a toy that made little annoying clicking sounds.

But now it was Saturday morning, Kayleigh's special time with the alpha, and he had broken their bargain, even though she had faithfully continued to be the most adorable and loving dog ever to touch down on planet crazy. It was completely unacceptable! She continued to avoid my eyes, whimpering softly. Staring fixedly out the glass door at the exact spot where the alpha had last been spotted, determined to coax him back from the ether with her X-Ray vision.

I drew a deep breath and launched into the Course's creation myth, explaining that in the beginning there was only one dog, seamlessly fused with Daddy dog in ways we can no longer really wrap our heads around here in the condition we think we're in as many different dogs. "In that original ontological instant in which we took the preposterous idea that we could flee the one kennel seriously," I continued.

"You're an ontological instant," the ego said.

"I don't recall asking for your opinion," I replied.

"You're the one talking to a dog."

Seriously. Although I accepted the Course's story that all suffering stems from our repressed belief that we have separated from our one true self and source, our moment-to-moment decision to reinforce that belief by dreaming up a world of many bodies in perpetual conflict yet complicit in triumph over one mind, a lot of the time it still felt like my savior had just abruptly turned his back on me and walked out that proverbial door.

In truth, I had once more awakened that very morning longing for something I couldn't quite name. Someone who would really "get me," always laugh at my bad jokes, follow and agree with my often cockamamie ideas and opinions. Appreciate me all the time, know me in all my vast frailty and still want to hang out with me. And yet, I understood, believed, and had even known in every fiber of my one true being (when willing) that my salvation comes only from my one real capital M Me. Or is it Us? Oh, never mind.

As *A Course in Miracles* workbook lesson 70, "My salvation comes from me," informs us:

> All temptation is nothing more than some form of the basic temptation not to believe the idea for today. Salvation seems to come from anywhere except from you. So, too, does the source of guilt. You see neither guilt nor salvation as in your own mind and nowhere else. When you realize that all guilt is solely an invention of your mind, you also realize that guilt and salvation must be in the same place. In understanding this you are saved. (Paragraph 1)

But we don't really understand. We believe our happiness, our emotional and physical survival, depends on finding another (and another and another) "out there" to meet our needs and eventually fail to meet them so we can continue to cherish the sad, sob story of poor, pitiful me. Although we convince ourselves our suffering springs from the failure of the object of our projection to deliver on its side of the bargain, our suffering actually comes from our refusal to see the situation as it really is instead of as we set it up. Our refusal to choose the inner teacher of loving forgiveness beyond all need and take responsibility for our unhappiness back to its source in the mind that dreamt it up, enabling us to remember it's only a dream. *My* dream.

The seeming cost of accepting today's idea is this: It means that nothing outside yourself can save you; nothing outside yourself can give you peace. But it also means that nothing outside yourself can hurt you, or disturb your peace or upset you in any way. Today's idea places you in charge of the universe, where you belong because of what you are. This is not a role that can be partially accepted. And you must surely begin to see that accepting it is salvation. (Paragraph 2)

We are in charge of the universe we made up to hang out in in our imaginary flight from eternal union. But we are also in charge of our return. The problem and solution lie side by side in the one mind. When we're willing to return to the mind and view them through the lens of the inner teacher of love we see there is really no problem at all and experience the boundless comfort of no need. But sometimes the puppy within is still too afraid of real comfort, still too mired in neediness, and so we are simply as kind and patient with ourselves and others as we can manage.

Recognizing her fear as my own, I sat down on the floor with Kayleigh and drew her into my lap, massaging her shoulders and singing the little lullaby I used to sing when she was so young and dangerously ill—*How much is that doggie in the window/The one with the waggley tail/How much is that doggie in the window/I do hope that doggie's for sale.* I held her paw, knowing all was well even as I recited a little story about how out of all the doggies in the world, I had chosen her to bring home, that little white lie.

She drove her muzzle into the crook of my elbow the way she used to back then. She licked my hand, finger by finger, inside and out. Then she shook her head, tags jingling, hopped off my lap, and resumed her sentry position at the door, softly whimpering.

Entertaining Absolution

I stood at the open door to his office and knocked softly.

He glanced up from the papers he was grading. "Hey," he said. "Long time no see with."

Tell me about it, I thought. "Got a minute for your favorite student?"

"Funny."

I sat down in front of him and folded my hands.

"Something on your mind?"

"What mind?"

He smiled.

But where to begin? "I was wondering if you might humor me." "I always do."

"Maybe we could just play pretend?"

"I thought that's what we've been doing?"

"A little role playing I mean."

"Ah." He pushed the papers away and folded his hands, too.

"I was thinking maybe you could play a priest."

"I don't know about that."

"You've got the look."

He patted his hair. "You think?"

"Totally."

He shrugged. "OK, so I'm the priest."

"And I'm the confessor. We're playing Confession, see? I tell you my sins, you give me penance to say, I say it, and then God forgives me and we go eat donuts."

He looked puzzled. "God forgives you," he repeated. "Seriously?"

"I am not making this up."

His brows shot up the way they do.

"Well, anyway, what do you say?"

"What am I supposed to say?"

"Not much, actually. I do the saying. The spilling of my guts I mean. Only not really, because most of my sins are *way* too pathetic or downright disgusting to go into so I generally make up some placebo sins."

"Placebos?"

"You know, minor substitutes for major infractions."

"Your own little criminal hierarchy, hey?"

"Exactly. But this time I'm really trying to tell the truth."

"The truth will set you free."

"Amen to that. Now turn away like we're in a confessional and there's a little screen between us."

He pivoted sideways in his chair.

"Right, just like that. Now open the little window right there by your head. Then I'll speak to you through the screen."

He slid the imaginary window open.

"Absolutely no peeking, OK?"

He nodded.

I bowed my head. "Bless me Father for I have sinned."

"Oh, come on," he said.

"You said you would humor me."

He sighed. "Okey dokey."

"Where was I? Oh, yeah. Bless me Father for I have sinned."

"Don't you mean brother?"

"You're not really taking this seriously, are you?"

"Well." His lips twitched.

"Hey," I said.

He cleared his throat.

"You're inwardly cracking yourself up this very minute, aren't you? And at my expense."

"I wouldn't go that far," he said, and cleared his throat again. "Anyway, go on."

"It has been forty years since my last confession," I said.

"Whoa. That doesn't sound good."

"Zip it, Father. Where was I? Oh, yeah, I accuse myself of," I began, but where to start? In lower case t truth, after a period of serene right-mindedness I was just absolutely infuriated with several recent costars (despite the fact that some of them had really very minor roles in the scheme of the dream) for their colossal failure to respond to my extremely reasonable, amiable, and justified requests. Deliver on their end of our thoroughly and justly negotiated bargains, leaving me with that same old feeling of utter helplessness that had haunted me all my life.

And yet, I knew from studying and practicing *A Course in Miracles* that it was really not his, her, or its broken promises that had set my blood to boiling but my refusal to see the situation as it was instead of as I set it up. Meaning, that a part of me I was not in touch with, addicted to specialness and afraid of real intimacy, actually wanted to see myself unfairly treated. This prevalent theme in my personal story of a unique, victimized self had been wildly manifesting for days in the classroom of my life in the form of imaginary others ignoring and failing to respond to my needs, proving the ego's secret agenda that I exist but it's not my fault. It's theirs. No need for God to punish me when he could have at much more despicable and deserving culprits.

"I'm angry," I whispered.

"Go on."

"But not for the reason I think." *A Course in Miracles* Lesson 5, "I am never upset for the reason I think," came back to me. "See, 'The upset may seem to be fear, worry, depression, anxiety, anger, hatred, jealousy, desire or any number of forms all of which will be perceived as different. This is not true.'" (From paragraph 1)

"So much for that little hierarchy of yours."

"No kidding. And 'there are no small upsets. They are all equally disturbing to my peace of mind.'" (From paragraph 4)

"So much for placebos."

"OK, I get it. The correction is simply applying the idea to each of them specifically. That's how I begin to see they all serve the same purpose of proving separation and denying responsibility for it, and can be given the new purpose of recognizing our sameness as your students. Beginning to see how everyone here competing to have their only real need met through impossible means shares the same mind split over the guilty thought that we defected from our eternally loving source and can never be accepted back into the one loving fold."

"So what you're really saying, Father, is it always all goes back to that tiny mad idea that my experiment in individuality had any real effects. My belief that I now need to hide out from God in this universe of colliding forms that always have their own interests at heart, that never even notice mine even though I do everything in my power to make them love me."

I was wearing what my father used to call my "Sarah Bernhardt" face. It was not a compliment.

Jesus busted out laughing.

I started to laugh, too, but we were not quite done with this yet. "Well, I'm glad we got that out of the way," I said. "I really should do this more often. Now it's your turn to give me some penance."

"Could you go over that whole penance thing again?"

"You know; prayers I need to say to exonerate myself."

Jesus bowed his head and thought about it. "OK, repeat after me," he said. "I will not take my imagination seriously."

"Oh, man. Couldn't you just give me a couple hundred Hail Mary's and call it a day?"

He smiled. "Let's go eat donuts," he said.

Healing My Mind About the Dream

The body is the central figure in the dreaming of the world. There is no dream without it, nor does it exist without the dream in which it acts as if it were a person to be seen and be believed. ... In the brief time allotted it to live, it seeks for other bodes as its friends and enemies. Its safety is its main concern. Its comfort is its guiding rule. It tries to look for pleasure, and avoid the things that would be hurtful. Above all, it tries to teach itself its pains and joys are different and can be told apart. (From *A Course in Miracles* Chapter 27, VIII, The "Hero" of the Dream, paragraph 1)

In the sleeping dream, I am in my early twenties, visiting an old friend now living in a large city that resembles San Francisco, only oversized and sprawling, like photographs I've seen of Hong Kong. She is out of town and I am having her boyfriend and a woman friend of his (both much older than I) to dinner. I have apparently just had a book published and the woman interrogates me about it, dismissing it as just another piece of juvenile fluff. I start to say something that contradicts her. She rolls her eyes and changes the subject, further conversing with the likes of me clearly beneath her.

In the next scene my husband appears at his current age, although I still magically inhabit the body of my younger self (dream on, dreamer!). He has some kind of business- or family-related crisis, and needs my help. We start walking in pouring rain on the verge of snow—highly unusual for California—and there are children sledding past us on flows of slush rushing down the sloped pavement, being called home by frantic parents. A female relative we have long been out of touch with shows up and we forge on together, walking and eventually driving, trying to get somewhere to resolve the problem, thwarted at every turn by traffic, weather, construction and a seemingly ever-expanding, increasingly threatening urban landscape.

I suddenly remember I have forgotten the books for a book signing I'm supposed to do later and need to go home to pick them up. My husband is angry. The female relative offers to drive me but he needs her to go with him. I tell them I'll take a cab and start walking toward a street corner but everything around me grows vaster and vaster (rendering me smaller and smaller by comparison), the challenges seemingly insurmountable. I am navigating some kind of elevated sidewalk, gazing down at mostly vacant streets (no cabs in sight), crawling with gangs of sinister-looking characters chasing each other around, brandishing weapons.

I follow a detour up a hill, finally spot some cabs in the distance, start running and shouting to hail them; but they ignore me. I run into bleachers above a stadium full of soccer hooligans blocking me from the street. I realize I can't make it home in time and will have to miss the signing. Desolation sets in. I have failed to help my husband for nothing, failed to meet my obligation, and am now lost, farther from home than ever. The rain picks up, pelting my face. I awaken in my bed to my dog licking me, the hooligans' cries fading, the dream habitat gradually receding like an image in a rearview mirror.

Only a few years ago a dream like this would have left the body I believe I inhabit madly scrambling to unravel its meaning based on circumstances in my waking "life." But what struck me most about this sleeping dream was the absence of emotion. The lack of reactivity in the dream figure I identified with in response to other dream figures' criticism, impatience, fear, anger, and seemingly nonstop impediments to my arriving at my destination. I felt no pull to assign intent to the actions of others or analyze events that appeared beyond my control. I just kept traveling.

Until the very end of the dream, that is, at which point I realized I couldn't make it home again by myself, i.e.; as this discrete body I identify with on her own "special mission." This body, whose age in the illusion of time matters, whose accomplishments and ability to manipulate dream characters to meet her needs defines her. In short, I realized that although I knew on some level that I was dreaming, I wasn't yet ready to awaken, to approach our one and only home filled with kindness in my heart toward everyone and everything, certain that none of the differences among fellow actors or constantly changing dream sets and scenes amounted to anything at all but *my* fear. Ambivalent about awakening from the dream, I remained lost, straining to attribute my predicament to outside forces even though I knew better. Aware I had a choice but still unwilling to make the "sacrifice" of me I still believed it entailed.

This is where many of us find ourselves after years of sincere longing, commitment, and wavering willingness to live *A Course in Miracles*. It is a painful place to be. This dream revealed just how resistant I remain to growing up with this Course. To leaving behind the toys of specialness I use to defend my belief in guilt over an imaginary defection from our one source that never really happened. How I continue to project the guilty thought of it outward onto a vast world of imaginary, largely diabolical, past and present forms seemingly blocking my every move rather than choosing for the comforting abstraction of right mind. How risky that choice still feels. How reluctant I am to relinquish the seemingly endless dream my unconscious investment in separation realized continues to manifest, nourishing a fantasized cycle of sin, guilt, and fear that appears to pit us against each other in an ever-expanding, confusing arena of external obstacles to inner peace.

In my waking dream, too, I have unearthed a new-found layer of resistance to relaxing my grip on the guilt I secretly cherish because, although I now recognize it as the cause of all suffering, it nonetheless preserves the concept of me. And who would I be without this dream figure lost in an ever-expanding world of insurmountable challenges? This perennial child unable to attain her just rewards because of the insensitive, if not downright unlawful, nature of all these other forces rigged to thwart her?

Our self-accusations (just like those we level at our seeming adversaries) protect the guilt that preserves the idea of a personal self. Our present (unconscious) decision from moment to moment to take that guilt seriously preserves the story of a special me which in turns protects the belief in the sin of separation. We can only begin to heal as we begin to recognize, by turning to the perspective of the lucid dreamer within, that we are dreaming all the time. Reminding ourselves (as Ken Wapnick often does) when tempted to finish the sentence "I'm upset because of _____" with an outside cause, that we have merely mistaken the dream for reality again; ourselves for its hero, completely forgetting we are "the dreamer of the dream" who created these symbols to prove we exist but it's not our fault.

Our sleeping dreams are really no different than our waking ones, except that we choose to believe in the latter to perpetuate an elongated (from the ego's perspective) experiment in individuality that in truth—given its impossible nature—was over before it began. Although it hurts us, this allegiance to a will other than our own, it is simply a fearful error in perception, a passing, childish whim that had no effects on reality.

When we find ourselves in that painful place of holding onto the thought of guilt within that's keeping us stuck, we need to respond with the same kindness we are learning to offer others whose call for love we've begun to recognize as our own. Fearful people deserve comfort, not condemnation. The less we judge ourselves for resisting, the more self-compassion we can muster, the more quickly mind-healing happens and inner peace returns, regardless of what seems to be up in the dream.

The answer to our sense of failure always lies in simply observing our robotic attraction to guilt, including its "hugging close" within, and learning to check in, despite our fear, with a mature part of our mind that hears only calls for love over the ego's hooligan shrieks. This part of our mind is *always* certain that life beyond the dream offers everything we really want and will lead us to become the one grownup Self we have been seeking and never finding for such a long, exhausting time.

... The hanging-on to guilt, its hugging-close and sheltering, its loving protection and alert defense,—all this is but the grim refusal to forgive. 'God may not enter here' the sick repeat, over and over, while they mourn their loss and yet rejoice in it. Healing occurs as a patient begins to hear the dirge he sings, and questions its validity. Until he hears it, he cannot understand that it is he who sings it to himself. To hear is the first step in recovery. To question it must then become his choice. (From *Psychotherapy: Purpose, Process and Practice*, 2, VI, paragraph 1)

Holy, Wholly, Moly

I stood at his open door, about to knock, but he wasn't inside. Strange, I'd called ahead, made an appointment even. He had never been late before but the holidays were upon us, after all; what self-respecting fragment of the whole couldn't quite literally feel their weight? His phone had probably been ringing off the hook. Then, too, it was almost the end of the semester; lots of other students melting down, no doubt. I would just have to curb my impatience, "make it about them," as Ken Wapnick likes to say on that CD set I can't seem to stop listening to even though I really hate it when he says that.

I ventured into the semi-darkness, placed the plate of Christmas gingerbread cookies I'd made him on the desk, plunked myself down in the chair, and wiggled out of my heavy coat. I watched the sleet fall in sheets outside the beveled windows just beginning to coat the bare trees with an icy film, and began reviewing the topics around which I came seeking his counsel. The all-too-familiar overwhelmed feeling the holidays always triggered in the little s self I still see in the mirror each morning. The same old sense of failing to measure up a bad online review of one of my books had fueled. The book signing that had left me mentally whining about my introverted tendencies again, the nagging sense of being exposed as an imposter any public appearance seems to reactivate. Twinges of regret over past mistakes, Congressional and media babble about an impending fiscal cliff, continued chatter about the approaching end of the world in a couple of weeks, and the weird little bug that had infiltrated my body leaving my head aching and stomach churning, seriously compromising my ability to whittle down an ever-burgeoning to-do list.

And yet, what I really wanted to discuss with my imaginary inner teacher was not so much these apparent story lines that seemed to be thwarting the progress of an imaginary Susan but a new-found *unwillingness* to swallow them. A part of me was just so sick of the whole damn thing. A part of me just found the emotions required to defend them too freaking exhausting. I couldn't seem to muster the required fear and judgment, couldn't seem to keep the anxiety necessary to nourish them going. None of the problems seemed all that important compared to healing my mind about them. Then, too, they truly had taken on a boring sameness. I watched myself reviewing them, but couldn't seem to identify with the self they appeared to be happening *to*, which left me wondering about the reviewer's inability to assign meaningful importance to any of it.

I sighed, and looked down at my watch. Ten minutes had come and gone, the way whole years seemed to, lately. I bit my lips the way I do, re-crossed my legs. Where was he? How could I be expected to make sense of this by myself? I uncrossed my legs, closed my eyes, and drew a deep breath, recalling what Ken Wapnick had to say about beginning to see that the cause of *all* our seeming problems: a willingness to indulge the thought of separation from our one and only Self and source to support the belief in separation from our inner teacher and make the specific seeming consequences of that belief in our "individual" lives special.

Every seeming problem disguised the secret belief that our imaginary flight from eternally, whole love really happened and deserved punishment, proving we pulled off the "crime" of existing as unique entities. But it's not our fault. There are guiltier others "out there" much more deserving of God's wrath, intent on compromising any hope of my sustaining inner peace. These holiday demands, the book review, the book signing, the fiscal cliff, the approaching end of the world, the stomach flu, all kept me so busy vying for survival that I had no time left to heal.

And yet, I was more deeply conscious this week of the weight of that original belief. How I longed to simply drop it, to feel the buoyancy of a Self unencumbered by a body simply through choosing to side with a part of our one mind that doesn't believe in it. In truth, despite my continuing resistance, the ego's continuing body of evidence, a part of me didn't really buy it anymore. In spite of myself, I'd been drawn to the definition of The Holy Spirit in *A Course in Miracles'* Teachers Manual, Clarification of Terms, as described in paragraph 4:

> The Holy Spirit abides in the part of your mind that is part of the Christ Mind. He represents your Self and your Creator, Who are One. He speaks for God and also for you, being joined with Both. And therefore it is He Who proves Them One. He seems to be a Voice, for in that form He speaks God's Word to you. He seems to be a Guide through a far country, for you need that form of help. He seems to be whatever meets the needs you think you have. But He is not deceived when you perceive your self entrapped in needs you do not have. It is from these He would deliver you. It is from these that He would make you safe.

I thought about how I had actually managed to finally drop my neediness for a special relationship to go or be a certain way over the past year, the deep comfort, release, and possibility for real communication that decision offered. I thought about how the decision to show up at the book signing without needing it to go or be a certain way—to make it about being kind and open to everyone else there instead of the personal self's story of unworthiness—had left me completely relaxed, unfettered by the anxiety and nausea that had plagued me, actually able (I cannot believe I'm saying this) to *enjoy* the experience.

I opened my eyes and checked my watch again. Another twenty minutes had passed, and no sign of the bearded wonder. What if he didn't show? How was I supposed to make sense of it all? I closed my eyes again and thought about how I had never really connected with the Course's concept of the Holy Spirit. It sounded so freaking lofty, to smack of such specialness, and just seemed to reinforce my belief in an individual in need of super-natural intervention. Encouraging me to engage in the same old game of trying to entice spirit to deliver the goods to a personal me in a real world, to fix up my body and the circumstances of my life rather than heal my mind about the idea of a world, a body, and a life apart from God.

But now, waiting for my imaginary Jesus, I recognized that my resistance to the Holy Spirit was really a resistance to the idea that I—just like everyone else wandering this earth seeking for herself where she can never be found—am mind and not body; completed abstraction rather than incomplete form, ever connected with a part of our one mind available from moment to moment to help us make sense of things.

It occurred to me in a welcome flash that left me smiling my inner teacher's smile that he wasn't going to show. Nevertheless I had passed another test. Maybe I really was at least *beginning* to grow up with this Course, I thought, rising and slipping back into my coat.

I eyed the plate of cookies, reached down, grabbed one, and bit off the tiny, little cookie man's head. Then again, maybe not, I thought, and forged back out into a cold, dark world.

The Holy Spirit is described as the remaining Communication Link between God and His separated Sons. In order to fulfill this special function the Holy Spirit has assumed a dual function. He knows because He is part of God; He perceives because He was sent to save humanity. He is the great correction principle; the bringer of true perception, the inherent power of the vision of Christ. He is the light in which the forgiven world is perceived; in which the face of Christ alone is seen. He never forgets the Creator or His creation. He never forgets the Son of God. He never forgets you. And He brings the Love of your Father to you in an eternal shining that will never be obliterated because God has put it there. (Paragraph 3)

✓

Listen

As a college student one summer, for reasons I still can't quite fathom given my colossal lack of experience, I somehow landed a job working as a case aide in a social rehabilitation center in upstate New York, part of an on-going effort to release long institutionalized patients into alternative settings such as halfway houses, and eventually into independent-living venues. Various public mental health institutions bused their patients to our facility daily for occupational, group, music, and art therapy, as well as training in the life skills necessary to take care of themselves on the "outside."

In retrospect, the administration must have been desperately understaffed because they charged me with responsibilities far beyond my expertise. I ran a Weight Watchers' group, for example. All 110 pounds of my 20-year-old self earnestly advising mostly middle aged, often heavily medicated, obese people—many of whom had spent most of their lives on the "inside"—on portion control and the value of exercise, even though they often saw their heavy-on-refined-carb diets as the only real comfort in their lives. Why someone didn't deck me (or worse) on the spot is truly a miracle in form!

Although it troubled me—especially learning that some of these "clients" had been abandoned as children, transferred to these facilities not because of their condition but because there was no other place to put them—I loved the work, and found myself (perhaps because of my age at the time) particularly drawn to the adolescents to whom I was assigned as a kind of mentor. One young schizophrenic woman whose unpredictable behavior and angry outbursts the staff found especially challenging took an inexplicable shine to me. We started spending a lot of our unstructured time together and, in ways I couldn't begin to explain, I felt a sense of closeness to her I had not experienced before in any of my relationships with family or friends.

She spoke mostly in gibberish, and, at first, rarely made eye contact. But she would sit or stand beside me, very close. I started really listening to her, began to notice patterns and connections in her speech, and eventually, I think, understand a lot of what she was saying. Like immersing oneself in a new language, a foreigner in an unfamiliar land, the process required humility and patience, a willingness to follow instead of lead, opening to unfamiliar symbols assigned to the same human content we shared. I even began conversing with her, using her language. She started really looking at me, and responding, and seemed delighted that I had somehow broken the code.

We began to have truly joyful—spoken and unspoken— exchanges. A kind of wink, wink would pass between us, as if she knew, I knew, it was all a game, the unique, elaborate vocabulary she had crafted to express her unique, elaborate, reality, to keep herself safe (as we all struggle to in one way or another) by keeping others away. The more closely I listened, the more I immersed myself in her "culture," the more enjoyable our time together grew. Most astonishingly, she began to get better. The outbursts ceased. By the end of the summer, she had made real strides in therapy and was beginning to converse in "our language," engage in "our culture." Her psychologist and caseworker had new hope about the possibility of releasing her to a halfway house in the not-too-distant future.

I attended summer school back in Boston the following year so I could graduate early, eventually moved far, far away, and lost track of her. But for a variety of reasons she came back to me recently while listening to a Ken Wapnick CD in which he again mentioned an experience he had as a graduate student hearing a recorded therapy session between a renowned psychologist and a schizophrenic patient in which you could not tell one from the other.

Much like Jesus, that memory of our true, non-dualistic identity *A Course in Miracles* uses as a *symbol* to meet us here in the condition we think we're in, the therapist had met the psychotic patient where he thought he was, recognizing the patient's problem as merely a reflection of the same problem we all share regardless of how we express it, the belief that we separated from our eternally united identity and will never be accepted back into the one loving fold. Projecting the guilty thought of it outward thereby creating an imaginary world in which to hide from an angry God while blaming our secret guilt on others to establish our relative innocence. "Proving" through our isolated uniqueness that we exist independently—helpless victims of our own hallucinations—but it's not our fault.

"It is in the instant that the therapist forgets to judge the patient that healing occurs," *A Course in Miracles Psychotherapy: Purpose, Process, and Practice,* explains (3. II. paragraph 6). And while specifically addressing the professional psychotherapy-patient relationship, its teaching—that we begin to heal our mind about our relationships as we recognize there is only one mind in need of healing and that would be mine—applies to everyone and everything.

I have been noticing lately that when I communicate with anyone from a place of making our differences real, attempting to fix them or change them or even help them as if I knew what they needed, as if we had different needs, the exchange—how shall I put this?—goes to bloody, freaking hell! But when I begin to completely relinquish my need for the relationship to go or be a certain way, become willing to truly listen to the other person and meet them in "their culture," I realize that despite differences in vocabulary, the message is always the same.

Everyone here roaming this world secretly yearning for a forgotten union they believe they squandered and no longer deserve is acting out the same unconscious fear I have. *Every* self-identified fugitive from love shares the same split mind that begins to heal whenever I am willing to choose for the part of our one mind truly able to listen and see. The part of our mind that knows beyond all hallucinated melodies and chords of doubt that we are safe and wholly harmonious, completely heard and seen, understood, and loved.

And something else seems to be happening, too. Lately, as I listen to some people's stories, I find myself almost unable to concentrate on the details, the specifics, because the underlying, unifying call for love is so strong. It's a little unnerving, and yet, I can feel the gentle hand supporting us both, the divine, abstract comfort beyond all words passing between us. This disturbed me at first as the ego swooped in to rail about not paying enough attention to the form, until I realized that on occasions, when someone seems to need my attention to the details, it is right there, so close we cannot fail. In either case, provided I keep my attention on that openness to *not knowing* that invites the quiet, centered teacher of forgiveness, a loving response occurs, bypassing—thank God—the ever evaluating-on-false-evidence ego brain.

Something good must come from every meeting of patient and therapist. And that good is saved for both, against the day when they can recognize that only that was real in their relationship. At that moment the good is returned to them, blessed by the Holy Spirit as a gift from their Creator as a sign of His Love. For the therapeutic relationship must become like the relationship of the Father and the Son. There is no other, for there is nothing else. The therapists of this world do not expect this outcome, and many of their patients would not be able to accept help from them if they did. Yet no therapist really sets the goal for the relationships of which he is a part. His understanding begins with recognizing this, and then goes on from there. (Paragraph 5)

Judgment is the sickness.
Non judgment is the healing.

What Is Sin?

I lifted my head from the cradle of my folded arms resting on his desk, flexed my fingers, stinging with pins and needles from the weight of it. Hard to tell how long I'd been waiting here in the dark, since last night at least, maybe longer. I must have fallen asleep.

"Long time no see with," our imaginary inner teacher said, sweeping into his office and flipping on the light, battered briefcase slung over one shoulder. Same old flimsy robes and sandals despite the frigid temperatures out there.

I rubbed my eyes. "You really should bundle up." I said.

"No kidding?"

"Not that the cold actually causes viruses but it can weaken your immune system."

His eyes widened. "We've talked about this," he said.

"I am so not making this up. Well, at least not here on the level I think I'm at, anyway, if you know what I'm saying."

His brows shot up the way they do.

"Plus, people might think you're crazy."

He smiled. "Yikes!"

"Oh, never mind."

"Why are we whispering?" Ever willing to meet me in the condition I think I'm in, he whispered back, easing into his desk chair across from me and straightening the folders in front of him.

"I still have that cold," I said.

"Ah."

Plus, I'd nearly worn out my voice trying to shout down the ego, even though I knew better.

He nodded. "How was Christmas break?"

I sighed. Where to begin? Although I had coasted into the holiday season on a wave of merry right-mindedness, buoyed by weeks of benevolent awareness toward everyone and everything, somewhere around mid-December the seeming tide abruptly, dare I say, savagely, turned. And I found myself once more adrift in turbulent waters, thrashing about for my very survival, seemingly gripped by the ego's overwhelming undertow of sin, guilt, and fear, victim of a variety of sinister, elfin forces beyond my control.

Worse, I knew all too well, as any little s self-respecting *A Course in Miracles* student would, that this could not possibly be. I could not possibly be upset because of all these fruit-cakes out there, all these demands, obligations, and temptations; there being no actual "out there." I must have first chosen the inner teacher of fear in an effort to preserve the puny, "special" self I still see in the mirror. To prove I exist—a separate, sniveling, suffering, often (I am sorry to report) soundlessly swearing Susan—but it's not my stinking fault.

I knew I could—theoretically, anyway—see peace instead of this by aligning my perception with the inner teacher of forgiveness seemingly sitting across from me now, reflecting the memory of wholeness for all in my mind. The proverbial door to truth remained open. There were no real vacations from my forgiveness classroom except the derelict forays I chose to embark on, staggering back into the dream again, taking it all so damn seriously. I could have seen peace instead of this, but obviously preferred pain, however excruciating, and hated myself for it.

"I think I need you to play the priest again," I said, head bowed.

"The priest?"

"You remember—in the confessional. You pretend you're the priest and I'm the miserable, sinning parishioner."

"Ah, that game," he said. He swiveled in his chair and opened the little imaginary, screened window, just like I'd taught him.

"Bless me, Father, for I have sinned," I began, clasping my hands.

"We've talked about this," he said.

"You're not supposed to say anything yet."

"Sorry."

"OK, let's start over. Bless me, Father, for I have sinned."

He busted out laughing.

"Hey, Father, get a grip; I'm suffering here, remember?"

"Right." He cleared his throat, did his best to look serious. "Go on," he said.

"I've been identifying with the body again," I breathed.

"How do you know?"

I thought of my daughter driving home from college for winter break over a treacherous pass in a snowstorm, how I'd sat at my desk for hours paralyzed with fear. Now and then torturing myself by tapping into the Department of Transportation web cam focused in harrowing detail on the blizzard that left cars inching along one lane of a normally three-lane highway. As if I could will her to stay on the road; keep SUVs and trucks a safe distance away from her compact car through the sheer power of my X-Ray vision.

I thought of the unrelenting work demands that left me feeling breathless as I tried to keep up while also meeting the expanded holiday schedule of social obligations that seemed to completely deplete my fragile, introverted nature. I thought of a special relationship that appeared to have once again trampled my boundaries (as if), leaving me apoplectic, the toll indulging in red meat, butterfat, sugar, and wine seemed to have taken on my physical well being, the virus that left my throat raw, head pounding. I thought about the way I kept conjuring imaginary, idyllic ghosts of Christmases past, how guilty I felt, having made healing my mind through applying this Course in my life my highest priority, and yet, apparently unable to accept the benefits.

How did I know I'd been identifying with the body instead of the mind? "Sin seems real," I said.

"Ah."

"And I've been dealing with this one alone," I said, eyeing the ego's noxious fumes in my peripheral vision. "And it isn't pretty."

"What one would that be?"

"I see what you're saying," I said.

"You always do."

"If there is no sin, there is no guilt. If there is no guilt, there is no ego. If there is no ego, there is nothing to fear. But I've been acting like there is again. Acting like my sinful choice for the ego thought system in my seeming daily life just like my sinful choice to believe the 'tiny, mad idea' that I could separate from our one Self and source in the seeming beginning had real, sinful effects. Harshly judging myself for siding with a nasty idea that seems to have a life of its own but in truth has no life at all. It's like it says in the second part of the workbook, 4. What is Sin?:

> Sin is the home of all illusions, which but stand for things imagined, issuing from thoughts that are untrue. They are "proof" that what has no reality is real. Sin "proves" God's Son is evil; timelessness must have an end; eternal life must die. And God Himself has lost the Son He loves, with but corruption to complete Himself, His Will forever overcome by death, love slain by hate, and peace to be no more. (Paragraph 3)

"I couldn't have said it better myself," he said.

"Ha! The trouble is a part of me I'm not consciously aware of is still afraid that, because love was truly slain, only this substitute, sinful, mortal self exists. And while it's no great shakes, it's a hell of a lot better than being cast into the primordial goo. It's the unconscious nature of all this that makes this damn Course so hard to learn, isn't it?"

"You think?"

"But it's *not* a sin, just a mistake." Suddenly, I believed my own words. My self-worth did not hinge on what I did or didn't do, on all my human foibles, but on my uninterrupted union with an all-inclusive love that never has and never will fail us. My sinlessness was guaranteed by God, an eternal innocence hard-wired into our true and only nature.

The funk of the last few weeks abruptly lifted. Like the Grinch poised at the top of Mount Crumpit catching the chords of that enduring Who song wafting up from Whoville, my heart expanded, grew light. I wasn't going to need any penance, after all. No one was guilty here. Dah who freaking dor-aze!

"Maybe I'll just stay here with you from now on," I said.

Jesus continued to smile. He really didn't make a very good priest at all. "Where else could you possibly go?" he asked.

He had a point, God bless him. He always did.

How long, O Son of God, will you maintain the game of sin? Shall we not put away these sharp-edged children's toys? How soon will you be ready to come home? Perhaps today? There is no sin. Creation is unchanged. Would you still hold return to Heaven back? How long, O holy Son of God, how long? (Paragraph 5)

I Do Not Know the Way to You

My little dog Kayleigh had been up six times during the night, apparently again suffering from the mysterious intestinal distress that had plagued her entire puppyhood, threatening her tiny, little life back then. Damn. It was Sunday, my only day off this week. I'd been looking forward to a lunch with friends, but apparently my curriculum had shifted overnight. I called the after-hours vet, was told to bring my dog in, and warned to expect a long wait.

I shot the lunch hostess a quick email explaining the situation, grabbed a Course book written by a friend I'd been struggling to find time to read, wiggled a weak and wary Kayleigh into her little parka, and blundered out into the single-digit morning air, cup of Joe instantly chilling in my hand. At the pet hospital, we weighed all 5.8 pounds of my darling doggie in. We waited on a hard bench a while—Kayleigh burrowed in my jacket—before the receptionist whisked us into a private exam room to wait some more.

Kayleigh stared up at me with her ancient eyes and shuddered. She remembered this place all too well from those early days when we'd camped out here regularly, the cold metal exam table, the cavernous torture chamber waiting behind those steel doors from which, even now, the cries of fellow poked and prodded pets emanated. I had failed to intervene as she had hoped back then, too. She buried her muzzle in the crook of my elbow.

I had hoped at this point to close my eyes, breathe deeply, and check in with our inner teacher about the rubrics for this current pop quiz but found it difficult to do so because of the video playing on the open computer screen on the counter. A treatise on all you ever wanted to know about canine dental disease and so much more streaming nonstop for patient and human parental enrichment. Triggering waves of guilt about my continuing failure to brush Kayleigh's teeny weenie teeth on a regular basis, as I'd been instructed to do, way back when.

After a while, a nurse came in, interrogated me about Kayleigh's condition, and vanished, leaving us to contemplate the vile consequences of advanced periodontal disease that might have been avoided by a responsible pet Mama's faithful brushing. I turned on my phone and checked my emails. The lunch's hostess was urging me to come if we got out of the vet's in time. I glanced at my watch. An hour and a half had already transpired; the festivities would commence in an hour, and I hadn't even taken a shower yet.

I had been here before. Early on in my *A Course in Miracles* practice I caught myself trying to make living the Course my life's work by sequestering myself in my office, the better to immerse myself in its teachings. Completely forgetting that whatever appeared to be happening in the classroom of my life *was* my work, the complicated relationships that lay just outside the closed door *were* my curriculum. I would not find my way home by merely studying the big, blue book and then isolating myself with a handful of other Course students who shared my understanding of it, but by learning to extend the unwavering kindness it teaches to everyone and everything wandering this world secretly frightened and alone.

I recalled complaining to my beloved external teacher Ken Wapnick (in one of my interviews with him) about why I couldn't seem to catch a break from the unrelenting forgiveness lessons seemingly bombarding me at warp speed. He'd responded by quoting (internationally renowned priest and author) Henri Nouwen who had said something like, "I kept getting interrupted in my work and then I realized my interruptions were my work."

Ken often reminds us not to make the Course our life—attempting to avoid the troubling, messy situations, problems, and relationships that trigger us—but rather to live our lives fully, assigning them the new purpose of healing our mistaken belief that anything outside our mind could disturb or enhance our peace. Learning to forgive my misguided wish to have my day go my way rather than allowing it to reveal my only real wish:

remembering our one, united identity by changing my mind about the purpose of my interactions with others. Learning to recognize every seeming call for love as my own and respond with the gentle compassion I am always truly seeking as I join with our inner teacher of forgiveness, who sees only our shared interest of remembering our unaltered union within.

In my lap Kayleigh gazed up at me with such longing. I nestled her back into my jacket and held her close. She had been troubled lately by my daughter's coming and going, the packing to return to college following winter break already well underway, our family's preoccupation with work and social obligations that left us charging off in different directions without her. But her sickness had drawn me back in. Like my human daughter, Kayleigh did not always find it easy to accept my affection, but she did so now, rolling on her back and offering up her upset belly for comfort and adoration.

I turned off and put away my phone, slipped the book I had hoped to begin back into my purse, and merely held her, stroking her soft fur and warming her paws in my hand. Another hour came and went yielding additional, fascinating insights on canine dental disease. The exam and tests eventually revealed bacterial and parasitic issues requiring the usual medications. I paid the bill, bundled my dog back up, and headed back out into the cold, grateful again to be happily wrong about, well; I suppose that would be everything.

And so today we do not choose the way in which we go to Him. But we do choose to let Him come. And with this choice we rest. And in our quiet *hearts and open minds, His Love will blaze its pathway of itself. What has not been denied is surely there, if it be true and can be surely reached. God knows His Son, and knows the way to him. He does not need His Son to show Him how to find His way. Through every opened door His Love shines outward from its home within, and lightens up the world in innocence.* (*A Course in Miracles* workbook lesson 189, paragraph 9)

The Need of Every Heart

Last week, I once more found myself in that rawest of places, judging several imaginary "someones" and "somethings" harshly, holding them responsible for the steely taste of anger arising in my throat, yet painfully aware it could not be. I was too far along with this Course *not* to realize that perceiving myself a victim, experiencing ill will toward anyone wandering this world guilty, vulnerable, and alone for any reason, must mean I had again chosen the inner teacher of separation, conflict, and differences, rather than the inner teacher of peaceful wholeness that seemed to have taken yet another sudden, unexplained sabbatical.

I knew—truly, madly, deeply—that I could see peace instead of this, as *A Course in Miracles* insists we always can when willing to gaze on our perceptual temper tantrums without judgment through the clear, kind lens of the inner teacher of truth in our mind. But I was equally conscious of my stubborn resistance to doing so, my kneejerk desire to keep the story of Susan rolling, upheld through the stories of all these people and situations that appeared to thwart *my* attempts to satisfy *my* needs. The ego's 24/7 broadcast of justified specialness blasted away in my head but, try as I might, I couldn't seem to change frequencies.

This seemed particularly confounding because over the last year I had finally dropped my story that a close personal relationship (what the Course calls a "special relationship") was responsible for my suffering, and largely released my outrage over its failure to meet my needs. (As if anyone or thing seemingly "out there" in a dream of our own dreaming could convince us we are loved and loving when we secretly condemn ourselves for having pulled off the bogus crime of separation from our source.) I guess I had expected that becoming more right-minded about this long-standing, difficult relationship would have a ripple effect, resulting in more sustainable peace overall, somehow disabling the power of other illusions in my personal hierarchy to upset me. Not so much.

While the initial release of my neediness *had* resulted in heightened, elongated awareness of our universal innocence, over the last few months the ego seemed to have somehow once more hijacked the journey home to the one loving heart we never really left. In the absence of the attention the special relationship seemed to command in my forgiveness practice for so long, issues I had with less important relationships and more minor seeming irritations rushed in to fill the void. Revealing to me all too graphically that there really is no hierarchy of illusions, as *A Course in Miracles* asserts. All of the external problems I perceived—from an acquaintance's seeming insensitive comment to the juvenile behavior in Congress to my body's bizarre symptoms to an overwhelming work schedule—seemed equally impossible to see through the eyes of eternally certain, all-inclusive peace.

Try as I might to find it, the quiet center within remained elusive. I flipped through the big, blue, battered book in vein, hoping to find a sentence to shift me back from the default ego position I found myself stuck in. And then, while listening to the Ken Wapnick CD set *Rules for Decision*, a brilliant discussion of the Course's text section of the same name found in Chapter 30, the answer came in the form of Ken's response to another student also discouraged over her inability to make inner peace her primary goal.

Ken explained (and I am paraphrasing) that the effort to make experiencing sustainable peace our goal dooms us to frustration and a sense of failure. Secretly believing the "tiny mad idea" of separation had real effects, as we clearly do, striving to perceive we exist apart from each other and our creator but it's not our fault, it's theirs, apparently stranded in bodies designed to uphold that perceptual error, we can't help but experience profound ambivalence about wanting the peace of God. After all, we believe we threw that peace away in the seeming beginning. Our one mind appeared to split over the guilty thought of it, leaving us unconsciously at war with ourselves about what we *really* want. Yearning for real, special love that will never fail us while invested in a personal self that blocks our awareness of the shared, abstract love for all we are truly seeking, within which we actually remain, our dreams to the contrary notwithstanding.

To say we want the peace of God, as *A Course in Miracles* workbook lesson 185 points out, is one thing, but to mean it is quite another. Because, while the conscious part of our mind genuinely yearns to reunite with the enduring wholeness of our true, indivisible nature, another part we're not aware of actively works to undermine that possibility. This other part works tirelessly to convince us we are really good, spiritual people; it's all those other nutcases that deserve to be damned. And keeps us so distracted by a seemingly endless parade of imaginary external problems that can never be permanently solved that we completely forget we could once more choose to remember our Self by aligning with a healed point of view.

A much more comforting, realistic, and mind-healing approach? To begin to see our lives as a classroom in which we honestly own our resistance to experiencing the peace of God in all the forms in which it seems to arise. Patiently learning to refrain from judging ourselves by joining with the part of our mind fully aware that our fantasy of running away from home had no real effects and there is, therefore, nothing real (and certainly nothing sinful) to judge. Not in "my" body and not in "yours." Not in the seeming beginning when the preposterous plan first arose, and not in the gazillion imaginary reflections we projected (and continue to perceive outside the mind) in an external reality that never existed.

Today devote your practice periods to careful searching of your mind, to find the dreams you cherish still. What do you ask for in your heart? Forget the words you use in making your requests. Consider but what you believe will comfort you, and bring you happiness. But be you not dismayed by lingering illusions, for their form is not what matters now. Let not some dreams be more acceptable, reserving shame and secrecy for others. They are one. And being one, one question should be asked of all of them, "Is this what I would have, in place of Heaven and the peace of God?" (*A Course in Miracles* workbook lesson 185, paragraph 8)

Despite our apparent defection from our non-dualistic nature, we remain one child of God, held forever within that warm embrace. Learning we are happily wrong about everything by learning to patiently accept but refrain from siding with our negative emotions, observing the dream of our so-called lives through the lens of the lucid dreamer within that always has our back and knows beyond all shadows of ego doubt that we nonetheless remain loved and loving. We cannot fail to awaken to truth once our fear completely dissolves through our moment-to-moment willingness to see its futile manifestations as they are (silly attempts to prove the lie of individuality) and not the way we set them up (as real crimes we must continually deny by seeing them in others to support our case for relative innocence).

Denying our resistance will not get us home but neither will berating ourselves for experiencing it. Only honestly *looking* at our anger, frustration, doubt, anxiety, fear, and annoyance with that champion of sanity within that knows we have nothing to gain or lose by our honesty will help us learn to claim our rightful role as dreamer instead of dream figure. Allowing the memory of the peace of God we already have and are to gradually dawn on us and extend to others as our formidable but nonetheless groundless resistance subsides.

It is this one intent we seek today, uniting our desires with the need of every heart, the call of every mind, the hope that lies beyond despair, the love attack would hide, the brotherhood that hate has sought to sever, but which still remains as God created it. With Help like this beside us, can we fail today as we request the peace of God be given us? (Workbook lesson 185, paragraph 14)

Dreaming Dreamy Dreams

In my sleeping dream (within the seemingly "awake" dream we call life) I had apparently won a trip to a tropical island that included lodging at a bed and breakfast a good friend of mine had once visited and raved about. The several-storied, New England, shingle-style house, complete with wraparound porch, hovered above a manicured lawn shaded by pineapple, lemon, and coconut trees. An elaborate, lush garden in back featured stone walking paths, alcoves and gazebos (presumably suitable for sitting and fanning oneself), gurgling fountains, and a small pond of fish, coppery fins glinting in the dappled sunlight. A high, cement wall surrounded the compound, exit and entry through locked gates controlled by an armed employee in a sentry box up front.

The interior décor exuded Edwardian charm. Along with a spacious dining room adjacent to the central sitting room and main staircase, the lobby also contained a small shop where the proprietor sold locally made clothing and a couple other closed rooms reserved for staff. I admired a heavy, intricately embroidered robe, running my fingers over the ornate filigree, but the price tag far exceeded my budget.

It turned out the brochure had omitted the unfortunate reality that the B & B lay adjacent to a war zone. A pervasive, palpable sense of danger arose every time I left the grounds on a sightseeing mission to visit the currently dormant volcanic area, the fascinating ruins of ancient civilizations, and museums teeming with archeological relics. Gunfire thundered through the hillsides, while smoke poured from rooftops clinging to jagged cliffs. At some point, toward the end of my visit, my friend, who had recommended the venue, appeared. The proprietor of the shop recognized her and, learning we were friends, lowered the price on the robe I'd been coveting enough that I could afford it.

Then I found myself in a big city again, a place I thought I knew that just kept growing more cavernous, unfamiliar, and frightening. It was night, and I walked the wide streets swinging a bag containing the robe and other possessions in the pouring rain, certain of my destination but not entirely sure I was going the right way. Other people, too—some with backpacks, some with children on their backs or leading the elderly—were traveling like me. Although we didn't speak, I somehow knew we were headed toward the same place: home.

I ducked into an open doorway on the ground floor of an apparent apartment building, glad to find my husband safely inside resting on a cot in a dimly lit room. I tried to convince him to come with me but he said he was tired and didn't want to go on. I told him I needed to go, but would try to come back and get him. Realizing with regret that I had lost my bag somewhere back in the fray, I forged on, but my fellow travelers seemed to have morphed in my absence into a threatening group of strangers on the verge of coalescing into a mob. I ducked down a side street to find a safer, parallel route, but the streetlights were gone and I could barely see. The rain grew torrential, flooding the empty street and rushing around my ankles. I saw a couple of children and, concerned, called out for them to walk with me, but they didn't respond.

Now I was running, conscious of being chased by a menacing, invisible force. I somehow ended up back on the island in the B & B's backyard, lying on the ground in fetal position, wet and shivering. A woman friend who had inexplicably severed all contact with me some years ago—an estrangement that confused and saddened me—came out the back door of the house and told me she was going to take me home. I started to cry, overwhelmed with gratitude. I told her I couldn't find my things. She said I wouldn't need them and led me back into the house to dry off. I went into the lobby with her and she gave me a towel as a man in a beautiful robe, some kind of visiting priest or spiritual leader, floated by us. He opened a door, stepped in, and closed it behind him. I dried off and my friend handed me the robe I thought I had lost to put on. I started to cry again.

I awoke lying on my back in my bed to the whirring of the air filter in the corner mingled with the sound of my own drawn breath, eyes still shut, trying to will myself back to sleep, consumed by a deep longing to return to the dream and find the home that had eluded me for so long. I had seemed so close to breaking the code to all waking and sleeping dreams. Standing there wearing *my* special robe, reunited with *my* estranged friend; the door behind which I sensed salvation at last almost within reach, if I could just drop back into the dream, turn the knob, and step into the sacred place where the priest had gone.

And then, I had to laugh at the way applying the Course's unique forgiveness in the classroom of our lives messes with our heads (in a good way), its metaphysical symbols beginning to permeate our thinking, our waking and sleeping dreams. Its clues to right-mindedness revealing themselves everywhere we look, seemingly sprinkled from above like divine fairy dust but, in fact, carefully placed by our own dreaming mind to point us again and again back onto the only path we are all really traveling. The road from mindlessness to mindfulness that will eventually lead everyone wandering this world feeling lost, alone, and critically endangered, back to the same, awakened awareness of the oneness joined as one we never really left. Once more alive with the melody of the one forgotten song we never really stopped singing, despite our mute dreams of exile.

And I realized, staring at the faint demarcations of my bedroom ceiling, reviewing my sleeping dream gently with the inner teacher of wholeness available in our one mind, that my wish to will myself back into my sleeping dream, to once more become what the Course calls the hero of the dream rather than the dreamer, mirrored my wish to remain in my waking dream.

We are always willfully (although largely unconsciously) rooting ourselves in our dreams. Indulging a futile desire to dream a happy ending, find an eternal home, *within* the dream, rather than taking our inner teacher's proverbial hand—always extended in the guise of our friends, our partners or spouses, our foes and fellow travelers—and allowing him to lead us home. Benign or threatening, robed and unrobed, in whatever costumes they may appear, on the road or still unaware there is a road. Allowing him to lead us out of the dream of differences to all we ever really wanted and dared to imagine we lost to the kind awareness of our sameness that precedes the experience of uninterrupted whole- ness as we retrace our steps back up the ladder our belief in sep- aration seemed to lead us down. Finally arriving at that awakened state beyond form in which we are completed within completion, beyond all dreams of beginnings and endings; home within our one full, forever beating heart.

You came this far because the journey was your choice. And no one undertakes to do what he believes is mean- ingless. What you had faith in still is faithful, and watches over you in faith so gentle yet so strong that it would lift you far beyond the veil, and place the Son of God safely within the sure protection of his Father. Here is the only purpose that gives this world, and the long jour- ney through this world, whatever meaning lies in them. Beyond this, they are meaningless. You and your brother stand together, still without conviction they have a pur- pose. Yet it is given you to see this purpose in your holy Friend, and recognize it as your own. (Chapter 19, IV. The Obstacles to Peace, D., i., paragraph 21, The Lifting of the Veil)

Surrender Susan

I was just so frustrated again. Still nauseated, in fact, by the seeming stupendous insensitivity of a costar in the movie of my so-called life, a special relationship I thought I had forgiven once and for always that nonetheless seemed to be right back in my face. Prompting the unwelcome realization that although recognizing that this relationship was not the cause of the conflict and drama in my life had been a huge step toward right-mindedness, it was by no means the end of the road to healing.

Acknowledging that this person was not the cause of my problem was not the same as truly answering my own desperate call for love presenting itself in disguise, responding from a place of open, honest empathy beyond all need to have things go my way (as if I even knew which direction that might be). In truth, I knew I was pushing love away again because it scared me. I still wanted to prove the lie of a me capable of fleeing from love because at least I knew what happened in that sad story, while I had no idea what true joining with the only real relationship within for any sustained period might mean.

"Surrender, Susan!" the ego, currently impersonating the Wicked Witch of the West of *Wizard of Oz* fame, wrote in the sky above my empty, little head. "Turn back, my pretty, before it's too late!" she shrieked, hovering on her broomstick in my peripheral vision, seemingly unbidden, in an effort to terrify me back in line.

"Sickness is a defense against the truth," I countered, quoting *A Course in Miracles* workbook lesson 136. Referring not just to the wretched stomach flu I appeared to have succumbed to, but also to the sick strength of my desire to hold this person—who just never seemed to change his confounding, clueless, boundary-trampling ways—responsible for my emotional and, likely, physical distress. A belief I knew sprang from the lie that our true, united, indivisible nature could have somehow separated from its source. Fragmented into a gazillion unique pieces competing in exile for scant resources, hard-wired to project the unconscious, albeit ever-resurfacing guilt festering in their minds outward in an exhausting, maddening, *sickeningly* futile effort to prove themselves innocent victims, just like me.

Despite this basic understanding of, and professed allegiance to, all things *A Course in Miracles*, I had stewed in my own toxic juices the day before—bitterly wallowing in self-pity as I lay on the couch sipping ginger ale and watching back-to-back re-runs of that deliciously soapy British concoction *Downton Abbey*. Completely unwilling to check in with the inner teacher of forgiveness patiently twiddling his fingers in a right mind that, at the moment, seemed more light years away than I had a numerical vocabulary to name.

"You're a defense against the truth," the wicked witch cackled.

"Funny," I said.

She narrowed her blood-shot eyes, lifted her whiskered, green chin. "Never!"

But even if I wasn't yet ready to smile gently at the absurdity of my hallucinations, I at least knew I did not have to listen to her witchy ways. She'd been trying for weeks to scare me off this path, impersonating the movie character that had invaded my nightmares as a child, skywriting her all-too-personal warning everywhere I looked. But I was not a child anymore. And even if my fear of returning to the scene of the imaginary crime of separation currently overpowered my desire to take the hand of the inner teacher of kindness, I was at least far enough along with this Course to know the fear would pass. When it did, I would once more find myself holding the proverbial hand of the guide that was leading me out of this bad dream sans yellow-brick road to our one and only home that had nothing, thank God, to do with Kansas.

And so the pale, limping, pathetic, bed-headed person I still think I am stormed off to a tai chi class to get her juju back, my bumbling beginner body following fellow students who'd been practicing far longer than I through the 108-move series. Acutely aware as I struggled to follow the hypnotic dance that I had made all this up, this classroom in a renovated theatre filled with earnest Americans learning an ancient Chinese martial art turned healthful, body, mind, and spirit practice from another earnest American. This special relationship and menacing ego I seemed to be fleeing, the car I drove here in and the road I drove on, the radio reports of more bombings in places the person I see in the mirror couldn't even pronounce—every last bit of it.

At break I was told in answer to my question that tai chi began as a self-defense system developed by Buddhist monks a couple thousand years ago to protect themselves and their possessions from the raids of marauding bandits—ha! Holding love in their hearts as they created a way to defend the little s robed selves they still mostly thought they were from invasion. (OK, so maybe I threw in that last part.)

Rejuvenated by the end of class, feeling well enough to stop at my favorite neighborhood coffee shop for a half-caf Americano to go, I realized, while waiting in line, that the emotional sickness at the root of the physical, my robotic compulsion to prove myself victim of the world I see by identifying my favorite objects of projection as the invading marauders responsible for poisoning the love in my heart, had passed. Walking back to the car beneath a cobalt sky free of warnings, I encountered the inner teacher of true forgiveness disguised as an acquaintance I had frequently caught myself judging in the past. Now I recognized in his distraught account of his problems in a special relationship my own uncertain self—longing for reassurance that despite the nature of my current dream, I couldn't fail to find the comfort and completion of our one loving home—and responded with genuine warmth.

In the car, Jesus, that sneaky *symbol* of the part of our mind that never took the "tiny, mad, idea" of separation seriously, had changed back into his robed-marvel costume and settled in beside me as I sipped my coffee, miraculously going (and staying) down, praise the Lord.

"Where have you been?" I asked.

His brows shot up the way they do.

"Just kidding," I said, realizing again that taking his hand always meant first taking the hand of the ones we love to hate, however minor or major their role in our dream appears. And I thought about how, for the longest time, I magically believed that if I were doing this forgiveness business right, I would somehow get up in the morning and see the special object of my projection transformed into a perfectly compliant, unwaveringly supportive version of the one I'd dreamed up, with whom *I* could blissfully enjoy *my* ever-awakening state. For the longest time, I still believed changing my mind from the ego as my teacher to the inner super savior would result in a classroom in which all my lessons had already been learned and I could simply sit back and rest on my graduate laurels.

For the longest time, I thought it was the classroom that needed to change, that a conflict-free life would prove I was making real progress with this Course, that I could awaken as "me," have this Course and the person I see when I look in the mirror, however imperfect, too. You know, without all those difficult others "out there." Somehow, that thought had wormed its way back in and I was furious that the objects of my projections were still hanging around, doing the same, old infuriating things. Worse, that wicked witch of the ego thought system knew it and was pitching it as evidence not only that I would never get home, but that, if I refused to turn back, continued on this path to sanity, I would end up as flying monkey food.

Surrender Susan, the wicked witch wrote in the sky of my brain over and over, cackling away, seeking to convince me once again that the home I was seeking was not in the mind but back in the dream. Where I could align with its good and evil defenses against the truth, its ever-winding yellow-brick-road to nowhere that, however dangerous, would at least keep the idea of a seeking, dreaming, monkey-bait Susan going.

The fact that I had released my belief that this special relationship was the cause of my conflict did not mean I had completely let go of the robotic need to project the guilt and fear still alive in my mind on my favorite target. I was not always willing to see peace instead of reacting to this person doing the things this person does in this script of "otherness" I'd chosen to review. The details of which I am choosing from moment to moment to continue to believe, reinforce, and support, or question, release, and heal my mind around, depending on which inner teacher I am willing to follow.

I am not always ready to choose again, but at least now I know I always have a choice. I have felt the peace beyond mortal understanding that mirrors the peace of our real home before, and will always feel it again once my fear in the form of anger, sickness, anxiety, irritation—whatever—subsides. At least now I have faith that no matter how miserable I am choosing to make myself at any given moment in a misguided effort to preserve the idea of me, the indivisible love I am really seeking is still so close I cannot fail.

From the level on which we meet it *A Course in Miracles* is a process. Until all the secret guilt in my mind is undone, I still need the classroom of my life in which to learn and the teacher of forgiveness, ACIM-style, to learn from, lending the statement, *Surrender Susan,* a completely different, welcome twist. The promise that if I step back and am willing to follow, I *will* make it home to the one love we are, sooner or later, having never really left it in the first place.

I started the car. "I see what you mean," I said, back on the road again.

Jesus, go figure, just smiled.

And I knew, truly, madly, deeply, all I really needed, right now, to know.

The Choice for Completion

In looking at the special relationship, it is necessary first to realize that it involves a great amount of pain. Anxiety, despair, guilt, and attack all enter into it, broken into by periods in which they seem to be gone. All these must be understood for what they are. Whatever form they take, they are always an attack on the self to make the other guilty. (*A Course in Miracles* text, Chapter 16, V. The Choice for Completion, from paragraph 1)

I sat in his office in front of his desk, still processing the confounding events of the last 48 hours, including the eventual recognition that seemed to have instantly propelled me back to this chair in the classroom of the mind. Following a particularly consuming, harrowing episode in the dream in which I had once more experienced myself completely at the mercy of a special relationship, who, from my perspective, had failed to deliver on his end of what the Course calls our "special relationship bargains."

My imaginary Jesus, in signature nubby robes and sandals, sat humoring me, as always, bless his forever-beating heart. I hadn't seen him since Saturday morning when, alone in my kitchen, inexplicably filled to the brim with love for all sentient and insentient beings while blasting the song *You Get What You Give* by the New Radicals, he popped right in to join in the festivities. I handed him another invisible microphone and we sang, more like screaming, really, in the best possible way, at the top of our lungs. "You've got the music in you!"

For several days prior, I had not (I am sorry to report) had the music in me, instead siding with the discordant inner teacher of special love gone missing in the form of my cherished daughter off at college. I'd been feeling the hollow ache of her absence again. A more pronounced, cavernous version this year in which—understandably and rightly more involved in the whirlwind of campus life—she wasn't visiting on breaks, often crashing here with her friends, the way she had freshman year. I'd been asking for help in seeing this differently through the wacky, pink, right-minded shades of you know who to no avail when, suddenly, blasting this CD collection my daughter had burned for me as a birthday gift a few years back, I felt the music in me welling up again, the mistaken sense of lack eternally filled. Bathed and enveloped once more in the memory of that same old forgotten song that, in truth, has never stopped playing in anyone, the hymn of our forever supported, completed, loving, undifferentiated union.

One of the less observed (but nonetheless truly endearing qualities) of hanging out with Jesus? It offers all the benefits of being alone, without *feeling* alone. By that I mean you can do anything you freaking please, go as wild and goofball as you wish, with absolutely no fear of being mocked. In fact, he didn't miss a beat, now, as I continued to belt out the lyrics, jumping up and down and all around the room like someone, well, *his* age.

Afterwards, I had him help with the dinner I was preparing for two dear women friends coming over that night, the Mario Batali turkey meatball and Martha Stewart spaghetti sauce recipes I had chosen, the latter of which I couldn't resist tweaking by adding white wine and extra chopped basil. Because, I mean, who better to indulge an underlying authority problem with than Martha Stewart? Or, well, Jesus, for that matter.

When we'd finished, I took him to my tai chi class and had to laugh watching him stumble around, secretly thrilled to have found such a good-sported, if invisible foil, someone worse at this practice than me!

I paused in my reverie, sighed.

Jesus continued to fiddle with the little snow globe I'd given him for Christmas that never failed to crack him up.

I snapped my fingers. "Pay attention," I said. "This is important."

He did his best to look serious but, frankly, acting (unlike singing and dancing), is no more his forte than tai chi. He cleared his throat. "And then?" he asked.

"And then we drove home," I resumed, remembering.

And I found myself feeling victimized again, this time in the form of an absence of expected communication from another special relationship who appeared to have completely disregarded me anew, leaving me feeling once more unloved and, in rightful retaliation, unloving. I will spare you the gory details that, in retrospect, make no real sense at all. Suffice it to say, the joy of my time spent playing with the inner robed marvel, hearing and singing and dancing to the tune of that forgotten song, must have scared the crap out of the part of me that clings to the coveted IV of my special identity. Because I found myself suddenly alone again, stranger in a strange and threatening land within a dream of exile of my own making, fighting to reinforce and defend the terms of my special relationship bargain and longing to punish its perceived violator.

The special love relationship is the ego's most boasted gift, and one which has the most appeal to those unwilling to relinquish guilt. The "dynamics" of the ego are clearest here, for counting on the attraction of this offering, the fantasies that center around it are often quite overt. Here they are usually judged to be acceptable and even natural. No one considers it bizarre to love and hate together, and even those who believe that hate is sin merely feel guilty, but do not correct it. (From paragraph 3)

I spent the next 36 hours indulging my persecution fantasies, spinning my case, engaging others to agree with me, now and then asking for help to see myself and this person through the robed-marvel-seemingly-gone AWOL's right-minded shades, but unwilling to relinquish the self-righteousness required, despite the unbearable pain of clinging to having things my way.

It is in the special relationship, born of the hidden wish for special love from God, that the ego's hatred triumphs. For the special relationship is the renunciation of the Love of God, and the attempt to secure for the self the special-ness that He denied. It is essential to the preservation of the ego that you believe this specialness is not hell, but Heaven. For the ego would never have you see that separation could only be loss, being the one condition in which Heaven could not be. (Paragraph 4)

By the time I actually conversed in form with the object of my projection, the pain was too great to hold onto anymore. Although my mind on ego made several runs at blame, a part of me could not help but recognize that attempting to have this person behave the way I wanted, honor my special needs, had and would never bring me the sustainably peaceful, joyful love I was really seeking. Trying to steal the love I was looking for and believed I lacked from another dream figure never had or would work. We continued to talk, our differences apparent but, our need to change each other somehow disarmed. I wasn't exactly happily wrong. But I wasn't unhappy, either, just willing to let the hurt go.

And then, standing there speaking with this other person I heard the phrase, "you are my fear of God." And stood, momentarily breathless from awareness that I'd been using this relationship in one form or another for probably a gazillion lifetimes to prove I exist but it's not my fault. To prove love had failed me (to cover the belief that I had failed *it*) through my decision to experience individuality and get away with it by burying the guilt in him. Only this time around, the other body refused to play the game. I had used that refusal for so many years to imprison myself, to nurture my guilt and fear and feed my bitterness, but now I saw it offered my way out of prison, the open door I'd been looking for as long as I could remember, since the dawn of illusory time.

Whenever any form of special relationship tempts you to seek for love in ritual, remember love is content, and not form of any kind. The special relationship is a ritual of form, aimed at raising the form to take the place of God at the expense of content. There is no meaning in form, and there will never be. (From paragraph 12)

This year is thus the time to make the easiest decision that ever confronted you, and also the only one. You will cross the bridge into reality simply because you will recognize that God is on the other side, and nothing at all is here. It is impossible not to make the natural decision as this is realized. (Paragraph 17)

You are my fear of God, I thought, only you're not here, and neither am I. Nothing ever happened to divide us. Not the moment we chose to believe we were other than one with God and each other, not in all these lifetimes spent acting out that belief, and not now. Using this relationship to prove my innocence by limiting love has never worked. But using it to release me from the bondage of this special relationship bargain made to uphold the lie that exclusion from real love is possible—dropping all my doomed-to-failure-anyway needs for you to be or act a certain way to make me feel safe, withdrawing the power I have given you to in any way affect my inner peace or our continuing connection—will.

We talked a while more, reaching no real agreements, forming no new bargains, and yet, somehow, it seemed, each feeling heard. Peace not of this external world's bottomless neediness, born of the freedom available when we recognize only our sameness, washed over me.

"And then," Jesus, whispered, smiling, even though he knew.

"And then, I was here again. Right here with you."

"Ah." He handed me the tissues.

I dabbed at my eyes.

"I know what you're thinking," I said, after a while.

"You usually do."

"They grow up so soon."

"Ha!"

"One more question?"

"Anything."

"Could I get a commitment from you?"

"A commitment?"

"Yeah, I mean, this on again, off again thing is killing me."
He threw back his head and laughed.

I had to laugh, too. There was really nothing else whatsoever in this whole seeming world left to do.

The Appointed Friend

Anything in this world you believe is good and valuable and worth striving for can hurt you, and will do so.
Not because it has the power to hurt, but just because you
have denied it is but an illusion, and made it real. And it
is real to you. It is not nothing. And through its perceived
reality has entered all the world of sick illusions. All belief
in sin, in power of attack, in hurt and harm, in sacrifice
and death, has come to you, for no one can make one illusion real, and still escape the rest. For who can choose to
keep the ones that he prefers, and find the safety that the
truth alone can give? Who can believe illusions are the
same, and still maintain that even one is best?

The big, blue book lay cracked open on my desk to Chapter
26, VI. The Appointed Friend. I had come a long way on this
imaginary journey back to the place we never really left. I did not
slam the book shut, throw it against the wall, or fantasize backing
over it with my car as I once might have after reading a passage
like this. Because, even though the ego would rather have a root
canal then listen to one more word, a part of me had begun not
only to believe it, but to *trust it* from the inside out. (On a good
day anyway.)

Over the past year, and in an ever-deepening way the past few
months, I had learned that every time my need for anything in
this world to go or be a certain way surfaced, including (dare I
say, *especially*) the need for my closest relationships to behave a
certain way, acute suffering followed. While union with our true
and only friend within appeared to vanish, leaving me engulfed
in a bottomless pit of loneliness. Any time I tried to make a single
exception to this rule—to literally make something out of nothing through the alchemy of my "personal," infantile will—all hell
broke loose. Yet every time I just came clean about my neediness
with the inner teacher of kind forgiveness beside me, I could no
longer perceive myself entirely alone, and the profound relief of

completion I'd been seeking in all the wrong places eventually returned. Leaving in its wake only healed compassion for everyone and everything likewise mistaking need for Self.

I had been listening to the Ken Wapnick CD set, *Intimacy: Love without Needs*, in which he talks about the importance of keeping our attention focused on the only *real* relationship available to us here in this dream of conflict vanquishing eternal peace: the memory of all-inclusive love still shining in our mind. Within which our only heart has never stopped harmoniously beating. Our relationship with our kind, inner teacher who patiently waits for us to exhaust our interest in our trinkets of specialness—our bodies, our relationships, our jobs, the roles we play, our ambitions, our achievements, our failures, our governments, our ever exploding and imploding universe. The heavy baggage of forms we accumulate to anchor ourselves in this dream of specialness that nonetheless quite literally amounts to a nothing to which we have merely sacrificed our *awareness* of the weightless everything of our true nature.

The inner teacher of fearful separation we've been siding with all our lives reads horrendous loss in passages like this. Counseling us to run like hell from the idea that the details of our special existence are all the same in their unreality, fights quite literally to the death to convince us we have missed out on both the special love and special punishment our special selves deserve, simply as a result of our fantasized uniqueness. Nonetheless, the ego, born of the lie that we could separate from indivisible wholeness or would possibly want to, remains simply a figment of the one child of God's twisted imagination.

However much we might magically wish our fantasy real, ideas really cannot leave their source. We have never left our united home in the mind. Despite our hallucinations, we remain one child of God, merely dreaming of exile. A dream we come closer and closer to awakening from as we begin to experience ourselves as its dreamer rather than hero, taking responsibility for its cost back to the decision-making mind, choosing again to share the inner teacher of unity's lucid vision.

Lead not your little life in solitude, with one illusion as your only friend. This is no friendship worthy of God's Son, nor one with which he could remain content. Yet God has given him a better Friend, in Whom all power in earth and Heaven rests. The one illusion that you think is friend obscures His grace and majesty from you, and keeps His friendship and forgiveness from your welcoming embrace. Without him you are friendless. Seek not another friend to take His place. There *is* no other friend. What God appointed has no substitute, for what illusion can replace the truth? (Paragraph 2)

There is no other friend! All conjured substitutes will fail in the end because I made them up; along with the "me" they were meant to fail. When I stay focused on our only real friend within, the part of our mind that sees everyone and everything seemingly "out there" as equally deserving of unconditional friendship, the needs of the self I see in the mirror completely recede. And the insanity I have for so long insisted on seeing outside me vanishes in the sanity of our enduring, inclusively loving reality within.

A Course in Miracles begins with the statement "There is no order of difficulty in miracles." Meaning, we eventually learn, as we grow into understanding the Course's non-dualistic meta-physics through practicing forgiveness ACIM-style, that one illu- ✓ sion is no more real, important, or therefore impossible to forgive (change our mind about) than another. And yet, although we may believe this, we each lug around a personal Pandora's Box of illusions we treasure and conceal from our right mind.

We spend a long time, as Course students, willing to concede that some of the world around us is unreal even as we insist on clinging to other facets. My belief in the reality of my daughter and husband, for example, the body I believe I inhabit with its special plans, desires, ambitions, weaknesses, and failures, is so split off from my everyday awareness that it seems almost impossible to begin to collapse that personal hierarchy of illusions. And yet, we have a built-in relationship we can rely on 24/7 to illuminate the nothingness of even the illusions we hold most dire or dear, if we will only pivot toward its ever-blazing light.

As I write these words, I have to smile, glancing down at my little dog, curled in her bed, at my feet. One eye open, watching me, focused as always on my every move. So sure of the special part she plays in her master's life, so certain her safety lies in her place within her adopted pack.

My human daughter visited yesterday, bathed and coddled her, and made a little bun of our dog's ears on top of her head. Consumed with delight over the entire family gathered together on the couch for a change, Kayleigh hopped between our laps, licking every inch of our fingers and hands, inside and out, tail beating like a metronome, demonstrating her unwavering devotion. Insuring the special place she has marked forever in our hearts that, in truth, requires no such sacrifice. I pick her up now and hold her to my chest, again overcome with gratitude for the all-encompassing, everlasting friendship within, from which no man or dog is ever held apart.

> Make no illusion friend, for if you do, it can but take the place of Him Whom God has called your Friend. And it is He Who is your only Friend in truth. He brings you gifts that are not of this world, and only He to Whom they have been given can make sure that you receive them. He will place them on your throne, when you make room for Him on His. (From paragraph 3)

Choose Once Again

I sat at my desk on yet another Monday morning, staring at the computer screen, the proverbial blank page I still sometimes see in my dreams, as white as the newly, fallen snow outside my office window, beckoning my inner child to fill with angels. A space I once believed filling with words might reveal the answers I was seeking, coaxed from the faraway recesses of enlightened mind. A space I have simply dedicated in more recent years to observing and reviewing my individual wishes to experience individuality seemingly realized with the inner teacher of true forgiveness of what never was within. Joining with him to retrace these symbols back to their source: the false belief in many conflicting bodies triumphing over one ever-tranquil, loving mind. A story without plot or characters, heroes or villains, lights, camera, or action, nonetheless always met with ever-expanding applause.

It had been a week in which events within the imagined movie of this so-called life had left me rocked by an intense experience of déjà vu, a heightened awareness that I had seen these films before, ad nauseam, actually. Their recurrence offered the self I still mostly think I am a fresh opportunity to use them for the purpose of healing my mind, instead of grounding myself more deeply in this dream of exile. To remember I was their producer, writer, and director, rather than their star intent on delivering an Academy-Award-winning performance.

Hollywood's Academy of Motion Pictures had delivered its awards to its best and brightest the night before and the industry's pageantry, the flash of the Red Carpet, lured. The couture gowns, the jewels, the gaffes, the potty-mouthed, talking Teddy bear, Barbra's surprise performance of that beloved anthem of the special relationship, *The Way We Were,* the blood, sweat, and tears the self I luxuriate in vicariously indulging beckoned. And so, I texted my inner teacher, the imaginary bearded wonder within available 24/7 for consultation. I asked him to meet me in the viewing room for a little retrospective of another episode in *The*

Sorry Saga of Suffering Susan. And suddenly found him sitting beside me, wearing the cardboard, 3-D glasses he had pinched from me a while back and found so entertaining—upside-down, no less—not an easy feat! (Obviously, form has never been his forte, and no glasses will ever enable him to literally see my hallucinated, 3-D world.)

Nonetheless, to humor him, really—a favor I owe him, *big time*—I turned them over and placed them back on his face. "We need to talk," I said.

"Time for popcorn?"

He was getting used to this. I patted his arm. "It's a little early for that," I explained. "Cup of Joe, instead?"

He shook his head. "Trying to get off the stuff."

"Ha! Flax-seed muffin?"

He held one up to his glasses, rotating and examining.

"You want to eat the top," I said, demonstrating how to twist it off intact, a skill for which I am justly famous. Within a pretty small circle of fellow nut cases, but still.

He followed my lead. "What about the bottoms?" he asked.

"No real texture, superfluous really. If you're in a bad mood, just hurl them, like this."

"Far out," he said. But he must have been in a good mood again because he just put his down on the little side table conveniently built into our imaginary, especially plush and comfy, theatre chairs.

The lights dimmed. The credits rolled. And we were once more watching another scene in *The Sorry Saga of Suffering Susan* in which I again found myself lamenting the many ways in which a costar seemed to have invented his own damn script, improvised his own plot and lines. Rather than delivering the one we'd been rehearsing in my mind, the one I'd been trying to get him to play since the apparent dawn of linear time. Only now, about to throw another internal diva hissy-fit, I found myself pausing. Not merely aware there was a better way, but actually unable to deliver the reactive performance that would lead to the tragic outcome

I once craved as a substitute for the comedy I secretly believed I didn't deserve. *We* didn't deserve.

I grabbed the remote, hit the pause button. "Right there," I said.

Jesus tilted his head, adjusted his glasses, as if to obtain a better view.

"The thing is, I'm tired of this role," I said. "Tired of the whole damn series, really."

"Why?"

As if he didn't already know. "Because it hurts, too much."

He nodded.

"See, every scene in every movie of our seeming, individual life offers the chance to choose again for healing our mind instead ✓ of reinforcing the idea that I exist but it's not my fault. It's that award-winning costar's. It's the sorry plots and scripts. And we'll keep taking our role in the same tragic scenes seriously, mistaking the character we hired on to play for *what we are*, the drama we're acting out for our actual *lives*, until we're ready to see things differently. You know, the way *you* see them, as opportunities for healing our mind of the thought of separation realized instead of driving ourselves deeper into the movie-making business. It's like you said in Chapter 31, VIII. Choose Once Again:

> Trials are but lessons that you failed to learn presented once again, so where you made a faulty choice before you now can make a better one, and thus escape ✓ all pain that what you chose before has brought you. In every difficulty, all distress, and each perplexity, Christ calls to you and gently says, "My brother, choose again." (From paragraph 3)

"See, in content, if not form, it's like that movie *Groundhog Day* where Bill Murray keeps living the same day over and over but eventually learns he doesn't have to step in the metaphorical puddle again. He can eventually learn to avoid the victimized and victimizing mistakes he made and replace them with kinder responses. Simply by reviewing them with his right mind and realizing they're hurting him. Keeping him imprisoned in an endless, frustrating, groundhog-obsessed day."

Jesus nodded.

I was on a roll now. "Or, it's like the introduction to the old *Dick Van Dyke* show, where he walks into his living room and trips over the ottoman for a couple of years before he finally learns, toward the end of the series, that he could choose to remember his mistake and step around it."

There had been other scenes from *The Sorry Saga of Suffering Susan* revisited over the last week, too; itchy evidence of another spider bite, the creepy perpetrator mysteriously at large, and my failure to once more reach my stealthy daughter—away in the mountains in a snowstorm over the weekend—by phone. My complete inability to cohabitate with a box, or five, of Girls Scout cookies (invited into the house by a rogue costar) for example, without succumbing to a seemingly involuntary urge to consume every last one of them in order to eliminate the possibility of future temptation, resulting in a crabby sugar hangover. I *know*.

And yet, in each case, there arose in my mind the certainty that I just didn't want to hurt myself again like this, and didn't have to (even as I kept doing so). The awareness that holding any one or thing seemingly "out there" responsible for destroying my peace—including the Cookie Monster I still seem to see in the mirror—would cause me to suffer. And I didn't want to suffer anymore. Besides, it was getting so freaking boring!

"And so, I chose again, for you," I concluded.

Jesus and I gazed up at the screen. The credits rolled. And it went blank again.

We sat in silence for a moment, or a lifetime, who the hell knows?

"Do you mind if I eat the bottom of this thing, too?" he asked, after a while, raising his muffin.

I thought about it, surprised to learn I really had no opinion whatsoever on the subject. I shook my head, and smiled. "Knock yourself out," I said.

The images you make cannot prevail against what God Himself would have you be. Be never fearful of temptation, ✓ then, but see it as it is; another chance to choose again, and let Christ's strength prevail in every circumstance and every place you raised an image of yourself before. For what appears to hide the face of Christ is powerless before His majesty, and disappears before his holy sight. The saviors of the world, who see like him, are merely those who choose His strength instead of their own weakness, seen apart from Him. They will redeem the world, for they are joined in all the power of the Will of God. And what they will is only what He wills. (Paragraph 4)

Let Us Not Fight Our Function

I sat across from his desk, waiting a long while in the semi-darkness on a stormy, late winter morning, staring at the tiny torpedoes of wet snow detonating on the sidewalk outside his office window. He breezed in at last, my imaginary inner teacher, sandals slapping the hardwood floors, the scarf I gave him tied around his waist—go figure—snowflakes still clinging to his hair and beard. There really was just no convincing him to take the reality of our Colorado seasons seriously.

"Long time no see with," he said, flipping on the light and slipping into his chair across from me. Trying to cheer me up, I suppose. Good luck with that.

After days of right-mindedness in which I found it relatively easy to run with the ebbing and flowing events and situations in my so-called life without compromising a sense of inner peace and compassion for all, I had suddenly awakened (for lack of a more accurate term) in a complete funk. The ego's snarky, 24/7 ode to the many ways the world had failed me (and I had returned the favor) stuck, like an unwelcome song, in my head. Once more seemingly prey to a barrage of external problems bombarding me with the random rapidity of asteroids in a video game that my aging reflexes could never move fast enough to deflect.

There was the all too familiar pain in my neck—gift of an ancient injury—nagging anew for attention, the throbbing in my deformed and apparently newly inflamed foot and toe, a to-do list longer, and seemingly more doomed, than the Congressional debate on the sequester, and the matter of that gloomy weather "out there." That already had me obsessively googling the 10-day forecast only to learn of a snowstorm barreling down on Denver from Saturday night into Sunday morning, when I was scheduled to fly to San Diego to attend a week-long Academy class with Ken Wapnick at the *Foundation for A Course in Miracles* in Temecula. My worry seemingly justified, given the fact that a little more than a week ago a storm had dumped nearly a foot of snow here in a whiteout that resulted in the always thrifty Department of Transportation (DOT) holding off on even their usual minimal plowing of residential neighborhoods until Sunday night, followed by the subsequent cancellation of untold numbers of flights out of DIA.

Then, too, because my husband was out of town for the week, scheduled to fly back from Utah late Saturday night in that same predicted snowstorm, I fretted about him making it in. Concerned about him getting stuck, of course, but also selfishly worried he might not arrive in time to provide *me* with a backup plan for how to get to the airport should he be detained in Salt Lake City. He had the SUV and the nerves to use it in extreme conditions that would normally enable that to happen, while my vehicle lacked the clearance to navigate the DOT's fiscally responsible, albeit infuriatingly, hands-off approach to snow removal.

"Don't worry," the ego said. "They'll cancel your flight long before you need to leave for the airport."

"I can't hear you," I countered, at least aware that any dubious comfort extended from the inner teacher of separation realized was not in my best interests, to say the least.

"And if it's a big storm, you probably can't reschedule."

"I'm not listening," I lied. What if the flight *was* cancelled? I *really* needed this workshop. I'd been looking forward to it for months. After all, the last Academy class I attended had left me feeling ambivalence-free for weeks. Totally aligned with that one quiet center within the one mind (the Course talks about) no fantasized external obstacle can ever rattle. How I yearned to enter that quiet center again. I had to make it to Temecula!

"Yeah, right," the ego said. "Well, listen to this, sweetheart. Remember that March snowstorm that hit ten years ago and shut down the city and airport for five days?"

I sighed. Only, too well.

"Or a couple years later when you tried to fly your parents out for one of those nice, family Christmases you've been seeking but never finding since time began and they got stuck in Dallas and had to turn around."

Who could forget? I could feel myself tearing up anew, even after all this time.

"Wasn't that what led them to stop flying out to see you ever again? Pity."

I am never upset for the reason I think, I reminded myself. And even if I wasn't ready to choose peace instead of this, I didn't have to sit and listen to the inner teacher of fear's case for specialness designed to prove I individually, importantly, and tragically exist, but it's not my fault. It's because of the weather, the DOT, the injuries, the deformities, the parents, the husband, the vehicle.

And yet, there really was the matter of the manuscript I'd been working on all last week to incorporate final copyedits in preparation for passing on to be formatted for printing that seemed to have gone AWOL. No matter how many times I searched my Word files, I could only find the previous version.

"Sans the hours of corrections you labored to enter," the ego was only too happy to add. "Could be another sign that this little project of yours—hmmm, how do I put it?—just isn't quite ready for prime time?"

A bad word flew out of my mouth of its own volition. I covered my ears. There has to be a better way! I thought. And I was back in this office again, right here in this chair, waiting for you know who to return and flip on the proverbial light.

"So why do you?" he asked, sitting across from me, now.

He had a point. "I know what you're thinking," I said.

"You always do."

"It's like you say in workbook lesson 186, paragraph 2: 'Let us not fight our function. We did not establish it. It is not our idea. The means are given us by which it will be perfectly accomplished. All that we are asked to do is accept our part in genuine humility, and not deny with self-deceiving arrogance that we are worthy. What is given us to do; we have the strength to do. ...' Meaning, how any of this turns out in form is irrelevant. The point is remembering that my *only* function here in this dream of constant conflict is to learn and practice true forgiveness, to see things differently by choosing you as my inner teacher instead of the ego. To recognize I am not the ego, but the decision maker, capable of choosing from moment to moment to side with the strength in my mind, instead of the weakness of my imaginary body."

Jesus shrugged, nodding.

"And so, true humility means siding with your vision that sees past all these blocks to my experience of love's uninterrupted, united, and all-encompassing presence. I need only accept your plan for salvation, until I remember it is my plan. Devoting the purpose of my life to learning the lessons of forgiveness with you as my teacher, using the content of my life as a curriculum in which I learn to look at everything that seems to happen as just another opportunity to heal my mind of the belief that anything external could possibly threaten the uninterrupted peace we share within."

He smiled.

"I know what you're thinking," I said.

"I know you do."

"Get back in that classroom."

He nodded. "Break a leg, kid!"

"Ha!" And I was back at my computer, snow gently falling outside my office window, once more happily wrong and ready to begin the day's only real work.

> And so we find our peace. We will accept the function God has given us, for all illusions rest upon the weird belief that we can make another for ourselves. Our self-made roles are shifting, and they seem to change from mourner to ecstatic bliss of love and loving. We can laugh or weep, and greet the day with welcome or with tears. Our very being seems to change as we experience a thousand shifts in mood, and our emotions raise us high indeed, or dash us to the ground in hopelessness. (Paragraph 8)

These unsubstantial images will go, and leave your mind unclouded and serene, when you accept the function given you. (From paragraph 10)

The Fear of Redemption

I'd awakened again, a tangled, sweaty mess, the air conditioning unit in my hotel room once more inexplicably malfunctioning, unsuccessfully trying to will myself back to sleep with my secret, warrior-woman powers, even though I knew I was doomed. Opening my eyes with yet another sigh, I surveyed the ceiling, the lamp in the parking lot just outside my window casting a ghoulish spotlight through a crack in the drapes on the disabled cooling device. And then, as my eyes adjusted to the room's prevailing darkness, I spied him—the bearded wonder—sitting cross-legged on top of the desk in the corner. His hands resting on his knees, thumbs and index fingers touching the way I'd taught him the last time I dragged him up to the yoga retreat in the mountains I sometimes flee to, eyes squeezed shut.

"What are you doing here?" I asked.

One eye popped open, then the other. "Why are we whispering?" he countered.

"Because it's the middle of the night, for Christ's sake," I said. Ugh. "Sorry, but I mean, people are sleeping." Somewhere; on a planet far, far away.

"Seriously?"

But I was in no mood for levity. "Anyway, you need to leave."

After all, it was not like I'd invited him. Honestly, the last thing I needed after a day like this was my imaginary Jesus dropping in, unannounced, smiling more like the Cheshire Cat, in my opinion, than the face of innocence. Although I'm in the habit of checking in with the inner teacher of forgiveness on a regular basis throughout my days, lugging my satchel of dark illusions du jour to his classroom for the review that always, eventually, anyway, enables me to see things differently, since I'd boarded the flight to San Diego that would take me to the weeklong Academy class with Ken Wapnick at the Foundation for *A Course in Miracles* I'd been looking forward to since my previous visit, the robed marvel had not once crossed my mind.

In fact, not much had traversed that barren wasteland since I'd arrived in Temecula two days earlier. Unlike my last visit, in which my thirst was joyfully, endlessly quenched by every drop of wisdom shared, I was having severe difficulty focusing on Ken's words, alternating between extreme restlessness and sleepiness. Now and then consumed with fantasies about various junk food products I didn't even really like anymore and hadn't ingested in decades that I just had to have right now. Finding myself, at one point; absolutely captivated by a vivid image of a life-size Twinkie dancing in my peripheral vision. (I am not making this up! Oh, well, never mind.)

My brain lay leaden in its skull, neurons ground to a halt. The constant awareness that this was yet another clever bout of resistance flu did not make the experience any easier. I knew I was listening to the inner teacher of fear instead of the inner teacher of love, but his name rested on the tip of my tongue, stillborn. And even though he now seemed to be sitting right here in this room with me, I had zero desire to utter that name or look upon that face.

Despite the unpleasantly elevated room temperature, a sudden chill came over me. My frozen heart raced. Like Ebenezer Scrooge in *A Christmas Carol* at the sudden appearance of his deceased partner Marley, rattling his death chains, I pulled the covers over my head in a wave of dread I couldn't comprehend. He had come for me, I was sure of it, and I wasn't nearly ready yet. He had no right. I had *not* invited him. He needed to leave—now!

"Please get out," I pleaded, from beneath the covers. I waited a minute or two for him to scram before peeking out again. But there he still sat, smiling that unalterable smile.

"I said, leave!" I had raised my voice, consumed now with anger. This was *my space*, after all!

And then, I must have fallen asleep again because I found myself in a kind of carnival fun house, stumbling around in the dark through a maze of corridors with false floors, walls, and ceilings, only to find, to my horror, an illuminated Jesus popping out at me around every corner and behind every door, his smile and girth enlarging and decreasing in those bloody trick mirrors that had terrified me as a child.

Although I somehow made it out of that den of horrors, I then found myself in the old *Laugh In* TV show of my youth, standing before the psychedelically painted wall of small doors I felt compelled to open, as if searching for something. But instead of the heads of cast members popping out with a moronic joke to tell, the joke was on me! Because only Jesus' smiling face stared back at me, every time.

Next I was transported to one of those confusing, cavernous cities I often find myself lost in within my sleeping dreams, winding my way down densely populated sidewalks in which every passerby, despite different bodies, wore the face of Jesus! I started running, only to find myself back in my own kitchen in Denver, standing in front of the refrigerator door, heart pounding. I drew several deep breaths, and opened it. There, to my horror, nestled among cartons of Greek yogurt, eggs, and avocados, he stood, my tiny, smiling, inner savior, serenely gazing up at me. I screamed, a child's scream, slammed that door, turned on my heels, and raced off into the dark.

I awoke to find myself back in my hotel room again, covers still drawn over my head. Aware in a way I have never been before of just how deeply a part of me doesn't want to take his hand, learn this Course, follow him home. And I realized I don't really want to see him *everywhere*, in *everyone* and *everything*. Christ, maybe I don't want to see him at all!

And then I was back in that classroom in the mind, sitting across from him at his desk, the big, blue book propped open before me to Chapter 13, III. The Fear of Redemption, paragraph 2:

> Under the ego's dark foundation is the memory of God, and it is of this you are really afraid. For this memory would instantly restore you to your proper place, and it is this place that you have sought to leave. Your fear of attack is nothing compared to your fear of love. You would be

willing to look even upon your savage wish to kill God's Son, if you did not believe that it saves you from love. For this wish caused the separation, and you have protected it because you do not want the separation healed. You realize that by removing the dark cloud that obscures it, your love for your Father could impel you to answer His Call and leap into Heaven. You believe that attack is salvation because it would prevent you from this. For still deeper than the ego's foundation and much stronger than it will ever be, is your intense and burning love of God, and His for you. This is what you really want to hide.

"OK," I said. "I get it. I just became afraid of love again—truly, madly, deeply terrified. But I can't help it. I'm doing the very best I can with this, making it my true purpose, looking at all my reactions—OK, *most* of them—with you, and reminding myself I'm never upset for the reason I think. Asking you over and over to help me see everyone and everything the way you do. But just so you know, there's not going to be any leaping into Heaven going on any time soon."

"I can see that," he said.

"I'm just saying."

He nodded.

"So what do I do?"

He looked into my eyes. I hate it when he does that. At least his old smile was back, not a shred of mockery—just that abiding faith I so longed to curl up in—faith in me! Ultimately not the little m me I see when I look in the trick mirror of the ego's eyes, although I could tell, even that, was OK, for now.

"It's just that I'm not a hundred percent sure there's a better place than this, you know? A better *me*. Even though I'm beginning to see this world holds nothing I really want, I'm just not there yet."

He shrugged. "Yeah, but you will be."

"If I just keep looking with you, you're saying, even when I'm afraid of you?"

He nodded.

"Especially when I'm afraid of you?"

That smile again—the good one.

I yawned. "I'm just so tired."

He took my hand. OK, *actually*, I took his. And I was back in my bed in the hotel, right mind restored, resting in love, merely dreaming of exile.

... Here is both his pain and his healing, for the Holy Spirit's vision is merciful and His remedy is quick. Do not hide suffering from His sight, but bring it gladly to Him. Lay before His eternal sanity all your hurt, and let Him heal you. Do not leave any spot of pain hidden from his light, and search your mind carefully for any thoughts you may fear to uncover. For He will heal every little thought you have kept to hurt you and cleanse it of its littleness, restoring it to the magnitude of God. (From paragraph 7)

Devotional Pose

I rapped softly on the mottled glass of the ajar door to my imaginary teacher's office, a courtesy; really, since I could tell he was not inside. Not inside and not outside either, on a day like this, as far as I could tell. But I no longer fully trusted these observations of mine, and was willing, for once, to wait. I pushed the door open and paused, soaking in the lingering starlight of his presence, unencumbered by the bare overhead fluorescent light, currently switched off. He deserved a better office, I thought. Note to little s self; see what you can do about that.

I stood a moment longer soaking up that inexplicable sense of infinite space unfettered by the cramped walls. His desk and empty chair, facing the always-open door, fit snugly in front of the beveled windows. The chair I liked to call *mine* looked out at the stately brick buildings across the courtyard, those hallowed halls of higher learning obscured here and there by oak tree branches that had been around the block, nonetheless about to bud anew.

Squeezed between my chair and the door on an area rug that had seen better days I found just enough space to unfurl my yoga mat, and sat a few minutes in lotus position, eyes shut, breathing those full-bodied breaths I had learned to calm this body's ever-addled nerves. Simultaneously filled with longing and growing gratitude, I then assumed the position that best expressed the reason I had come. Bent knees beneath me on the mat, I curled my torso around them, allowing my forehead to touch down, arms fully extended in front of me, imagining him standing at my feet, the object of my embryonic humility, accepting this offering.

In yoga, devotional pose, also called child's pose, symbolizes the respect due revered teachers and elders. Despite years of dabbling in Eastern traditions that often involved one form or another of bowing to gurus, I had eschewed the practice on the basis of the wildly unsupported (in my actual experience) conviction that God was not embodied, but somehow within. Or, more likely, in ways I could not comprehend or express correctly, we were contained within God. The mere suggestion of which would have had me ejected from the pew of the Immaculate Conception church in which I knelt as a child, swallowing my grave doubts even as I tapped my fist to my chest, obediently uttering mea culpa, terrified to raise my eyes toward the alleged habitat of a God that might smite me dead at any moment for my silent, renegade opinions.

In any event, I knew no priest or guru was going to help me find my way to the awareness of that gentle intersection of self and God I craved, within which all doubts disappear. No one had a special corner on divinity, I blasphemously, if clandestinely, dared to presume. I was somehow already there, the cesspool of my hateful thoughts notwithstanding, just like everyone else, if I could just somehow remember the code. Just somehow feel and thereby allow that love to express itself through me all the time, to everyone and thing I encountered. Besides, gurus had led too many friends into cults never to be heard from again. I would not be one of those. I would find the directions to our one home my way, or, you know, not at all (admittedly the most likely scenario).

A Course in Miracles has given me those directions. It has explained the inexplicable guilt within that left me feeling secretly unloved and unloving so much of the time—blaming it on external causes only to feel even more guilty—and exposed the dynamics of my secret wish to remain separate and unequal to others. A result of taking the "tiny, mad idea" that we could separate from our eternally loving, all-inclusive Self or would possibly want to seriously, and projecting the guilty thought into an entire universe of forms vying for survival. Each attempting to prove they exist but it's not their fault; it's someone else's, each trying to find in an imaginary someone or something "out there," a guilt-free ticket home.

And yet, even though I now intellectually know for certain that the path and its destination are not separate from me, I am not yet there all the time in my awareness, to say the least. The dreaded clouds of guilt in my mind seeded by that secret, false belief in separation still cluster on the horizon, seemingly stacked against my will. Sometimes disguised in the faces of those I love to love and hate, sometimes disguised as the deeply flawed person I see in the mirror, seemingly obscuring my vision of the road before me, let alone the end I seek. And I am, at times like these, overwhelmed with a longing to fall to my knees at my teacher's feet. To receive his blessing, his forgiveness, an absolution I still can't fully offer the self I still think I am, on my own. Filled with such deep yearning to know that innocence he knows once and for always, hoping to absorb it through some kind of celestial osmosis from his imaginary touch on my imaginary, bowed head.

I lay there a few moments longer, breathing, before I sensed his presence again in the room. But he wasn't standing over me, as I'd expected. His office had somehow expanded to include room for a yoga mat beside me in which he also lay in child's pose, deeply breathing. I wanted so badly to bolt, and yet, as if obeying a distantly familiar beat, my lungs slowly expanded and contracted in unison with his to the tune of the forgotten song we have never, in truth, stopped singing.

"I think I get it now," I whispered, after a while.

He continued to breathe, in, and out, rhythmically, beside me. Really, there was nothing left to say.

> There must be doubt before there can be conflict. And every doubt must be about yourself. Christ has no doubt, and from His certainty His quiet comes. He will exchange His certainty for all your doubts, if you agree that He is One with you, and that this Oneness is endless, timeless, and within your grasp, because your hands are his. He is within you, yet He walks beside you and before, leading the way that He must go to find Himself complete. His quietness becomes your certainty. And where is doubt when certainty has come? (Chapter 24, V. paragraph 9)

A Happy Outcome to All Things Is Sure

"I must realize that (when projecting) I am throwing Jesus under the bus and running over him again and again and again and it's not helping me," I read, for the billionth time, from the notes I had taken at the March 2013 Academy with Ken Wapnick I was finally getting around to typing up. Meaning, I have secretly chosen again *not* to remember the part of my mind represented in the Course's non-dualistic figure of Jesus, that never took the dream of separation seriously, whose unbridled awareness we can learn to join with every time we find ourselves feeling unkindly toward anyone or thing. Instead of reliving the ridiculous idea of separation realized again and again by projecting the guilty thought outside the mind, effectively pushing Jesus' love away and experiencing anew the pain of that decision.

The graphic reminder seemed especially salient this Monday morning as I sat at my desk gazing out at the particular gloom to which Colorado seems particularly prone this time of year. Gracious greenery busting out all over about to be pummeled by sleety rain segueing to snow. I was supposed to be writing a blog post, examining proofs for my book, answering emails and generally getting with the program another week in the dream of this so-called life required. Instead I sat transfixed, contemplating the fate of a tulip outside the window on the kamikaze edge of exposing her curled, coral head, consumed by guilt over that bus metaphor and the events of the last 48 hours.

My husband and I had taken advantage of the steady spring snowstorms by heading to the mountains for a day of skiing with friends. In or out of their pleasant company, I felt the steady presence of my imaginary robed marvel—that *symbol* of a love not of this world that embraces all and knows no opposites—beside me. Swinging his skis on the chair lift somehow fitted to those confounding sandals; whooshing down steep canyons beneath azure skies and cartoon-like clouds, robes flying. So close to me I could not fail. Not at the turns required in steep terrain on the mountain or the steep terrain on the seeming road home to the one love we never really left. Not at seeing clearly with him the beauty and innocence of everyone and thing, awash with boundless gratitude for all.

As my husband and friends peeled off toward more challenging runs, I experienced the wonder that often ambushes me lately of my hand secure within my inner teacher's, often accompanied by an inner power point presentation in which the lingering objects of my projections—upon whom I still pitch the repressed guilt in my mind over believing I exist at real, abstract love's expense—flash by, seemingly unbidden. Enabling me to experience the joy of true defenselessness that comes with seeing our sameness, the undifferentiated union we remain unaltered by past transgressions or future expectations.

And yet, by the end of a mind-healing day, over a leisurely dinner with friends, I found myself once more judging some of these same favorite targets I had seen correctly but hours earlier, silently and, even, aloud, differences between us again paramount in my perception, defensiveness on the rise. In short, I caught myself figuratively once more throwing Jesus under the bus, and taking the crime seriously. Even though I knew who I was really running over, the resulting, punishing pain to the personal self I still see in the mirror that would, and did, swiftly and inevitably follow.

And so I found myself this morning still feeling the crushing weight of that guilt, once more turned on the object of projection I find it most difficult to forgive: that very self I still see when I look in the mirror, too often hanging her head in shame over her addiction to specialness. Although I believe, as the Course tells us, that all bodies are illusions therefore the body I think I inhabit is no more real or culpable than the bodies I think it interacts with, I have to admit I still love to hate this body most of all. Still strive to preserve the "sin" of separation from our source at its seeming core that at least proves I exist in opposition to a God

I doubt could ever forgive my defection, ever welcome me back into the one, loving fold.

And yet, Ken also said at the March Academy that we must recognize that blame and self-blame are the same. All special relationships are venues we've imagined in which to act out our addiction to guilt. But, even when wracked with the pain our projections cause us, we can stop and reach for that inner teacher's hand. Even if we're not ready to receive its comforting pressure right now, we have felt it before, and can remind ourselves we will feel it again when our fear—regardless of the form it takes toward others or ourselves—subsides.

We can remind ourselves again and again when we slip back into the darkness of the ego thought system as we inevitably do following extended periods of kind right-mindedness; that feeling guilty means I first felt innocent. Which proves I'm not really guilty, after all, just frightened, and therefore don't exist apart from eternal, all-inclusive innocence, after all. A realization that still scares the crap out of a part of my mind that is not yet anywhere near 100 percent sure something better awaits it.

We can remind ourselves, when we slip off the true forgiveness wagon, that we're just not ready yet to remember we never really dropped that hand. Despite our story that we have thrown real love under the bus, nothing has really happened to interrupt the oneness joined as one of our true nature. We just became afraid again and fearful people deserve comfort, not punishment. We're not there, yet, in our perception, emphasis on the word *yet*. But we will be, we really will. Ken said so and so did our inner teacher and, honest to God, they cannot tell a lie.

> God's promises make no exceptions. And He guarantees that only joy can be the final outcome found for everything. Yet it is up to us when this is reached; how long we let an alien will appear to be opposing His. And while we think this will is real, we will not find the end He has appointed as the outcome of all problems we perceive, all trials we see, and every situation that we meet. Yet is

the ending certain. For God's Will is done in earth and Heaven. We will seek and we will find according to His Will, which guarantees that our will be done.

We thank You, Father, for Your guarantee of only happy outcomes in the end. Help us not interfere, and so delay the happy endings You have promised for us for every problem that we can perceive; for every trial we think we still must meet. (*A Course in Miracles* workbook lesson 292: A happy outcome to all things is sure.)

Hunger Games

Another Monday and another snowstorm predicted to hover over the Denver area, dispensing its unseasonably frigid gloom through Wednesday. Icing rush-hour thoroughfares and nixing my plans to attend the tai chi classes upon which I had—after only a few months of practice—already begun to depend for restoring my ever unsteady equilibrium. Suffice it to say the world was too much with me. There was too much work to be done, too many emails to answer, too many projects to complete, too many inexplicably unkind plot developments to wrap my puny, little head around. And I was hungry, hungry, hungry again for that elusive something no food or substance known to humankind had, or ever could, really satisfy. And then, my husband called and told me to turn on the news.

I paused before asking him what happened; aware I had been here before too many times. Conscious of the delicious sting of adrenaline now coursing in my veins, the part of me that—even as fear spiraled up my spine—hungered for another tragedy to feed on, another reason to hold an outside force responsible for this inner, perennially unsettled and un-sated "human condition." The result of the constantly resurfacing repressed guilt in the mind over the unconscious but nonetheless robust belief that my wish to exist apart from our one creator had real—dare I say *dire*—consequences. Consequences that, fortunately for me, had once again appeared to express themselves in *outside* drama, thereby temporarily relieving the person I still think I am from that inside morality play.

Although I dimly recalled I had a choice about which inner teacher to look with as I stood, transfixed, clutching the remote, the decision to watch with the inner teacher of fear, to see through the vulnerable body's eyes the Boston Marathon bombings replay in slow motion over and over again on CNN, seemed a no-brainer. As I watched unsuspecting, innocent runners and bystanders inexplicably, brutally struck down while navigating streets still dearly familiar to me from my long-ago college days, how could I help but join in the crescendo of rising outrage with the residents and visitors to this city of my youth? Hungering to find those responsible even though I knew the outward hunt would never deliver anyone inner peace.

As the week and the story wore wearily on, revealing the victims' and the victimizers' heart-wrenching tales, culminating Friday in a hunt for the latter played out in the media like back-to-back reruns of the TV series *24*, I had never been more conscious of my resistance to stepping away from the screen. More aware of my lust to involve myself in the chase to apprehend the final surviving culprit, to identify with the citizens of the greater Boston area holed up in their dwellings, or to try to imagine what must have occurred to cause a 19-year-old kid to participate in what appeared to be a vicious, premeditated act of terror.

He was innocent, he was guilty, I thought, from moment to moment; one or the other, just like me. It mattered not to my mind on ego. One minute a victim, the next minute a victimizer; as if there were a real difference. Broadcasters on NPR kept saying this was a day for "collecting not connecting the dots." But like everyone else wandering this apparent psycho world in which seemingly random assaults could fell the body they think they are or the bodies of those they love in an instant, I had already connected the dots. And the bloody trail led firmly and satisfyingly far, far away from the body I think I am.

Meanwhile, I watched the body I think I am engaged in defending itself from the assaults of people in its "personal life" again intent on trampling its boundaries, disrupting its plans, failing to consult with it, and generally wreaking havoc with the trajectory of its earnest missions. And I was hungry, hungry, hungry again for something I couldn't name, an innocence that could only be tasted at someone else's expense and never fill me completely or for more than a nanosecond.

A Course in Miracles Chapter 19, IV. A. i. The Attraction of Guilt, talks about the "hungry dogs of fear" the ego sends out to seek out evil and sin and drag it back to its master. I have read this section many times but it only recently dawned on me, while "innocently" attending the March Academy class with Ken Wapnick at the Foundation for *A Course in Miracles* that the hungry dog of fear was *me*, when I choose the ego as my teacher, that is. A creepy realization I have been unable to fully disassociate since, despite my considerable talents in that direction. Last week, I could truly taste for the first time the concealed desire to kill the Course references, acted out in all our seeming relationships, along with the almost irresistible impulse to charge into the world to find a culprit to punish that I might experience—however briefly—some relief.

Fear's messengers are trained through terror, and they tremble when their master calls on them to serve him. For fear is merciless even to its friends. Its messengers steal guiltily away in hungry search of guilt, for they are kept cold and starving and made very vicious by their master, who allows them to feast only upon what they return to him. No little shred of guilt escapes their hungry eyes. And in their savage search for sin they pounce on any living thing they see, and carry it screaming to their master, to be devoured. (From paragraph 12)

I know. And yet, if I would only choose Jesus/Holy Spirit (that *symbol* of the part of our mind that remembered to smile at the "tiny, mad idea" of separation at the seeming beginning) as my teacher, look through the eyes of invulnerable, all-inclusively loving truth instead of fear, all hunger would disappear. And compassion for all, including the differentiated self I think I am, would deliver true fullness, a peace and innocence this world (dreamed up to destroy those very qualities over and over again), cannot possibly ever deliver.

The Holy Spirit has given you love's messengers to send instead of those you trained through fear. They are as eager to return to you what they would hold dear as are the others. If you send them forth, they will see only the blameless and the beautiful, the gentle and the kind. They will be as careful to let no little act of charity, no tiny expression of forgiveness, no little breath of love escape their notice. And they will return with all the happy things they found, to share them lovingly with you. Be not afraid of them. They offer you salvation. Theirs are the messages of safety, for they see the world as kind. (Paragraph 14)

The trouble is a part of me I'm not really in touch with *is* afraid of them. The world is too much with me, emphasis on the word *me*. I want the hungry dogs of fear that keep the chase for me going more than I want the little lambs of love that would set me free. I can't experience an eternal, all-inclusive love not of this world and me at the same time. And that's just not acceptable to the me I still think I am, still uncertain she deserves something better, still uncertain safety lies beyond the walls of this embodied self and the imaginary minefield of a world it appears to navigate. And, while I'm willing, when confronted by all this seeming external drama, to remind myself that I'm not upset for the reason I think, for a while longer, experiencing puny, insatiably hungry me seems more urgent than experiencing whatever the hell no me looks like. However painful, at least I know what to expect here in me land: another micro or macro tragedy, another phone call telling me to turn on the news, another apparent private or public disaster on which to, with guilty gusto, feed.

Although I know I could see peace instead of this, although I genuinely want to look through the eyes of love for all, I don't really want to see. I want to get home, but I don't want to go in the right direction, away from the body and its imaginary world and back to the mind. And so—still hungry, hungry, hungry— seeking for sustenance where a part of me knows it can never be found, I try to forgive myself, and wait for that little spark of willingness to choose a better way to return.

If you send forth only the messengers the Holy Spirit gives you, wanting no messages but theirs, you will see fear no more. The world will be transformed before your sight, cleansed of all guilt and softly brushed with beauty. The world contains no fear that you laid not upon it. And none you cannot ask love's messengers to remove from it, and see it still. The Holy Spirit has given you His messengers to send to your brother and return to you with what love sees. They have been given to replace the hungry dogs of fear you sent instead. And they go forth to signify the end of fear. (Paragraph 15)

Relate Only with What Will Never Leave You

My imaginary bearded wonder sat waiting at the base of the trail-head; right where I had left him God knows how many hours, days, or lifetimes earlier. Perched on the little camp chair I bought him recently so he wouldn't have to spend all this time waiting for me on his feet. So immersed in playing with the thumb sumo puppets my friend Peggy had given me for my birthday (abandoned in my haste to charge back onto the battleground) that he barely glanced up as I wound my way around the last few switchbacks of the hill below to stand before him.

The plastic sumo wrestlers on his thumbs concluded their little vaudeville routine, with a bow.

"You know they're supposed to be duking it out, right?" I said.

His brows shot up the way they do.

"Not auditioning for *Glee*."

He smiled.

"Anyway, we're burning daylight," I said. "Up we go."

"Where?" he asked, as if he'd forgotten.

"Home!"

His eyes widened.

"I can't take it anymore," I said.

"No kidding?"

I nodded. "It's a cesspool down there."

"So, I've heard."

"Honestly, you have no idea." I clapped my hands in an effort to get him moving.

But still he sat, thumb puppets standing at attention.

"Put those toys away." It felt kind of good; I have to admit, playing the adult for once in our life together.

Ever so gently, as if handling fine crystal, he pulled off the puppets and tucked them in the little net beverage holder on the arm of the chair.

"See, I'm ready to take your hand," I said, arm outstretched. "Together or not at all—remember?"

He allowed me to pull him to his feet.

"I know what you're thinking," I said.

"You always do."

"Hallelujah, right?"

He smiled. "So, let me get this straight," he said. "You think we're going home together?"

I nodded.

"Just you and me?"

I gave him a thumbs up. It had been another one of those weeks. I had never been more truly, madly, deeply ready to leave the ever-developing and morphing problems and expectations; my own endless-seeming needs, every nasty little speck of protoplasm, each illusive wave and particle of the whole unholy hologram, behind.

"We've talked about this," he said.

And then it came to me, with a sickening sumo punch to the solar plexus, knocking the wind right out of my proverbial heavenward-bound sails. "You mean we have to take *them* with us?" I asked, once my breathing sufficiently stabilized. "Are you freaking kidding me? Obviously you haven't met them, have you?"

"Why are we whispering?"

I glanced back down over my shoulder at the city fuming on every level, and in every sense of the word, in the valley below.

"You think they can hear us, don't you?" he said.

I covered my eyes with the palms of my hands, the phrase "together or not at all" from The Lifting of the Veil in the final section of *A Course in Miracles'* Obstacles to Peace unfurling itself, banner-like, across the vast, empty recesses of my scant gray matter. "So you're saying you mean that *literally*? I mean, it's not just another metaphor?"

He smiled.

"Jesus! Well, that changes everything, doesn't it?"

He shrugged.

I was never going to pass this Course! I fell to my knees in despair, at his feet, tucked into devotional pose, where it appeared

I was doomed to spend the rest of eternity. "Please don't make me go back down there," I pleaded.

He rustled back into his chair, rested his palm on my head.

But I knew all too well what he was saying. I had never felt more acutely the gaping divide of my split mind, the intense ambivalence with which I approached my life. The deep yearning to make a non-dualistic, all-inclusively loving Jesus my only real relationship, and the simultaneous desire to keep that love for myself, turn my back on those I silently accused of stealing it, forever.

But, since we are, in truth, so much more than the sum of our imaginary parts, it would never work! I could never be in true relationship with Jesus unless I was willing to see everyone and ✓ everything I had cooked up to upset me as he did. As sharing the same mind split over the belief in separation, the same terror of punishment, and the same longing to take his hand and make it back to the summit where the split mind heals and we disappear into God's heart. Not to be lost, as the Lifting of the Veil section so eloquently puts it, but eternally found, no longer seen, but finally known.

"So you're saying my only real relationship is my relationship with God, who doesn't know me as Susan. But until I don't know me as Susan either, as long as I see other persons out there that seem to affect me, I need to look at all my seeming relationships with you to learn that there is no me or them, only our one abstract we, still seamlessly embraced in one endlessly loving relationship."

It was not that easy to talk in this position. My knees and ankles burned beneath me. I sighed. Clearly, I wasn't there yet, but I would get there one of these seeming days. As long as I was willing again and again, for however long it seemed to take, to admit I was happily wrong about everything, and ask to be taught by a part of my mind that was happily right!

I sat up and dusted myself off and we were instantly transported back to that classroom again. Once more seated side by side, reviewing the recent developments in *The Sorry Saga of*

Suffering Susan on the imaginary screen. Sharing a tub of popcorn, a good laugh, and a wave of compassion for all that ever was and still is and could never be divided.

Relate only with what will never leave you, and what you can never leave. The loneliness of God's Son is the loneliness of his Father. Refuse not the awareness of your completion and seek not to restore it to yourself. Fear not to give redemption over to your Redeemer's Love. He will not fail you, for He comes from One Who cannot fail. Accept your sense of failure as nothing more than a mistake in who you are. For the holy host of God is beyond failure, and nothing that he wills can be denied. You are forever in a relationship so holy that it calls to everyone to escape from loneliness, and join you in your love. And where you are must everyone seek, and find you there. (*A Course in Miracles* Chapter 15, VIII., paragraph 3)

Living Prayer

When I was a child and my mother's mother visited, she would sleep in my double bed, regaling me with stories I later discovered had been lifted from *The Arabian Nights* before veering off into more intimate, romanticized terrain. Fondly describing her life growing up in the Midwest among legions of older, mischievous, albeit adoring brothers, later marrying my French Canadian grandfather, and eking out a living on a dairy farm hugging the New York/Canadian border, where they managed to raise seven children, seemingly undaunted by the ravages of two World Wars, fire, pestilence, polio, and poverty.

But each night, before these tales commenced, my grandmother would kneel on the hardwood floor in her flannel nightgown, gray head bowed, eyes shuttered, gnarled fingers worrying the beads of her pale pink rosary. I would kneel beside her, laboriously working my way through my own set of magic baubles, now and then sneaking peeks, mystified by her beatific countenance. Wondering how the hell repeating so many Hail Marys and Our Fathers could deliver such obvious relief from the troubles of this world when all the practice did for me was deepen my conviction that no amount of good behavior would ever restore me to God's inner sanctum.

However hard I tried to play the role of reverent Catholic girl, I seemed to have come in short the faith gene. Although I sometimes felt the clear strength and support of a force beyond the discernible, messy world of the 1960s—especially when I walked alone in the woods or climbed up on my dresser on summer evenings to peer out my screened window at the clotted Milky Way—I did not feel God's presence kneeling on the worn pews in the over-heated, incense-choked churches of my youth. Staring up at clumsily-crafted statues of Jesus (God's *favorite* child; what might he have in mind for me?) nailed to the cross, crowned with thorns, frozen in bloody mid-perish, and Mary in all her pastel virgin splendor, squashing a snake with her bare, white feet. Murmuring mea culpas, beating my sorry, sinful chest, and hoping to hell God had better things to do than eavesdrop on my blasphemous doubts.

Besides, prayer didn't work. The day they shot President Kennedy and Sister ordered us to our bony, little knees, I prayed my heart out, conjuring those pictures of Caroline and John John and Jackie with her little cake-like hats in *Life* magazine. We all know how that turned out. When the twenty-four-year-old cousin I adored suffered a cerebral hemorrhage—just months later—I prayed again, with similar results. My prayers did not stop my grandfather from dying or the Vietnam War from winding wearily on, leaving empty chairs at neighbors' dinner tables. By the time Martin Luther King and Robert Kennedy were shot, I had given up on prayer and the God of the church altogether, the need to shed the burden of hypocrisy worth the risk of possible eternal damnation and my parents' certain, deep chagrin.

And yet, even in my evolving, distrustful state, I yearned and yearned for a love not of this world that would never fail me. Even as I half-heartedly explored spiritual alternatives that never yielded the unwavering, unconditional comfort I was really seeking, the reassurance that I was not this sinful self, I sensed this presence of goodness right there, somewhere, just out of view. Moving ghost-like in my peripheral vision so that if I could just snap my head around quickly enough; I might catch it in the act of eternally, innocently *being*.

I appealed more and more—as life's disappointments piled up over the years as they inevitably do—to its awareness with the only real prayer I knew: "Help me, help me, help me." A prayer that assumed I needed help but did not presume to know what that might mean. Because, except in situations in which I felt in imminent peril (from the phobias I had developed toward lightning and flying turbulence, for example), it never occurred to me to ask for something specific when I had no idea what might relieve that inner longing. Having accomplished many things I started out to do, I only knew none of them had. Although I did my best (however imperfectly) to lead a morally upstanding life, nothing relieved the nagging sense of being secretly, shamefully unloved and unloving at my very rotten core, a victim of impossibly high standards to which no one could possibly live up, especially myself.

I bring all this up because I awoke this morning, heart once more heavy with the weight of my needs. Missing my daughter, who had just left to study abroad, and again yearning for a real love that will never fail me, as if it could go missing. Contemplating the nature of prayer as it continues to reveal itself to me now that I have chosen *A Course in Miracle's* forgiveness of what never was (the belief that it *could* go missing) to lead me home. To deliver me from a dream of mortal forms vying for survival in a dualistic world, to the abstract wholeness of our true, all-inclusively loved and loving nature. Free from the ephemeral substitutes for real love we clutch at. That oneness joined as one my brain cannot possibly fathom, except when willing to once more open from moment-to-moment to the awareness that I am thankfully wrong about everything. Nothing in this world can destroy or enhance the love I am really seeking (having forgotten I already have it). But resigning as my own teacher and joining with a completed awareness not of this world can.

And so, in growing faith, I bow my head again and ask to know true forgiveness of everyone and everything, including this personal, needy, judging, ever-lacking self that continues to believe it offers me anything I really want, despite rapidly mounting evidence to the contrary. Again and again for however long it takes, I ask to forgive my sense of a self at odds with a dream world of others. So that my life becomes a kind of living prayer in progress, a healing duet in which I ask to see through the lucid eyes of my new inner teacher beyond the blocks to real love's awareness I still cling to in my fevered, fearful dreams. And hear echoes of the loved and loving song in which I remain forever bound in God, one with eternal being, merely dreaming of exile a little while longer, awakening as close as my next breath; wholly harmonic and sure.

The secret of true prayer is to forget the things you think you need. To ask for the specific is much the same as to look on sin and then forgive it. Also in the same way, in prayer you overlook your specific needs as you see them, and let them go into God's Hands. There they become your gifts to Him, for they tell Him that you would have no gods before him; no Love but His. What could his answer be but your remembrance of Him? Can this be traded for a bit of trifling advice about a problem of an instant's duration? God answers only for eternity. But still all little answers are contained in this. (*The Song of Prayer*, I. paragraph 4)

I Take the Journey with You

"Just go ahead and say it. You think I'm a drama queen, right?"

The robed wonder smiled that same old, impossible-to-read smile, pressed the pads of his fingers together, and leaned back in his chair.

I was lying on the floor, inverted palm draped on forehead. Despite his tenure, he doesn't have a couch in that stark little office of his; it seemed the next best thing. "So, I've got an idea," I said. "Let's pretend you're the shrink and I'm the patient."

His brows shot up the way they do.

"No, I mean it. I think maybe I could use some analysis." (I had heard he was a Freudian, after all. I'd always meant to try a Freudian.)

"Oh, come on," he said.

"Humor me, please?"

He shrugged, still smiling. "Story of my life," he said.

"Ha! So, here's what I'm thinking, doc. You may have been right about a few things."

"You don't say."

"OK, so that would be everything."

"Go on," he said.

But, where to begin?

It had been a week in which I found myself once more veering into fear, this time over a presentation I had to make to a larger-than-usual Course audience on "The Lifting of the Veil," the final subsection of the final section of the "The Obstacles to Peace" in *A Course in Miracles* Chapter 19, the conclusion to "The Fear of God." Inspired by Ken Wapnick's profound CD set, *Forgiveness Now: Those you do not forgive you fear*, I longed to share his conviction that the journey without distance to the one, endlessly expansive, all-inclusively loving home we have never really left begins and ends *now*, in my present decision to see everyone and everything the same as me.

I had experienced this shift from wrong-to-right-mindedness the Course calls forgiveness many times, the deep release and relief from the heavy weight of the secret, guilty thought that I had separated from our one, loving source it provided. The rising above the perpetual "battleground" of the perennial attack-defense cycle merely admitting I'm not upset because of anything outside my one, decision-making mind it offers. "I'm never upset for the reason I think," workbook lesson 5 tells us. The nagging guilt I feel within and constantly attempt to project on you is a lie, a doomed attempt to prove I exist at God's expense but it's not my fault, it's yours.

I knew I had a choice from moment-to-moment to retreat to that quiet center within wherein I could see and hear only my own misplaced fear in our ego doing what it does in the dream: attacking, defending, judging, criticizing, excluding, complaining, invading, killing, maiming, needing, competing, comparing, craving, flattering, ingratiating, abandoning, infecting, disabling, falling ill. And respond with the only response our one, innocent Self we've forgotten still deserves: love. I knew I could remember that—whatever seems to be going on around us or between us or within us, whatever seems to divide us—we remain one ever-loved and loving, child of God.

I had tasted the nirvana of this awareness, the peace, not of this world, it delivers, its enveloping embrace of completion, often, and yet. Here I was again, seemingly smacked down by terror (a reminder of that original terror experienced the moment I believed the "tiny, mad idea" of separation from our source had real, harmful effects) that seemed to stem from this presentation I never in a million years should have committed to in the first place, given my long-standing phobia of public speaking.

And yet, the journey begins and ends now, I reminded myself. And so I decided to get to the bottom of this fear once and for all. Even though the Course tells us it takes only an instant to return to right-mindedness, I felt, at this moment—heart again racing in anticipation of panicking as I had only a few years ago in such situations—the need to sit and look at my fear with you know who, asking to see truly. And so, I closed my body's eyes and did just that, waiting for the blocks to my awareness of truth to subside.

My mind on ego did its little lounge lizard shtick for a while, presenting its smarmy case for fear, dredging up my personal past. But I just kept remembering my purpose: seeing beyond my fear with my right mind. After a while, a single thought did emerge in the little Magic-8-Ball screen behind my forehead, fresh off the pages of "The Lifting of the Veil":

"Those you do not forgive you fear."

And I realized I was afraid of the presentation because I was afraid of the audience. Because I saw myself as different from the possible attendees, some of whom I knew had different understandings of the Course I feared them, believing they would judge me. As long as I clung to my belief that the differences in our Course understanding (or anything else) meant anything real, could possibly jeopardize the uninterrupted union of our true nature, I would continue to experience fear around them, reflecting that original thought of separation realized. Effectively preventing the teacher of inner kindness we all share to heal our one split mind with truly helpful words for everyone.

I sat a few more minutes, basking in fear's opposite—loving sameness—that precursor here in the dream to the perfect oneness we will again experience when we have applied the Course's forgiveness in all circumstances with everyone and thing we have dreamed up to thwart us. Gratefully surveying the faces of those I had seen as so different, instead inhaling the irresistible scent of our sameness.

Although the fear recurred in the hours before the scheduled talk, it completely abated the moment I looked out on the faces around me, remembering only our one right mind addressing a beautiful section of the Course that distills its entire message in the phrase "Together or not at all." Referring to the way the veil on our vision of true union lifts through our present decision to extend our proverbial hands to each other. Thereby taking the only hand we really want to hold, ever ready to lead us all back to the only "place" we really want to go (and in truth have never really left): the oneness joined as one of our true and only nature.

Never mind that I then experienced the ego's predictable backlash the next day, this time in the form of bullying self-criticism for a variety of perceived, individual inadequacies also designed to prove our differences. I've gotten pretty used to that happening in one form or another following elongated holy instants in the light, and knew return to sanity would also follow, having never really left.

Now I got up off the floor, dusted myself off, and went back to my seat across from his desk. "I don't really need analysis do I?" I asked.

He smiled.

"But I still need a teacher, for a seeming while longer, sometimes imagined embodied, sometimes not. Until I see everyone and thing—however frightening and threatening they appear to the body's eyes—as caused by the same mistaken belief and worthy of the same loving response."

He nodded.

My smart phone pinged with new notifications, including a Facebook post by another ACIM teacher who, from where I seemed to sit, appeared to be rampantly contradicting the very core of the non-dualistic metaphysics *A Course in Miracles* leads us to. The familiar judgment began to arise. I started to laugh, in a good way. Jesus was watching me, or was it the other way around? I dropped my phone in my purse, reached across the desk, and took his hand once more in mine.

> I take the journey with you. For I share your doubts and fears a little while, that you may come to me who recognize the road by which all fears and doubts are overcome. We walk together. I must understand uncertainty and pain, although I know they have no meaning. Yet a savior must remain with those he teaches, seeing what

they see, but still retaining in his mind the way that led him out, and now will lead you out with him. God's Son is crucified until you walk along the road with me. (From *A Course in Miracles* workbook Review V, paragraph 6)

The Dreamer of the Dream

In the dream I had in the wee hours of the morning, the dangerous details of which I can't now recall, I lay sleeping in another bed in an unfamiliar place, aware of a vast, omnipotent force out to get me that seemed to have somehow invaded my very body, unleashing its boundless wrath without *and* within. I shook violently, as if possessed, for what seemed an eternity, consumed by a primal fear so formidable I expected at any moment to detonate.

It took a while after waking in my own bed beside my own little whimpering dog apparently deep in the throes of her own nightmare for my racing heart and quivering limbs to still. My brain to grasp it was only a dream, whose content, like all of our sleeping and waking dreams, reflects my unconscious, shameful belief that I somehow managed to defect from indivisible, abstract Love and so deserve annihilation.

I couldn't help but marvel at the way my current Course study seemed to have once more leapt off the pages of the big, blue book smack into the center of the interactive classroom of my so-called life, even permeating the tattered fabric of my sleeping dreams. Allow me to explain. In preparation for teaching my weekly *A Course in Miracles* class here in Denver, I had been reviewing Chapter 27, VII. The Dreamer of the Dream, that begins with the encouraging news that "Suffering is an emphasis upon all that the world has done to injure you," and goes on to say:

> ... Like to a dream of punishment, in which the dreamer is unconscious of what brought on the attack against himself, he sees himself attacked unjustly and by something not himself. He is the victim of this "something else," a thing outside himself, for which he has no reason to be held responsible. He must be innocent because he knows not what he does, but what is done to him. Yet is his own attack upon himself apparent still, for it is he who bears the suffering. And he cannot escape because its source is seen outside himself. (Paragraph 1)

Throughout the Course we're told that our waking experience is no more real than our sleeping dreams, and works according to the same unconscious principles. In both we experience ourselves engaged in an ongoing series of situations in which we interact with other dream figures in an ultimately futile effort to get our needs met, while enduring seemingly unprovoked, random, meaningless attacks by forces beyond our control. In both we have forgotten we imagined the whole thing, that our experience is "an outside picture of an inward condition," as the Course puts it, but a mirror of the unrelenting turmoil and drama we experience within. Awake or asleep, this denial of responsibility for our experience and stubborn refusal to acknowledge its cause reinforces our elaborate, uniquely detailed, individual stories of suffering while proving the ego's myth that we exist separately from our creator and each other but it's not our fault, it's theirs.

Because we unconsciously believe we pulled off the impossible crime of separating from our one, eternally, loving, united source, we mindlessly jockey for favor, attempting to establish our relative innocence in the eyes of a vindictive God hot on our trail, constantly experiencing ourselves unfairly treated by others more guilty and deserving of punishment than we. But it never works for long. Because the habit of blaming something external for an internal state merely nourishes the unconscious guilt within, forcing us to find another attacker (and another and another) "out there" to blame.

All week long I had been reminding myself that every moment offers us another opportunity to refuse to justify the ego's thought system in whatever form it appears in our dreams, to challenge *every* unkind thought as it inevitably arises from the ego's 24/7 automatic projector. To remind ourselves, as *A Course in Miracles* workbook lesson 5 tells us, that we're "*never* upset for the reason we think." To ask ourselves honestly whether this thought, feeling, judgment, or need, this thing I'm about to say or do, will root me more deeply in my dream of exile from abstract, all-inclusive love or help me awaken to it.

This practice yields astonishing results. Although the self I still see when I look in the mirror believed she had already allowed her greatest forgiveness opportunities to be healed, I saw that I was once again stupendously (and, eventually, at least, happily) wrong. By really paying *constant* attention from moment-to-moment to the contents of my mind in a disciplined way, I began to see how my first reaction to almost everything—from the state of the nation to the way my special relationships react to my attempts to "help them," from which bike route to take on a Sunday morning to what plans to make for upcoming summer weekends, who to invite to dinner, and what kind of fish to throw on the grill— still comes from ego. The part of my mind that insists on having things go her way and secretly rejoices when other dream figures appear to prevent that from happening.

As the week wore on, I saw how invaded I feel by some people in my life who appear to trample my imaginary boundaries, how harshly I judge their perceived "insensitivity," and how conversely abandoned I feel by others. I saw how these two paradoxical themes: smothered and abandoned, the intertwined melody and harmony of the whole sad song of Susan stuck for seeming ever in my reptilian brain, played on and on with or without my rapt attention, and started to smile at the absurdity of it all.

And I realized once again I was mistaken in believing I knew what the journey would look like, and, most importantly, what the journeyer looked like. *I* was not going home with Jesus (that *symbolic* memory of enduring wholeness in our mind), studying or teaching from this book, or practicing forgiveness as a discrete physical or psychological body, but as a decision-making mind; the dreamer of the dream outside the dream, not the hero.

As I kept practicing, asking myself again and again which thought system I was choosing to reinforce *right now* (as Ken Wapnick advises) over and over throughout my days, I began to experience the seeming ego attacks in other dream figures as indistinguishable from mine. Both springing from the same failure to "look upon the problem as it is, and not the way that you set it up" (from paragraph 2) caused by our refusal to recognize we are the dream's dreamer, not the innocent victim of other dream figures' attacks or refusal to meet our needs.

Recognizing over and over whenever I was tempted to stray back into the dream that everyone walking this earth secretly accusing themselves of abandoning God and deserving punishment shares the same ego, the same right mind, and the same decision maker—ever capable of choosing the inner teacher of love over fear—enabled me to experience and respond (at least, eventually) with true kindness born of a peace, not of this dreamy world. A peace always available to us when we connect with the lucid dreamer within by refusing to side with the victimizing and victimized plots we're continually dreaming up, *right now!*

You are the dreamer of the world of dreams. No other cause it has, nor ever will. Nothing more fearful than an idle dream has terrified God's Son, and made him think that he has lost his innocence, denied his Father, and made war upon himself. So fearful is the dream so seeming real, he could not waken to reality without the sweat of terror and a scream of mortal fear, unless a gentler dream preceded his awaking, and allowed his calmer mind to welcome, not to fear, the Voice that calls with love to waken him; a gentler dream in which his suffering was healed and where his brother was his friend. God willed he waken gently and with joy, and gave him means to waken without fear. (Paragraph 13)

The (Eventually) Happy Learner

The proverbial battlefield still smoldered above strewn, severed limbs as tangled as a Picasso painting, the sun a distant orb obscured by the bitter ash of betrayal. I lay writhing in pain in the middle of it all, apparently with just enough Hollywood strength left to wrest myself free from the bloodied, muddied carnage, grab a tattered, still mostly white cloth, and wave it in the air. The score rose in a final, Rococo crescendo as I staggered to my feet, coughing, the camera slowly panning out, house lights rising to reveal a lone robed and bearded figure seated out there in the viewing room, bringing his palms together in polite applause.

It took me a moment or two to fully grasp once more that it was only a movie I'd gotten lost in again, but another DVD excavated from my cavernous library of morality plays. This one, like all the others, designed in one way or another to prove Susan the victim of circumstances beyond her control. Beleaguered survivor in a field of devastation, the dubious story that I exist apart from uninterrupted wholeness but it's not my fault, it's theirs. You know, the ones who'd so cruelly thwarted me, the ones I'd made pay so dearly for it. Only the taste of victory was no longer even remotely sweet.

Consumed with horror, guilt, and downright *shock* that I had this much wrath still left in me after so many hours in the forgiveness classroom, I sighed, again disgusted with my little s self. This was getting really exhausting. As the credits rolled, I stumbled back out into the theatre still wagging that soiled white flag, dropped to the floor into devotional pose, and lay the emblem of my surrender at his sandaled feet.

"Hey," I said, forehead still pressed against the carpet to the unmistakable tune of his gentle laughter.

I could hear him clearing his throat, the familiar sound of him trying to act serious, to meet me in the condition I think I'm in, so to speak, no small feat.

"Popcorn?" he said, brightly, tapping me on the shoulder and offering me a half-eaten bucket. Or was it half full?

I got up, dusted myself off, and slipped back into the chair beside him where I belonged.

"I know what you're thinking," I said.

"You always do."

"Seriously?"

He smiled. "Eventually, at least," he said.

He had a point, he always did. "'You who are steadfastly devoted to misery must first recognize that you are miserable and not happy,'" I said, quoting from the first paragraph of The Happy Learner in *A Course in Miracles Chapter* 14. " 'The Holy Spirit cannot teach without this contrast for you believe that misery is happiness.' "

"Couldn't have said it better myself," he said.

"Ha! The thing is; I thought I passed that test a long time ago, right? Look it up in your records. I know misery when I feel it. I've tasted the real happiness of your way of seeing. I can tell the difference. I really do know that choosing you as my inner teacher brings peace and choosing that other smarmy bastard brings pain. But there still doesn't always seem to be a choice, you know what I'm saying? I mean, Jesus, it happens so freaking quickly."

"Go on," he said.

But where to begin? In the past week, a series of (in retrospect really quite minor) dramas with a couple of other costars in seeming, rapid, mind-boggling succession appeared to have rocked my world to the point that I found myself once more in full fight-or-flight mode, completely rooted in the fox hole of a primal brain, unable to resist feeling justified in defending myself based on the overwhelming conviction that I was right and had every right to prove it.

Not even the déjà vu-like awareness that I had played this role with these same costars one too many times with the same tragic, guilt-nourishing results could stop me from rushing out onto the battlefield in an effort to establish my territory once and for all.

Only this time, as soon as the explosion of anger dissipated, it immediately gave way to a guilt more seemingly bottomless than anything I had heretofore experienced (which is saying quite a lot!), without so much as a pause in between in which to savor a nanosecond of self-congratulatory triumph.

"So what you're really saying is I must exhaust my belief in the possibility that identifying with, let alone defending, *any* personal interest however seemingly justified will bring me anything but excruciating pain? And that my only choice when I catch myself doing so is to forgive myself. Recognizing that although I have made some real progress in at least associating the cause of my suffering or happiness with my choice of inner teacher, my mind is still split. My decision-making mind is still terrified of returning to the seeming cause of the split, the belief that the "tiny, mad idea" of separation from seamless union with our one and only source had real effects. While still captivated by the possibility that the self I still see in the mirror has anything to win or lose from *anyone* or *anything* else seemingly 'out there' in the many movies of my own making. It's like you say later in that same paragraph:

> Have faith in nothing and you will find the "treasure" that you seek. ... A little piece of glass, a speck of dust, a body or a war are one to you. For if you value one thing made of nothing, you have believed that nothing can be precious, and that you *can* learn how to make the untrue true.

I've just been making a big to do about nothing again, is what you're really saying. Not because I'm daft, just because I'm so afraid of giving up on finding love within the nothingness of my dream of exile, and looking for it where it *can* be found in you. I just need to stop beating myself up about the ultimate nothingness of still having an ego, and bring even my most shameful ego attacks to you to be unlearned together."

He nodded.

"So the way to become a happy learner is to look with you at how much a part of me still doesn't want to learn this Course, at least not in every circumstance, at least not with those that most push my buttons. To see the part of me that wants to be an unhappy learner and forgive it. To catch without judgment my mistaking the role I'm playing on the screen for reality again, and drag myself back to this seat to watch the movie I made with you."

He just continued to smile.

"Well, I guess that's a wrap, then," I said. "I'm so glad we had this little talk."

"Always a pleasure."

I grabbed the popcorn. "I am so going to ace this Course!"

His brows shot up and down the way they do.

"Eventually, at least."

He threw back his head and laughed.

I had to laugh, too.

... Learn to be a happy learner. You will never learn how to make nothing everything. Yet see that this has been your goal, and recognize how foolish it has been. Be glad it is undone, for when you look at it in simple honestly, it is undone. I said before, "Be not content with nothing," for you have believed that nothing could content you. *It is not so.*

If you would be a happy learner, you must get everything you have learned to the Holy Spirit to be unlearned for you. And then begin to learn the joyous lessons that come quickly on the firm foundation that truth is true. (From paragraphs 5 and 6)

I Rest (Once More) in God

In the sleeping dream I was back in college again (will I *ever* stop dreaming I am back in school?) in a foreign-seeming land, pursued for unknown reasons by some kind of authoritarian regime intent on killing me for a crime I vaguely suspected I'd been involved in but couldn't quite recall. Apparently many other people had also participated, and, at first, some tried to help me. But the regime seemed intent on making me the scapegoat and that arrangement seemed to work quite well for the others, too.

I made it back to my vacant home, but they followed me, and I holed up inside. A guy I knew in the dream made it inside, too. I told him they were after me and he said they were following him, too. The pursuers started dumping gasoline around the perimeter of the house. Before they could set the fire, we dashed out the back door with some kind of cockamamie plan to distract them, and I ended up fleeing, alone again, to hide in another house. A father and grown son with Eastern European-sounding accents straight out of a central casting for vintage James Bond flicks followed me.

Meanwhile, I had apparently missed the first day of a two-day class back at school and would now have to take it pass-fail, or forfeit credit completely. The guy I'd holed up with earlier reappeared while I was in hiding and said I needed to go back and finish the class because he hated to see it mess up my GPA, or, worse, prevent me from graduating. Needless to say, I found this bizarre; the least of my problems!

The father and son came inside and I knew they'd been sent to bring me back and have me killed. They followed me into town in my car to await a formal execution. No one, including the guy or the friends that had earlier tried to help, attempted to intervene. The sacrifice of me seemed absolutely inevitable, beyond further discussion. I waited alone in a friend's house, frantic and terrified, and sat at a computer typing out the words: "Help me God!" over and over again.

I awoke in my own bed, thinking of the Course lines: "An angry father pursues his guilty Son. Kill or be killed," from the Manual for Teachers, 17. paragraph 7, a perfect summary of the ego thought system. Spawned by the belief that the "tiny, mad idea" of separation had real consequences, fragmenting the one child of God into a gazillion fugitives holed up in an imaginary fortress, each piece intent on proving I exist, but it's not my fault, it's theirs, in a desperate effort to avoid God's punishment. Nonetheless, the jig was apparently up!

My racing heart screeched to a halt in sickening slow motion. I rose and went downstairs to my office, grabbed the big, blue book, and opened it to *A Course in Miracles* workbook lesson 109, "I rest in God."

> We ask for rest today, and quietness unshaken by the world's appearances. We ask for peace and stillness, in the midst of all the turmoil born of clashing dreams. We ask for safety and for happiness, although we seem to look on danger and on sorrow. And we have the thought that will answer our asking with what we request. (Paragraph 1)

Are you freaking kidding me, I wondered, and slapped the book shut, entirely unable to swallow these words. After all, it had been a week filled with doubts and worries around every role—mother, daughter, wife, friend, writer, student, teacher—I seemed to be playing in my waking dream. As another birthday loomed, uncertainty about the future of the little s self I see in the mirror and the world I seem to interact with appeared at an all-time high, my faith in any of it at an all-time low.

Worse, I was seriously questioning the time, effort, and money I had poured into teaching and writing about this Course, and whether or not I could possibly afford to continue. Although I had been asking for help from the inner teacher of inner sanity and light to look at these doubts, darkness nonetheless prevailed. The bearded wonder appeared to have taken another unexpected sabbatical. And so I charged out the door, my little dog in tow, to walk it out. If I couldn't find inner peace, endorphins would just have to do.

The haze from the fires burning around Colorado still hung heavy even in the morning air as I huffed up and down the uneven, pollen-coated sidewalks, Kayleigh panting at my feet, still inwardly begging to look at these thoughts, this dream, through the inner eyes of love instead of fear. Finally, rounding a corner fragrant with roses and clematis hopefully entwined around a wrought-iron fence, the thought emerged that maybe doubting *me* was not such a bad thing after all, there being, in truth, no real me or here, here. What if losing faith in everything to do with my seeming self was actually a giant step toward faith in our capital S Self, that oneness joined as one of our true nature? What if profound doubt was just another symptom of withdrawing my misplaced confidence in a special self capable of making her way in the world, finding the special love and success, health and security she still believed she could get if she just gave a little more, worked a little harder, a little smarter, a little more faithfully.

Now on the verge of a run, despite my bad knees, powered by the possibility of an end to the thought of pursuit of all kinds, I kept reminding myself I don't know what I really want, and asking to connect with that presence in our one mind that does. Until I came to the end of the literal and proverbial road, the welcome recognition that giving any meaning/purpose to any of my "doing" in the world (including my "doing" with the Course) beyond the healing of my own mind split over its faith in the lie of separation would never bring me real peace. Or fill the bottomless lack resulting from that misplaced faith. But continuing to doubt and bring those doubts to real faith within the healed mind would.

I stood a minute beside the grassy gulch, inhaling the perfume of right-mindedness. I would continue to do what I do here in the dream, and if I had to do something else, so be it. But its purpose would always be the same. Helping me learn to side with our unbridled unity within, instead of shackled individuality without. To my little dog's relief, we walked home at a normal pace more suited to her tiny legs, freed of the need to rush toward yet another destination or dodge another imaginary bullet. Back home I sat down again at my desk, Kayleigh curled up in her bed at my feet, and, well, rested, I suppose you could say, in you know Who.

"I rest in God." This thought will bring to you the rest and quiet, peace and stillness, and the safety and the happiness you seek. "I rest in God." This thought has power to wake the sleeping truth in you, whose vision sees beyond appearances to that same truth in everyone and everything there is. Here is the end of suffering for all the world, and everyone who ever came and yet will come to linger for a while. Here is the thought in which the Son of God is born again, to recognize himself.

"I rest in God." Completely undismayed, this thought will carry you through storms and strife, past misery and pain, past loss and death, and onward to the certainty of God. There is no suffering it cannot heal. There is no problem that it cannot solve. And no appearance but will turn to truth before the eyes of you who rest in God. (Paragraphs 2 and 3)

I Want to Hold Your Hand, But ...

Our Love awaits us as we go to Him, and walks beside us showing us the way. He fails in nothing. He the End we seek, and he the Means by which we go to Him. (*A Course in Miracles* workbook lesson 302, from paragraph 2)

When I was a kid, our road-trip vacations inevitably began with my mother—staring straight ahead, shoulders hugging her ears—saying something like this, in a flat voice, about ten minutes into the drive: "Do you know if I left the iron on?"

Followed by my father, replying with something like this: "Jesus Christ!" in a voice, not so flat, before peeling off in the other direction with a squeal and jerk that left my brother and I gripping the backseat door handles for balance on our opposite sides of an imaginary, yet heartily defended, demilitarized zone. Wise enough to zip our ever-flapping lips as my parents returned to the scene of the possible crime to ensure one or the other's carelessness did not inadvertently seal our family's ever-wobbly fate.

"Did you lock the door? Did you put the cat in? Did I turn off the stove, close the windows—take the God-damn laundry off the line?" By the time I made it to junior high, I no longer so much as glanced up from whatever book I was deep into as my parents dutifully repeated the lines of their script, responding to the magnetic pull of a distracted lifestyle here in the dream by performing this little obsessive-compulsive ritual I now considered normal, along with all the other neurotic behaviors I'd observed over the years in others and myself.

I bring this up because I've been once more noticing these sorts of rituals in myself and—with help from our new inner teacher—at least seeing them as they are, as the Course puts it, and not the way I set them up. As detours back into the dream of separate selves vying for survival in a harsh environment designed to keep me away from the decision-making mind and the outstretched hand of said inner teacher ever willing, ready, and able to lead me back to the only home I really want to return to. As mindless wanderings back onto the battlefield in a futile attempt to right wrongs that can never be righted. Attend to ever-morphing, nonsensical situations that appear to demand my full attention to defend against eternal, all-inclusive abstract love. A love I crave, but am not yet certain I trust not to turn on me for the defection from its metaphorical arms I secretly accuse myself of, and therefore feel obsessively compelled to flee again and again.

Ironically, the more I work with this Course, the more aware I become of my compulsion to trade the realm of the decision-making mind where the choice for true comfort abides for the body's bogus refuge. The more committed I become to healing my mind through the process of catching myself attributing my unsettled inner state to external circumstances, the more I witness this seemingly involuntary urge to bolt. The more I recognize I have chosen the ego as my teacher and choose again to look through the lens of the part of my mind that truly sees only the oneness joined as one of our true nature, the more aware I conversely become of the many excuses I cook up to justify dropping the hand of the only teacher I really want. *Jesus Christ!*

And yet, the more I work with this Course, the more vital the character of a non-dualistic Jesus as my guide home becomes. Maybe it's my reaction to my Catholic upbringing that is being healed through practicing forgiveness, along with all the other outside forces I believe have bullied or thwarted this personal me over the years. Honestly, I didn't realize the extent to which I had turned my back on the figure of Jesus long before I left the church as a teenager until I started confronting my resistance to the Course's use of this character to symbolize our inner teacher. But fairly early on in my study, and much to my surprise, I experienced a kind of inner vision of Jesus standing at the base of a trail on a bald, rocky hill; hand extended, and somehow knew this was not my grandmother's savior. No trace of the biblical story of sin, guilt, fear and specialness clung to his robes. Somehow I knew I could trust him completely to help me find the unwavering love that seemed to have gone so horribly missing within.

And so I took his hand, gazed into those completely accepting eyes, and burst into tears. I leaned my head on his shoulder. I started to walk up that hill with him but then, you know, there were so many things I needed to take care of "down here" first. And so I ran away again. I continue to meet him on that trail, take his hand, walk a few right-minded steps with him, suddenly wonder aloud if I left the oven on, and charge back into the dream.

Unlike my bodily father, though, he only smiles and waits as I race back down the hill, promising to come right back. Smiles and waits as I exhaust another possibility that solutions to a seemingly inexhaustible set of personal problems can ever be found where the problems never existed. Until I once more return to this trail back in the mind, again willing to take a few more steps with him, hand in hand.

I see him standing there more and more these days in my mind's eye, patiently waiting for me on that trail home, and am just beginning to forgive myself for this constant racing back and forth from mind to body, body to mind. Somehow I know that one day I will have exhausted all the nothings back down in that dreaded valley of separate interests and, fear finally worn away, be ready to take his hand once and for all and steadily climb.

Until then, he gently reminds me salvation is inevitable by saying something like this:

"I am so close to you we cannot fail." (*A Course in Miracles* workbook, Part II, Introduction, from paragraph 6)

And I reply with something like this: "Are you freaking kidding me?"

"We cannot fail," he repeats.

But he must be mumbling again. "Speak up," I say.

He shakes his head, and smiles more broadly. "We cannot fail. The end is sure."

Jesus Christ! I think, sighing, and reply with something like this: "Just wait here one more minute, OK? I think I might have left the front door unlocked."

And he responds; bless his ever-beating heart, with something like this:

> ... The Holy Spirit has one direction for all minds, and the one He taught me is yours. Let us not lose sight of His direction through illusions, for only illusions of another direction can obscure the one for which God's Voice speaks in all of us. Never accord the ego the power to interfere with the journey. It has none, because the journey is the way to what is true. Leave all illusions behind, and reach beyond all attempts of the ego to hold you back. I go before you because I am beyond the ego. Reach, therefore, for my hand because you want to transcend the ego. My strength will never be wanting, and if you choose to share it you will do so. I give it willingly and gladly, because I need you as much as you need me. (*A Course in Miracles*, chapter 8, V. paragraph 6)

The End

Made in the USA
Charleston, SC
11 April 2015